It wasn't that easy

THE TOMMY GODWIN STORY

To Roger Bugg:

Without your support and enthusiasm the work would never have reached completion. My thanks to you and your encouraging and committed wife.

Tommy

It wasn't that easy

THE TOMMY GODWIN STORY

Tommy Godwin

JOHN PINKERTON · MEMORIAL PUBLISHING FUND

First published 2007
Reprinted 2011

The John Pinkerton Memorial Publishing Fund

Following the untimely death of John Pinkerton this fund was set up in his memory.
The object of the fund is to continue the publishing activities initiated by John on the development of the cycle and its related history.

ISBN 978-0-9552115-5-3

Designed by David Hibberd
Printed by Information Press, Oxford

Front cover: Tommy Godwin in his heyday winning the BSA Gold Vase outright, 1951, and displaying the three gold trophies to celebrate his 80th birthday, 2000.
Back cover: Tommy in Team Manager days holding up Hugh Porter prior to a lap of honour at the World Championships, Leicester, 1970.

Contents

List of Illustrations

My sporting heroes

I have known about Tommy Godwin all my life, or else I seem to have known about him all my life. I grew up with a mom and a dad and a nan and a granddad who were avid sporting fans. Football, especially Aston Villa, was the most important sport of all but each of them was also keen on other athletic pursuits, from boxing to running, from cricket to tennis, and from rugby to swimming. Family gatherings were dominated by talk about sporting heroes. My Granddad Perry was a Blues fan but always reckoned that the best half back line that he ever saw was Gibson, Talbot and Tate of the Villa - although he quickly declared that the Brummagem had the better goalies, such as Harry Hibs and Gil Merrick. Our Nan's favoured player was George Cummings. A very tough full back, she reckoned he was the only defender that the famed Stanley Matthews was afeared of.

There were others that Our Nan held in esteem – Pongo Waring, Mush Callaghan, and Billy Walker amongst them. As for Our Mom, she was another Villa fan, well she did come out of Whitehouse Street, Aston Cross and had no choice. Stan 'the Wham' Lynn, Trevor Ford and, of course, Johnny Dixon and Peter McParland were the names that she held up high for me and Our Kid. Why of course? Well Peter MacParland had scored the two goals in the 1957 FA Cup Final that had given the Villa the victory against the much-fancied Busby Babes of Manchester United, and Johnny Dixon was the captain who had grasped hold of that cup that we still yearn to win. I was nine months old when the Villa come back to Brum in triumph. Our Mom went back down the Old End to join in the celebrations. She stood in the club room of the Albion pub on the corner of her street and the Aston Road North and held me up to the window as the team's coach drove past amidst the cheering throngs. I hope one day that the Villa will lift the cup and I can recall it!

Now football was a big thing for Our Dad as well but perhaps in our younger years he was more of a boxing aficionado. He'd boxed himself as an amateur, seen the great Randy Turpin fight down in Walford Road, Sparkbrook, and in the midst of the night he'd harked to the commentaries on the wireless of the fights of the likes of Don Cockell. He'd taken on the fearsome Rocky Marciano in 1955 for the heavyweight boxing championship of the world and was stopped in the ninth round in controversial circumstances. Our Dad also told us about meeting the young Garry Sobers in the late 1950s at the St John's Restaurant in Deritend, where the West Indians of Birmingham used to gather. Dad's oldest sister was married to Johnny Brown, a chap from Kingston in Jamaica, and Dad always said what a thrill it was to be in the same room as a wonderful West Indian cricketing side that included the three 'Ws' - Frank Worrall, Clyde Wallcott and Everton Weekes.

There were other names that the older members of our family held close and talked of with pride, such as Roger Bannister who had broken the four minute mile, and Jim Peters, who had failed heroically to take the gold in the marathon in the Commonwealth Games in Vancouver in 1954. Me and Our Kid, Darryl, grew up with these and other names as icons. Amongst them was Tommy Godwin. That's why I have always seemed to have known him.

Tommy was another of whom we were proud – perhaps even more so because he was one of us, a Brummie. We all knew that Tommy was a wonderful cyclist and that he had achieved great things, and of course, that he had his shop in Silver Street, near to where we lived.

I was fortunate to meet this sporting hero. A few years back Tommy came on to my BBC WM radio show and we spent over an hour talking about his life and taking calls from listeners who, like me, wanted to let Tommy know how much they thought of him. The response took Tommy back a bit and it led to me asking him back on my show again. During my chats with him I realised that there was more pulling me to Tommy than a pride in his achievements: he had grown up in Aston close to the street of Our Mom and Our Nan; he had gone to St Mary's School, where they had both been pupils; and he had worked at Powell and Hanmer's, as had Our Nan and many of her family. As much as was my pleasure at these connections, more was the joy of meeting someone who really was a sporting hero. Modest, polite, dignified and always solicitous to the well being of others – that is Tommy Godwin. He is the epitome of an English sporting gentleman and Birmingham and England should be most proud of him.

Carl Chinn
Community historian, broadcaster and writer

Preface

I would like to express my sincere thanks and appreciation to the many very close friends who have encouraged me through the years to continue what has been a long drawn out intention.

Talking of the past has always been part of my life. My experience in many instances can be matched by many of the readers of this book. But some are very personal, and emotions are overcoming at times, beyond belief in many cases, and I know people have been surprised when I show them. I do not apologise in any way for this, sincerity and love of other people is in my make up.

If I have compiled a reading of interest, I am very happy.

The writing has finished days before my eighty-sixth birthday, a 'Life Story' indeed.

Tommy Godwin
Knowle
April 2007

Foreword

I have known Tommy Godwin for around forty-five years. He was the British team manager at the World Track Championships in Liege, Belgium back in 1963 where I made my debut, and the following year he was our boss at the Tokyo Olympics.

Tommy, or TCG as some of us would refer to him, was the first national coach. Every day was the best day of his life and he ran the Olympic squad training sessions with unbridled passion. He was a strict disciplinarian, a virtue I very much admired and followed during my career.

We enjoyed highs and lows throughout our sporting involvement together and shared many a humorous moment, sometimes reducing us to tears.

The memories are many and priceless, far too numerous to mention in the Foreword. But the one I feel I should recall occurred on the plane between Hong Kong and Tokyo, the concluding leg of the long flight to the 1964 Olympiad.

Tommy surrendered his seat, well, perhaps after a little persuasion, to allow a lovely lady to join me. That Yorkshire lass later became my wife and is still my best friend today. She is of course Anita Lonsbrough the Olympic gold medal winning swimmer Rome 1960.

Friendships crafted through sport are very special and as the years have rolled by Tommy and I have remained pals to this day. I could spare his blushes for, despite being a big fella with fists like lump hammers, his emotions often speak volumes with a tear or two in his eyes. I hope everyone who is privileged to read his life story will enjoy it.

Hugh Porter MBE
Four times World Champion
April 2007

Acknowledge-ments

All the pictures reproduced in this book are from Tommy Godwin's own collection. Apart from some of the family snapshots, the photographers are unknown but we salute and acknowledge them here. Those pictures which first appeared in *Cycling* are reproduced by courtesy of *Cycling Weekly* whose kind permission is gratefully acknowledged.

Preface to the Second Edition

Since the first Edition appeared in 2007 Tommy's love of and work for cycling has continued unabated. This year he has received an honorary degree from Loughborough College for Services to Sports Science. On a recent visit to the Olympic Museum in Lausanne, with staff members from Loughborough College, he was interviewed about his career and this is now on record for visitors to the museum, available at any time and forever. The torches for the 1948 Olympics were created and made at Loughborough College and Tommy is active in the Loughborough Flames Project, motto 'Honour the past but look to the future', in which the College, together with the British Heart Foundation, is lighting the way to the 2012 Olympics by inspiring young people to live physically active lives. In the run-up to the Games Tommy has been invited to carry a torch in the relay to the Olympic stadium. He is Ambassador for the City of Birmingham to the 2012 London Olympics. These are fitting tributes 64 years after his double Olympic medals in the last Olympics to be held in this country.

R D Bugg
Breadsall, October 2011

CHAPTER 1

1920

My American upbringing

The year 1913 was when a young Englishman, aged twenty-seven, felt the urge to travel. The young man was my father, Charles Arthur Godwin, and his idea, along with many others of that generation, was to improve his quality of life. Still single, but full of ambition and enthusiasm, his destination was the fast-developing United States of America. Young people from many nations were hastening to answer the call of the 'New World'. Each nationality was attracted to the areas that had similar interests and culture to the country of their origin.

To young Charles Arthur, the Eastern Seaboard, as it was called, or the New England States, offered what he was seeking: engineering and industry, a mechanical environment. The firm he had left to make his way in the world was the Delta Metal Company, located in Aston, Birmingham. He had commenced work as a boy of thirteen, breaking pig-iron to be smelted down and used for the making of baths, basins and cisterns.

Dad as a young man

His family home was a small terrace home typical of the period, and was situated a mile and a half from his workplace. He had been born in 1886 of ordinary working class parents. His father was a factory worker and his mother kept a huckster's shop, as they were known in those days, the shop being in the front room of the house. Ma Godwin brought up seven children, six boys and one girl.

Charles settled in Bridgeport, Connecticut, and made friends from all over the world, but his dreams came to a temporary halt when war was declared in 1914. His immediate thoughts were to return to his home country and volunteer for the army. This he did, only to be told he could not be accepted for active service on medical grounds. It was then vital that he got work and he found a job assisting in the making of munitions at the Wolseley Sheep Shearing Company in Witton near Aston. Then, unexpectedly, he met the young lady who was to become his wife, Dora Evans. They married during the war and on June 5th 1917 their first child, a girl, Irene, was born.

When the war ended in 1918 Charles' mind returned to thoughts of America and he convinced his wife that this was where their future lay. Once again he crossed the Atlantic and looked forward to a family life in a new and vibrant country. Four days after their arrival, the second child of the marriage was born, another daughter, Gladys. The family faced difficult circumstances for they had little money and could only rent a couple of cheap rooms. With no furniture to speak of, they used upturned orange boxes as seating and slept on a mattress on the floor. Hard work, determination and the will to succeed pulled them through and they soon began building a home and future together. Some eighteen months later a third child, Thomas Charles, was born on 5th November 1920. The first son of the marriage was to provide Charles with a great deal of satisfaction, and as the years rolled on he learned of his father's intense enthusiasm to make a sportsman of his first male offspring.

There was the constant encouragement to make me first a good runner. Time after time Dad would race me over perhaps fifty yards or so, but my style was not conducive to good running. I ran rather pigeon-toed, and regularly tripped myself up at speed. Attempts were made to cure the problem. There was a slight improvement but no great response from me, in spite of Dad's enthusiasm. Determined to keep my mind focussed on sport, Dad took me on regular visits to watch Irish v Scottish teams playing soccer on Sunday mornings. Great fun, but not a true American sport. This was for the 'Limeys', as all British people were known. I enjoyed the half-times when segments of oranges were handed out and I listened in awe to the Irish and Scottish dialects. They were all hard men, giving their all in a Sunday morning of fun! But again, I was witnessing the effort needed in sport. Dad, I knew, enjoyed the company, but at home he would tell me fascinating stories of sporting endeavour. There is no doubt in my mind that in these early years I was being well groomed to succeed in sport.

By this time Dad had made contact with some boxing enthusiasts. He felt drawn to the atmosphere of the training gym, renewing an interest that he had

Above: Mom with
Irene, first born, 1917
Right: Grandad
Goodwin

experienced as a young man in England. He may well have entered the sport of
boxing, except that in one unfortunate family argument with his brother Tom
he lost his temper and the result was a broken nose, not good for family rela-
tionships. Grandad Godwin immediately confiscated all of Dad's boxing gear,
burned it and laid down a ban on boxing. This form of immediate reaction,
which was something he carried through his life, was something that I inher-
ited. It was obviously in the genes.

I can well remember being taken to watch and meet this hard-training bunch
of guys, all trying to maim each other. The next step was a routine for me to follow, skipping, exercises and punch bag work. The punch bag was an onion sack
filled with old clothes and hung in the cellar. Night after night came the warm
up then the punch bag, hands bound with tape, and a session of jabbing, in-
fighting, moving around, ducking and weaving and fast foot movement. The
session would finish with Dad on his knees and me, around eleven years old,
trying to punch my way through an adult's experienced guard. Often after getting smacked around the ear, I would be told-off for losing my temper and trying to rush in, swinging like hell.

Dad and Mom had a great circle of friends, enjoyed parties, and went out
fairly regularly on Saturday nights. On these occasions I was honoured by being
allowed to sleep in my parents' bed, on Dad's side, until they came home in the
early hours of the morning. One night I was awakened by Dad as he lifted me to
take me back to my own room. He asked, "Are you going to run in the Olympic
Games for me?" I have realised since that the year was 1932, an Olympic Games
year. My reply was, "Yes," anything to get back to sleep. He then asked, "Which
event, the 100 yards or the mile?" I must have thought quickly and said, "Oh, the
mile." I hoped it might please him more.

Mom and Dad in
Bridgeport with two
of my sisters

Apparently when Dad was a youth in England he was quite good sprinter.
Young men would gather on a canal side and run races over approximately 100
yards. They would collect small sums of money and have handicap races. They
had heard of talk of the famous Powderhall Handicap Races held once a year
in Scotland, where professionals ran for big purses. The whole story is now
beginning to unfold, with my Dad's strong desire to make me a good sportsman. There had obviously been no encouragement for him to further his talent. Obviously, at that time in my life, and certainly in my father's, neither of
us could imagine the possibilities, but the seed had been sown. My father must
have seen the signal. He had implanted an idea into my young mind. I, on the
other hand, felt that I must try to honour that promise.

Dad and I were inseparable. All our time together was either running or boxing. Then swimming came into it when my sister swam some half mile across
the local reservoir. She was then instructed to teach me to swim. Further sports
entered when one of Dad's pals, Jim Thorp, supplied a baseball. I had just
received what was known as a first base mitt. Dad and I spent hours throwing
the ball, me catching low balls, high balls, fast balls, some thrown to the left,
some to the right, some high, some low. I was going to be the best short stop in
America, according to Dad. Always the emphasis was on training and practice,
always aiming high. What a wonderful way to develop a young mind!

My schooling in America was very good. My scholastic ability was recorded
on a regular monthly report card, as was the practice in schools at that time. I
regularly had marks ranging from 82% to 100% in numerous subjects, History and Spelling being my highest grades. I still have my last report card. My

ability at school had made me aware of the High School system (14-18 years). These four years prepared young people for colleges, such as Yale and Harvard, which were equal in status to Oxford and Cambridge in England. There were, of course, other colleges, but, to youngsters in Connecticut, Yale was the dream.

I learned that the method for accepting students was to select those with high academic ability for the top places and those with lower qualifications were accepted for lesser subjects. Sports scholarships could be gained by those with high sporting ability but lesser grades. Even perfect attendance for four years in High School despite lower academic performance would get a very keen person into the hallowed halls of Yale. I began to think how with luck, encouragement and dedication I could possibly make it in some way. My eldest sister was already in Warren Harding High School (WHHS), the school for 14-18 year olds, similar to the grammar school in England. She was in the sophomore year, the second year, and doing well. She could well have inspired me if fate had not reared its ugly head – more of this later.

With the thought of eventually going to WHHS, I was a regular visitor to any part of the High School that I could gain access to. As it happened, the easiest place to get in was the sports field at any time throughout the year. There were continual practice sessions for athletics, track and field and baseball coaching. American gridiron received intense coaching because of the success of WHHS in this sport. Indoors, the gymnasium was in constant use, training basketball players to a very high standard. The swimming pool had numerous coaches. It was in this era that the famous 'Tarzan' films were first shown, and Johnny Weissmuller showed the very fast crawl stroke now called 'freestyle'. The coaches were trying to find youngsters with the ability to adapt to this new craze.

Little did I realise at my young age how all this witnessing of young people being educated in sports development would influence my thinking in future years. I look back now on this wonderful American way of life, the implanting of dreams, hopes, ambitions, pride, patriotism. The happiness that evolved from being encouraged by parents, and the pleasure of knowing that so long as you worked hard at whatever interested you and had some modicum of success, then you were assured of every bit of help you needed.

My memories of twelve years in Bridgeport include very seasonal weather. A true spring and Easter were very memorable occasions. Americans love special times of the year. Summers were regularly hot with blue skies. There were visits to the Pleasure Beach and Seaside Park and Sunday picnics out in the country in a Model T Ford, later a Nash. We had family days with friends at lovely freshwater swimming pools. Some days I went with Dad to watch the Bridgeport Baseball Team at Newfield Park, enjoying pop corn, Cokes and Mars Bars, rooting for the local boys. Then in my last two years, ten and eleven years old, the introduction to golf, where I became a registered 'B' class caddy, No 75B. At this stage I was carrying small cloth bags with Brassie, Spoon, Mashie, Mashie-Niblick, Jigger, and Putter for long handicap players. They were using Kro Flite, Spalding and Top Flite balls, some with square mesh, some dimpled, elastic wound, with a little black ball of white fluid in the centre.

During the summer this meant getting up at 5.30am, having breakfast or taking thick bacon and egg sandwiches to eat at the course. Then there was a journey on a 'Jitney' bus to the terminus at the city boundary and a walk of some one and a half to two miles, unless a farm truck came by. Then at Wheelwright Municipal Course I would sign on about 7.00am. Others were already there. When play started the Caddy Master would ring a bell for the number of caddies required. The Club House was some distance from the woods where we played while waiting for our turn. A certain ring would indicate if 'A' or 'B' class caddies were required. The fees for 'B' class caddies were 45 cents (about 2 shillings) for nine holes, 50 cents if you were good or the player had scored well, and 75 cents for eighteen holes, or even a dollar (about 5 shillings). Some days you would get one call. Other days there might be a second call late, which meant getting home around 7.00pm. Spare time was spent running around a beautiful wooded area or swimming in a natural rock pool of cold, clear water, utter bliss.

Autumn in America is something very special, particularly in the New England states, the Eastern Seaboard. The fall, as it is better known in America, is when all the tremendous wooded areas would offer a sea of colour, oranges, reds, yellows, browns and greens. Huge maple leaves would cover the ground, providing a fascinating carpet of colour, soft to walk on and eventually rotting away as the winter snows pushed them tightly into the ground to feed the soil with the best nutriment known to man.

For youngsters, winter's happiest times were sledding, skiing, snowballing and building snowmen. Snow was guaranteed every year, and very fast, light sleds such as the 'Flexible Flier' were a beautiful creation to own. After climbing a steep hill you would belly flop onto a wooden slatted top with polished 'T' shaped runners. The design allowed the runners to be moved in the direction you wanted to travel. Some of these thrilling moments took place by moonlight with a very enthusiastic father, who enjoyed his children's happiness. All this took place in the wonderful Beardsley Park.

Bridgeport had the name of the Park City. It is rather strange that my life in England since 1932 has been spent in the City of Birmingham, and this fine city is the home of perhaps more parks and open spaces than any other major city in England, also its tree population is second to none. But to get to Birmingham was certainly never even a dream, never mind an ambition. My life in America was full of interest, happiness and promise. I was, even at the tender age of twelve, quite sure what I wanted in this wonderful country in which I had been born.

I have forgotten to mention that when I was eight years of age, or thereabouts, a brother was brought into the world for me. I was given the responsibility of giving him a name. At that time there was a cult hero named Bobby Shafto, so my new brother was, and still is, Bobby, although christened Robert Frederick Godwin. Bobby was born in 1928. This was when Prohibition was brought in and the making and selling of alcholic drinks was banned. There have been many films made about this era, with the FBI clashing with Al Capone and

Brother Bobbie in
Jackie Coogan outfit

his feared henchmen, the gangsters. Speakeasies (illegal drinking premises) as they were called mushroomed the length and breadth of the country. Dad had always been a drinking man. In one visit to New York he visited one of these premises and met Dutch Schultz, one of Capone's top men.

As a young lad I witnessed my Mom and Dad making their own beer and porter stout, which I believed was allowed. The purchase of the ingredients was done in local shops, or stores as they are known in the USA. As kids my two sisters and I were encouraged to assist in the beer making and bottling. The brew was made in a large ten gallon glazed crock container. To bottle it meant that a rubber tube had to be pushed into the mix and the other end placed in your mouth and sucked until the beer came through. The end of the tube then had to be pinched while it was inserted into numerous bottles, filling each of them in turn. The two who were not filling the bottles had the job of putting the metal

Opposite: Passport
photo of family
leaving for England

caps on and then pulling the lever of the capping machine to ensure they were firmly fixed. Finally, labels with the name of the beer or stout were added and the date of bottling.

This I felt sure was all legal and above board and allowed for personal use. However, the next experience was to see what is called a still, a copper vessel with a conical top. This could be removed to put in some other ingredients which would become whisky. From the top a lead pipe ran down to a galvanised bucket, or pail in US terms. The pipe coiled around the inner surface of the pail and came out at the base. In operation a clear liquid created from heating and then condensing the ingredients would drip from the pipe for hours, finally filling a one gallon glass bottle with pure, neat alcohol.

It was definitely illegal but filling a need. To colour the alcohol to the golden hue by which whisky is known, Dad would heat a metal ladle filled with sugar until it turned brown and melted and then pour it into the container and shake it until the colour was right. Then it was my turn to become involved with my hand built scooter, an orange box nailed to a three foot plank, three inches wide and two inches deep with roller skate wheels nailed to the bottom. I was told to deliver some of the potent liquid to some of Dad's Italian friends, who would, in turn, send some bottles of homemade wine and grapes, always plentiful in season.

How I became a sportsman with this upbringing I will never know.

The terrible tragedy that awaited the world was the failure of the American economy and the banking world. During 1932 my father, rightly or wrongly, made a decision after seeing some children searching for food in a garbage can while on his way to work one morning. His decision was, that as a patriotic Englishman who refused to swear an oath against the King to obtain American citizenship, he would return to England, the place of his birth and infant nurture.

I expect, in retrospect, that it was quite a shock to his young family of four, but went unnoticed because Dad and Mom had obviously discussed the matter and agreed on a plan of action. We were told that we were sailing from New York to Liverpool on November 25th 1932 and due to arrive on December 5th 1932. Our ship was the SS Laconia, a Cunard liner. At that time all of their ships had names ending in 'ia'. I understood that it was a sister ship to the Mauritania and weighed 35,000 tons.

There was obviously a lot of excitement about the whole thing. Crossing the Atlantic was a thing youngsters thought about but rarely in those days experienced. The journey was full of surprises and when the weather turned bad and the seas were rough after only two days I was told by Dad that I might be sick Certainly all the ladies would be sick. However, he assured me that it was good to be seasick and it would clear out the system and I would soon recover. He was right on all counts and after one day I was over the worst. He encouraged me to eat my meals, get the sea air and I would soon be well. Mother had a terrible time and spent most of the journey in the cabin.

CHAPTER 2

1932

Getting used to the English way of life

Our arrival in Liverpool, after stopping at Galway and one other Irish port, was quite exciting and fun. We got out of Customs, found Uncle Tom waiting for us. He was my father's brother and had lived in the USA for some time and was very well liked by Charlie's brood because of his generosity and kindness. Uncle Tom had returned to England sometime earlier, as had Uncle George, another brother. Uncle George had served in the Marines and been to Rio de Janeiro and he would hold me fascinated for hours with stories of his life, the places he had been and the people he had met.

We travelled from the docks to the railway station in an English taxi cab. The black cab was quaint, with its little oval rear window through which I looked. I saw my first English 'Bobby', with a helmet which had a spike on it. I looked longingly back until he disappeared in the distance. I remember shouting and getting very excited. Of course, I had read of policemen and my father had told me stories of them and how tough they were. When he was a young man he was a member of one of the local gangs who used to go looking for fights with other gangs down at the 'Ten Arches' on Lichfield Road, Aston. Dad had scars from his fights where knuckle dusters were used. The tough Bobbies always walked in twos, and woe betide any young man who got caught. Dad always said that everyone had great respect for the police of that period. One tip Dad gave me was to carry a kid glove with me, a size too small, and if a fight was in sight to pull the glove on and make a fist as tight and firm as possible. Then get the first one in if you could, preferably to the solar plexus, and when the opponent doubled up to follow up with one on the button.

My Dad for as long as I can remember was a wonderful story teller. He always advised me to treat other people with respect, courtesy, kindness and helpfulness. However, if anyone set out for a confrontation, then I was taught how to handle myself, as 'The Old Man' used to say. So far as respect and courtesy were concerned, I had been treated at the age of about four or five to a Jackie Coogan outfit: knicker-bocker pants, a Norfolk jacket and a big baggy cap. I was told on Easter Sunday to stand on the sidewalk and as the ladies came past on their way home from church to tip my hat and say, "Good morning, Ma'am."

My father was always telling me, "Don't do as I do, do as I say." He knew his own upbringing was not ideal, and he himself had a life which included drinking, smoking and gambling. He wanted his son and future sportsman to learn from his mistakes. Another bit of advice was, "Listen to anyone and everyone, even a drunken man, because even he may say something sensible at times. Pick out what you want from conversation and forget the rest." He also used to say that book learning is good but the best education is travel because you learn so much from other people's lives. I expect he believed in being street wise, he was all of that, and now, recalling my life with him, I realize how capable he was in fending for himself and his family.

Our early years in England, particularly the first year, were degrading. The first house we visited was a terrace house, the home of my mother's parents, my maternal grandparents, Grandma and Grandpa Evans, 32 Chester Street, Aston, close to Rudder and Paynes wood yard. This was a tiny little house, with gas lighting, open fire with black leaded grate, a fender and a companion set, a small kitchen with just a gas stove and sink and the toilet up the yard. As a young boy, I know, I was almost ashamed to be there, remembering the beautiful home we had left in America. We had had a Hoover vacuum cleaner, electric light, central heating of a kind fed by a huge furnace in the cellar, and a Nash family car.

But what I remember vividly on entering Grandma's home was a black and white picture, a pencil drawing of two massive shire horses, which met you head on as you stepped into the tiny house from the blue brindle pavement. On showing an interest I was informed that my Grandad was responsible for the work of art, as I considered it. Apparently Grandad was in the printing trade and was good with his hands. I was introduced to my uncles Ernie, Fred and Bill, the last named lying on a sofa looking very gaunt and ill, the room full of smoke. He was in an advanced stage of consumption, as it was known then, but still continued to smoke BDV, Club or Woodbine cigarettes.

I found out very soon that I was going to live with Uncle Ern and Auntie Beat at No 11 Hubert Street, just around the corner. How we managed to live with two families in such small houses I will never know. My brother Bob went to live with Uncle Tom in Colebath Road, Billesley. I used to go and visit him on Sundays. That was good fun because Uncle Tom had a little shop and sold sweets. We always went back to No 11 with a good supply.

Life with Uncle Ern was very humble, but he and Aunt Beat were nice, inoffensive people. Uncle worked hard, had fishing as a hobby and did little else in life. The rear of the house opened onto a large brick yard, as did the other four houses. There was a communal brew house for ladies to do their washing, with a maiding tub, a dolly, a boiler and a mangle and the necessary scrubbing board. Also in the yard were four outside toilets, with ripped up newspaper hanging on a string. Everyone in the yard was very friendly and one man, George Davies, was to play a big part in the Godwin family as the years rolled on. He was the street bookie. Betting in those days was not legal, so betting slips were taken by a runner to the bookie. A lookout was posted at the entry to warn if police were seen, whereupon everything immediately closed down.

To survive at this time in our lives my parents had to be interviewed for the then called 'Means Test'. This was for people who were destitute and in need of help. They were given very meagre rations of sugar, bread, margarine, and small amounts of money to buy meat etc, usually belly draft of pork, or as Dad called it 'Pig's waistcoat with buttons on,' and sausages. Clothing and boots were supplied by the *Birmingham Mail* Fund, if needed. Our clothes from America lasted for sometime, so we did not call on the fund. Breakfast would be a bowl of porridge, some toast and a cup of tea. The main meal would be the meat mentioned, mashed potatoes and some greens. Uncle Ern did have an allotment, from which we had vegetables. After school there was a big piece of cottage loaf with rosemary lard, salt and pepper, or whatever else was going and a big mug of cocoa every night at bedtime. One person was working, my oldest sister Renie, aged fifteen or sixteen years, earning 12/6d a week at the Hercules Cycle Co at Aston Cross, Birmingham.

One thing I remember so clearly was being introduced to my male cousins, and being told by my Dad that I was going to Villa Park to see Aston Villa play. My father had always been a Villa fan and followed their progress whilst in America through the sporting columns of the New York Herald Tribune. This pleased me immensely, as I was watching professional men in sport.

As time went on my mother was lucky in finding a job at the big department store Lewis's as a pastry cook, having told a white lie that she had been employed as such in America at D & M Reads. This lie was found out some nine to ten months on, as one of the bosses knew of the American store and had written for references to give my mother a better job, only to be told that they had never employed anyone of that name.

My father after much chasing after jobs finally got a start at the Austin Motor Co in the tool room. From memory, we were perhaps twelve to eighteen months before getting a house so that all the family were together. There had been a move from our first rooms. We then had to rely on relatives on Father's side in two different houses: three children with Uncle George and Aunt Nell, and Mom and Dad with Dad's sister and her family.

Of course, I and my second sister had to attend the local school soon after our arrival, the St Mary's Aston Brook Church of England School. The shock of seeing the school really upset me. It was so old, so bare, dark and in need of repair, but a typical church school of that period. I cried many times thinking of the modern school I had attended in America. I could not grasp arithmetic with coinage or weight, or the system of teaching. History was so archaic, going back centuries with kings, aristocracy, wars with different countries and empire building. Great Britain had then conquered one third of the known world. Pink was all over the globe and every atlas. I knew American history from 1776, and could have answered questions on every battle, every battlefield, all the generals, all the presidents, the Boston Tea Party and the Battle of Bunker's Hill. Certainly, I could name every state and every capital city. But this I had to put to the back of my mind and focus on the British way of life, and all it was to mean to me in the future.

Needless to say, there was teasing because of my accent and my dress. I had arrived with a Lindbergh coat with lambswool lining, an aviator's helmet and knickers, or as they were dubbed by the Brummie kids 'Diarrhoea Bags'. There was the try on very soon by the school bully, Frankie Piper, pushing and shoving, demanding respect, until I responded with some of Dad's well rehearsed punches, A scrap ensued which took us all around the playground until the headmaster spotted us, came out, ordered us into his room. He gave us a very firm warning and told us any further fighting would take place in a ring under Queensbury Rules.

I got the respect of a lot of boys, including Frankie, and I was soon accepted in the swimming bath, in games and in the playground, eventually getting into the soccer team and an occasional cricket game. If they sent down a full toss or a bouncer up above the knees, I hit the ball as if playing baseball. But I could not defend my wicket, as I held my bat up high. I made the swimming team because

I used the basic crawl stroke, whereas English boys used breast or side stroke.

Whilst I was at St Mary's we used to be taken to Aston Commercial School for Metalwork. I soon found a great enthusiasm for metal, making trivet stands, twisted pokers, beaten copper work, soldering and even making moulds to pour molten brass into. The resultant object would clean up into perhaps an iron stand, very ornate and highly polished. This and model making with a Mr Bowen were the highlights of my school days in this country. I knew I could not go on to further education as I had missed the exam stage, which meant I was destined to leave school at fourteen years of age and get any job I could.

CHAPTER 3

1934
Starting work, starting cycling

My first job was at a firm by the name of Powell and Hanmer, a subsidiary of the Lucas Company. Their head office and works were at Miller Street, Aston. The company I worked at was situated not far from Aston Cross and in close proximity to the then famed Hercules Cycle Company on Park Lane. I was signed up by my father for an apprenticeship in the tool room for some seven years, commencing with 10 shillings a week in my pay packet.

The job seemed to be what I might be good at. I wanted to work with my hands, learn skills on turning lathes, shaping machines, universal grinding machines and, most especially, bench work. But I was soon to find that I was expected to make tea, clean out swarf bins, sweep the workshop floor and carry out all the mundane jobs to assist the craftsmen in any possible way. I also found that if I stood and watched any of the skilled workers on any of the machines or at a workshop bench I was soon told to "Bugger off."

I would be called upon to pull the truck when some press tools were to be taken to the press shop. But when I hoped I was to be shown how to set up the press tools, I was again sent back to the workshop. Tiring of all this I told my father that I was not happy with the way I was being treated. He explained that he had signed me up for an apprenticeship and if I wanted to talk to the boss about it, I must go into the office and explain how I felt. This I did, saying that unless I could get some insight into my future as a tool room engineer, I wanted to leave. The boss simply said that if I was not happy then I could leave, which I did.

I tell this start to working life, and my disappointment, because I had felt that this was my future. However, the job I went to from this early upset did not please my father at all. I got myself a job in a grocer's shop, part of a chain of stores called Wrensons. It was made clear to me that I was to be basically an errand boy, taking orders out on a carrier bike. A that time I had never had a cycle of my own, even in America. I had only learned to ride an Elgin cycle, which my close friend Sammy Creter owned.

My sister, who had a job at the Hercules Cycle Company, soon acquired a half-drop handlebar ladies cycle from Halfords for about £3-19-6d, with 10/- down and 2/- a week on HP. I occasionally had a ride on this when she was not around. However, the carrier cycle experience, a very heavy machine with a large delivery basket over the front wheel, soon got me very strong in the legs and filled me with determination when I had to climb up some very hilly roads to deliver groceries to customers.

But it was during this time in my life that the cycle bug bit, for the simple reason that one of the Wrensons customers, a Mrs Alice Bolton, was married to Charlie Bolton and they were both very keen tandem riders. They regularly had cycling books, *Cycling* and I believe *The Cyclist. Cycling* was, of course, the one that carried the racing features, track racing and time trialling, which I avidly read and started my first scrap book of Six Day events, IOM racing, TDF etc. But the highlight was seeing pictures of Denis Horn, Fred Tickler, C B Helps etc, all at the Worlds, and, above all, Arie van Vliet and Toni Merkens, winners at the 1936 Games in Berlin. I was at that time fifteen and a half years of age and

Me on sister's
Hercules – occasional
ride

most impressionable. Arie van Vliet was the man who caught my eye. Little did
I know that destiny would see me becoming a good friend of the man many
years after.

During my period at Wrensons the company had their own sports meeting,
which included a carrier bike race as well as ordinary bike races. I did not own a
bicycle but a Mr Len Williams, the First Assistant at our shop, had a BSA sports
bike, which he would travel round on to get orders for the shop. I very cheekily
asked if I could borrow his bike, remove the brakes and put on a fixed wheel. To
my surprise he agreed. That bike had cost the princely sum of £4-19-6d.

I then had the dilemma of getting both cycles to the sports ground some
seven or eight miles away from my home. Fortunately, a school pal, Wally Shur-
rock, agreed to ride the carrier cycle whilst I got used to handling the fixed
wheel. I did not know about toe clips and straps and was riding ordinary shoes
on BSA quill pedals. On the way to the ground I told Wal that I was going to

Toni Merkens,
1936 Olympics
– inspiration

try to sprint on a downhill slope, and I would wait for him along the Stratford Road. I sprinted and thought I had done quite well but, being aware that I left Wal behind, I turned to look over my shoulder to see how far he was behind. At the same time I automatically went to freewheel. The result, of course, was that I went straight over the handlebars, ripping skin from my hands, arms and legs. Wal got to me, very concerned, but I was determined to carry on for the next two miles or so to the sports ground. Whereupon I went straight to the First Aid tent, was cleaned up and bandaged and told not to ride.

I decided against the carrier bike race but took place in the one lap handicap. I was given 20 yards start because of my age, lack of experience and being heavily bandaged. I won my heat, although all the other riders had much nicer bikes and toe clips and straps. In the final I went back to the scratch mark, where it seemed all the other riders were assembled, and put my bike on the line. But I was told I had to ride from 20 yards. My reasoning was that it was not fair for me to have a head start. After some minutes of argument the starter said, "Okay, if that's what you want." So off we went. I on my cheap BSA with no toe clips and straps, and I finished third. The prize was a 7/6d Smiths Sports Timer, which went on later to come become the stopwatch my Dad used as I got into the sport.

The sports meeting was on the August Bank Holiday Monday, and Mom and Dad had gone to Matlock in Derbyshire for a few days holiday. When they came

6 Cycling   FEBRUARY 26, 1936.

Is it necessary

TO STRESS THE OBVIOUS?

Make your own comparison, where else
would you get such a specification?

Where else such an array of attractive
variations allowed at the all inclusive price?

SUN "WASP" is unique.

Built by one of the pioneers of upright
design by THE Firm that makes the actual
fittings to ensure constructional perfection.

The Sun "Wasp" obviates the one trouble
of an upright head by fitting the bottom
head ball race with larger bearings—3/16".

You must get that Sun Catalogue — and draw
your own conclusions.

The Sun "Wasp"
£7·12·6
(or easy payments).

SUN
CYCLE & FITTINGS CO. LTD. ASTON BROOK ST. BIRMINGHAM 6

Sun Wasp from
Cycling 1935

back I couldn't get to Dad quick enough to tell him. He was pleased for me in his
way, but cycling was not the sport he wanted me to be in. Soon after this, seeing
my growing interest in cycling, Mr and Mrs Bolton told me about a Sun Wasp
cycle with single freewheel, cantilever brakes, Accles and Pollock forks and a
Terry saddle, which was available for 27/6d. I had bought my first bike. It had
flat Lauterwasser handlebars, long spongy grips and a Lucas Challis bell. The
finish was black and chrome.

I started riding around the Midlands and after some time met up with a lad
I knew at St Mary's Aston Bank School. His name was Jackie Young and he was
the proud owner of a Dawes Marathon Cycle, with a lovely light green finish,
531 frame, Hiduminium handlebars, stem and seat pin and a Brooks saddle
– the real McCoy. Some days we would go to Cannock and back, thirty-five
miles for the return trip. We went through Lichfield where I saw a quarter-mile
cinder track in a park on which we had a ride. On the way back we thought we
were racing cyclists.

One day Jack said some friends were going for a long tandem ride on a Sunday and would I like to go? We were to meet at Aston Cross at 6.30am, which we
did. Plenty of grub in the saddlebags, cape and sou'wester, and away we went. I
was still only fifteen and a half and would not be sixteen till November. The ride
took us through Bromsgrove, Malvern, Ross-on-Wye to Symonds Yat. I found
out later that it was sixty-seven miles. During the day we walked, lunched, went
out rowing on the River Wye and then it was time to return home. We came over
the Malverns, and, around British Camp, we had rain. But we sang songs and
merrily swooped down towards Worcester, getting back to Brum about 8.30pm,
very tired but happy to have done a hundred and thirty four miles in the day.

Just before the period I write about, in 1934, when I was a boy of thirteen, I

Hubert Opperman
riding for BSA

read of the wonderful feats of endurance by the Australian trio of Opperman, Millikin and Stuart. This combination broke nearly every place-to-place record in the book, both solo and tandem. They were equipped with and sponsored by BSA Cycles, and this connection was due to the Australian manufacturer of Malvern Star Cycles, on which he used the then famous BSA components. There were continual references to the BSA in my early days of enthusiasm, but little did I realize the significant part the BSA Company was to play in my future in the sport. It is also surprising how I would gain close contact with Hubert Opperman and his connections during my career.

But my reason for mentioning the Australian riders was because of their feats in 1934. The BSA cycle which Opperman used was put on display at a cycle shop very near to where I was living at the time. My pal Jack and I used to go regularly to look at this red and cream bicycle, fitted with a Cyclo three speed derailleur. There were photographs and record details very professionally presented by the BSA advertising department. I expect that there were dreams of becoming long distance cyclists to emulate these great men.

During 1936 I started to go on cycle touring holidays when possible, the only trouble being that as I was in a shop working, I had to comply with working Saturdays. This meant that at Easter and Whitsun I could not always join my pals. However, one Whitsun one of my pals, Billy Evans, suggested starting our ride at about 10.30pm, riding as far as we could into the night, finding somewhere to sleep for a few hours and than proceeding up into North Wales on the Sunday. We rode from Birmingham to just outside Shrewsbury and, whilst in the country with no other vehicles, we switched off our lights and went along by moonlight. In those days even in day time you could ride for miles going to Llangollen, Betws-y-Coed etc and rarely meet a car or motor cycle. In fact, it was a pleasure sometimes to hear a motor coming up behind you. You knew that there were other people in the world and, if you happened to be in trouble, you might get help.

A Whitsun break included Monday and Tuesday, so after our ride through the towns mentioned above we proceeded to Llanduduno, Conway, Aberystwyth and finally back home via Machynlleth, Rhayader, New Radnor, Monmouth, the Malverns and Worcester. It was absolute bliss in those days. We had been managing to camp overnight, using a small storage tent we had borrowed to keep our provisions and clothing in. The tent we had found was not big enough to sleep in. It was a matter of laying our capes on the ground, putting a blanket over us and sleeping under the stars. In the morning we usually found our blanket wet with dew. Our food, most of which we had carried from home, we prepared over a 'Woollies' methylated stove made of tin. We would buy bread fresh and make sandwiches, or have jam. I had been given a couple of tins of fruit by Mr Farren, the manager of the shop where I worked.

On the day we were riding to Aberystwyth my pal had crashed and was fairly cut and bleeding. We approached a farm and asked for help, and were turned away without sympathy. I then took Billy to a nearby stream, with lovely fresh water running down from the hills. It was crystal clear, a pleasure to drink and no pollution. I washed Billy down, using handkerchiefs and any other rags to cover his wounds. I made some tea, and we had the last few morsels of food I had brought with me and got down for a good sleep.

The next morning a cup of tea and a couple of crusts were all we had. I then agreed to carry all the camping gear, putting a bag on the handlebars and one on my back, and we would try to get home as best we could. Billy struggled as he was in pain. I pushed when I could. The day was scorchingly hot. We had three small sticks of Llandudno rock, which I kept breaking up and sharing out in small pieces. This made us thirsty, of course, so we used the streams and brooks and water pumps or taps, which we found in villages and towns. Billy kept saying we would have to beg for help, but I was adamant that my Dad had always told me never to resort to begging. We pushed on to Birmingham, the total distance being some hundred and thirty-five miles, which we managed to do.

On getting Billy home, I dropped all the bags etc as I had about two more miles to cover. When I got to my home I got through the door and collapsed, apparently delirious. My Dad gathered from my babbling what had happened several hours later when I came round. Mother wanted to feed me quickly and get liquids into me. Dad, on the other hand, realized that I must be treated very carefully. He started by giving me liquids by spoon and wetting my face and body. As I became more aware he fed me a little and gradually brought me back to some reasonable state. He asked me some details and then got me tucked up in bed. The next morning food and drink were much easier to take, and I had to relate the full story.

I began to realize that if I wanted to be interested in cycling I must have weekends off, which meant leaving Wrensons. This I did, but with great reluctance. The man I worked for, Mr Farren, had given me a new meaning to life and work. He was a kind man, but insisted on everyone working hard, being clean, tidy and pleasant to people, and accepting discipline and being organized. In addition to taking errands, he taught me the grocery trade as it was then, boning sides of bacon, boning and rolling hams, serving butter from huge blocks, cutting and showing cheeses to the best advantage. I had to weigh up all different kinds of food such as dried fruits, nuts, sugar, tea, peas, beans, lentils – everything done by hand on brass scales. Then the art of window display, which was a job of patience and cleanliness.

I had worked for Mr Farren for only about eighteen months and I was under sixteen when I left. Yet, he had asked permission of the Wrensons General Manager if he could promote me to First Assistant, a job not usually offered to under twenty-ones. He was, of course, refused, but he had so much confidence in me and my abilities. It would, of course, have been more difficult for me to give my notice had I been so promoted. However, when I explained to Mr Farren he said he realised my interest in cycling as he had seen my pals waiting for me from time to time. So we parted on good terms.

CHAPTER 4

1936

I join the BSA
Company and
start racing

My Father, showing great concern about my leaving jobs, said he would get me a job at the BSA Company, where he was now employed. He wanted me to learn a trade and he thought electrical engineering was suitable. On enquiry, he found a boy must be sixteen to be accepted. He was promised that they would give me a trial when I was sixteen. In the meantime, Dad arranged a job for me in Production 'C'. The 'C' meant 'Cycle Components', so I was soon working in a section that made all the very popular racing components such as fluted cranks, 5-pin 1"x 3/16th chain rings of all sizes and hubs made from solid steel drop forgings. It was all absolute precision work, with hand viewing of every component and the BSA piled arms stamped on every one. The insert cups pressed into the hubs were lapped with emery dust and oil on an electrical motor turning at 4,500 rpm. The finished item was like glass, and this was my first job. Through my career, all my bearings had loving care – as taught.

The BSA in those days supplied cycle parts to every corner of the world. They were the components of the day. Later in my career I found the value and respect of the name wherever I travelled. When people found that I worked at BSA they all asked how they could get what they required for their racing machines, and on many occasions I was able to help. My life at BSA from my fifteenth birthday until 1950 when I left was full of interest, opportunity and learning, developing skills and meeting many wonderful craftsmen. I enjoyed working 47 hours in a normal week.

Upon reaching the age of sixteen I was immediately taken to meet Mr Wallis, the senior man in control of the electricians. It was obvious that Mr Wallis had made enquiries about my attitude to work and timekeeping from his questions. He was a very firm man and, to all intents and purposes, did not want a too friendly relationship with the people in his employ. I was, however, taken on, but not before being told the consequences of any misdemeanors. I was put to work with a man called Jim Heath to learn the trade of an installation and maintenance electrician. It was a 5-year apprenticeship, but even on reaching the age of twenty-one, one was not given full salary but had one more year proving one's ability before being paid the full rate.

The work throughout the rest of the time I worked as an electrician was hard physically and dirty because of the different workshops we worked in. It was unhealthy by today's standards, working in chrome plating and polishing shops. One with acid and steam filling the air and the other with polishing dusts. Above all, it was hard having to work on ladders most of the time and on concrete floors. All of these I found later in life were not conducive to correct preparation for a sportsman. But, then, at that time I was not even into sport, only in my mind and wild dreams were there such thoughts.

I think at this point I should mention that well after my retirement from the sport of cycling, at which I had found much pleasure and some modicum of success, I was told by my father that before I commenced work as an electrician he had spoken to the boss. He had told him that he wanted me to have all the hard, rough, tough, dirty jobs he could find for me as he wanted me to become a complete man.

In the days I write of every job was carried out as a physical action with no power assisted tools. The cutting and screwing of conduit (steel tubing) was done by hand. The conduit ⅝", ¾", 1", 1 ¼" and 2" would be cut by hacksaw, and the threads cut by hand with stocks and dies. One person was needed for the smaller sizes, but it took two to cut 2" threads. On a big installation some four to five hours a day was spent on this work. If the conduit was to run along a brick or concrete wall, the holes for the wood plugs had to be formed with a Rawlplug tool and hammer, a very tedious and arduous task.

Some of the hardest work was when laying HT cables. The very heavy cables, 3" in diameter were covered in lead and asbestos, which had to be physically pulled through underground pipes. This would entail two to three men feeding the cable from the six foot high drums to the underground entry and three to four men pulling on a fish wire attached to the main cable, very much a tug-of-war activity. There was then the movement of transformers into the sub-stations from the nearest point of delivery from the suppliers, sometimes a

My Gameson bike –
Dad pushing off

half-mile distance along the internal road system of large factory.

The staff in the electrical department was quite large, from memory I would say around twelve Electricians, each with a mate, plus staff working in the shop, rewinding motors and other bench work. In addition to Mr Wallis, who was the boss, there was Fred Humphries, the Foreman or Charge Hand, and Charlie Davies, the contact man with the installation and maintenance men.

There was a complete new building under construction in the 1930's, so every electrical requirement was being newly installed. The work was immensely interesting, working from blueprints and getting everything in the proper place. Of course, getting to and from the BSA was all done on my 27/6d bike.

In 1937, when I was sixteen, I saw the notices of the BSA Works Sports, which was always held early in July. There were all types of sports events, athletics, cycling, tug-of-war, egg and spoon and sack races, all of which made wonderful fun for the employees. I entered the 1-lap and 4-lap handicap races and waited for the day to arrive. On getting to the track I saw all the other riders with very posh, colourful machines, all with fixed wheels, no brakes and very smart racing clothing. Most of the riders were members of the 'SELCYC' Racing Club. The title name was 'CYCLES' spelt backwards. I had my old Sun Wasp with 26" Endrick wheels and ordinary road tyres. All the other lads had sprints and tubulars, so I was told, and the sprint wheels were made of laminated maple wood. The tubulars were Dunlop No 8's with a heavy tread to suit grass track racing.

In my first ride I was held and pushed off. I went into the first bend but because of a low bracket and very wide pedals, I caught a pedal in the ground as I leaned over, which caused me to turn sharply and shoot up the middle of the track, out of the Race in about a hundred yards. In the 4-lap race I was more careful and carried on for the whole distance, leading all the way until the home straight only to be passed by a number of the real racing men. It turned out that these guys were being trained by one of the Smith brothers from Australia, who had come to work at the BSA. Harold was the one who was coaching these boys, and these Aussies were prospective Six Day men and were professionals. Later they were joined by Joe Buckley, who rode the pre-war Six Days here and on the Continent.

When I got home at night my father, who had been at the sports to watch the athletics mainly, pulled my leg about my mishap, but then said he was impressed by my determination in the 4-lap race. He remarked, "You enjoyed yourself today, didn't you?" I replied, "Yes." His reply was, "If you behave yourself and do everything I say, I will buy you a proper racing bike next year." He started to lay down a programme of exercises and my bedtime was fixed. When I had been out for a ride he would tell me to wash down and rub myself dry and he would then give me a leg massage, as he had seen trainers do in other sports. He would then get me to bed by 9.00pm, bring me a mug of cocoa and then he would sit and tell me of the sportsmen he had seen, athletes and cyclists as well as boxers.

I must have given him a lot of satisfaction from July 1937 to March 1938 because one Thursday night he said, "Meet me at the gates." Of course, Dad worked at the BSA, as I mentioned earlier. "On Friday night we are going to see about getting your new bike." One of the popular frame builders then was Bill Gameson. The other one was Joe Cook, with his Imperial Petrels, but his machines were quite costly compared with Gameson.

We were introduced to Bill Gameson by a gentleman who had suggested to my Dad that he was the man to build me a bike. After a lot of talking, measuring me sitting on a bike already built, it was decided that I should have a 22½" frame with 73/71 degrees head and seat angles (these were the popular angles then), fitted with a Toni Merkens stem, Anglo-Italian handlebars, very wide and deep, a Brooks Sprinter saddle, Williams C34 cranks with 3-pin fixing, 1" x ⅛" transmission, Webb pedals with toe clips and straps, maple wood sprints and No 7 Dunlop tubulars. These were a tandem tyre, with very large section, very heavy and with a heavy file tread. The total cost was £10-19-6d. Dad had to pay a £2-0-0d deposit and 10/- a month. A promise of delivery was made for about four weeks, so that meant April 1938.

When the letter came telling me the bike was ready and that Saturday was suitable day to call for it I was absolutely thrilled. However, in those days few families had any means of transport, and we certainly did not have a car. I told Dad that I would go straight from work. Finishing time was at 1.00pm. A pal of mine said he would like to come with me. We were both on bikes and the idea was that I would ride my bike and push the new one along by my side, whilst my pal would ride behind to keep off any traffic. In those days cars came along only occasionally but not bumper to bumper, so it seemed it would not be difficult trailling one bike while riding another.

All went well for about two miles of the journey, but on nearing the Saltley Gas Works, a landmark in Birmingham in those days, I had to ride up a little rise and drop down the other side. But this was over a cobbled section of road, much of the city still had long stretches of cobbles. I got to the top of the rise all right, but on the downside the new bike being quite light in weight and the tubulars well inflated started to bounce. I was holding it by the handlebars and stem. It got out of control, so I picked the front wheel up off the ground then the whole bike just as I got to a junction where I had to make a right turn. Fortunately, my pal, seeing me in trouble, slowed down, put his right hand out and slowed any vehicles down. On getting around the turn, I managed to stop, still protecting my bike from damage. After I had stopped I sat there trembling, thinking of what could have happened to the new machine and me had I lost control. The next part of the road was a steepish hill, which I walked up with two bikes, one in each hand. For the rest of the journey if I rode it was slowly and if in doubt I walked. The excitement had left me, I only wanted to get home safely.

My new toy was safely cosseted. The home we were living in at the time was a large flat over a business premises in Lozells road. In fact, there were two attic rooms, which my father and I had. One room was a bedroom and the other was for my use as a homemade gym, now to house my new silver and chrome Gameson track bike.

CHAPTER 5

1938

Keeping fit,
training hard
and learning the
racing game – I
join the 'Rovers'

I mention my room used as a gym. I used to get up there to do some bends and stretches and abdominal curls. All very basic, but I had started reading *Health and Efficiency* and other books about physique. I was now searching for ideas to improve the body. The first one I remember was to expand the chest. You had to get a stool, lie on it on your back and, using two heavy books or house bricks, raise your arms up and slowly lower, breathing in and allowing the hands to go below the chest level and build up on repeats. This I did, finally getting two heavy cloth bags, filling them partly with sand, then increasing the weight by adding more sand.

I was now on the way, with daily hard work, exercises to develop my body, regular bike riding on my old bike and special visits to the W W Alexander Sports Ground. This was the home of many great athletes, some of whom won Olympic and World Championship Medals etc. Around the black cinder running track was a red shale, slightly banked cycle track, a very large 503 yards per lap. Training nights were Tuesday and Thursday. Some of the real top men of the Birmingham and Midland Centre NCU who arrived at the track were Tommy Blick, Eric Thornton, Fred Pollington, Jack Harrison, Alec Tennant and Stan Edwards. There were many other riders just making up the number, but hoping to develop into good riders who might win an occasional prize at some of the numerous grass track meetings which were so popular in those days. From the NCU handbook one could look through the pages of sports meetings, finding sometimes four to six meetings on the same day within a thirty to forty mile radius of Birmingham.

There were so many riders in those days that each meeting would have eighty to ninety riders competing. The handicaps were open to all registered riders, usually two handicaps at each meeting There would be heats, cross heats (or semi-finals), then the final – three rides to win one race. Then an invitation scratch sprint for selected riders, again a cross heat and final. There would be distance races of 3-mile point-to-point, Devil-take-the-hindmost and the programme would end with a 5-mile or 10-mile for some twenty to thirty selected riders. To break the programme up the athletes would run 100 yards, 220 yards, 440 yards, 880 yards and 1-mile handicaps. The shorter events were again with heats, cross heats and finals. A meeting would go on for 3-3½ hours, with crowds of up to 10,000 attending. There was plenty of tea, sandwiches, buns etc and just a few of the betting boys, all unofficial, but vital to the enjoyment of the day. Bets of 2/- and half a crown were usual. Any hot tip might see a 10/- wager, sometimes even £1-0-0d.

Back to my training, neither I nor my Dad had any idea of gears to use, so I just went down on the bike as I had picked it up with 23T x 8T x 1" (46T x 16T x ½"), equal to a 77" gear. I found later that this was the most popular grass track gear. Dad made me trail my bike down to the track, about one mile away. He forbade me to ride it on the road. Getting on the track was scary. All of the names I mentioned were big, big, mature men with a lot of experience. One, Tom Blick, had been Five-Mile National Grass Champion in 1936, and had been in the final trials for the Olympics of 1936, only to miss out on final selection.

Gradually getting in with some of the ordinary riders, I found myself enjoying the atmosphere. Week by week things got better. I could stand riding close and feeling other riders leaning on a bit, which didn't upset me. There would be line outs, then an occasional sprint. After a rest I would then watch the big boys going for sprints, being clocked for 220 yards. There was a steeplechase jump on the running track in the back straight, which seemed to be the point from where most sprints started, some 260 yards from home. The battles around the bend and then in the home straight were fascinating to me, and I found myself lifted by watching them and hoped one day to be somewhere nearly as good.

I was quite a loner then in my training and remained so through my whole career. But very early a man named Alec Tennant came to me. He too seemed a loner and said, "If I can be of any help, I would be very pleased to give you some advice." I told Dad and he talked to Alec, who was much older than me. They came to some agreement and I would ask for him whenever I went to the track. He advised me about gearing. I needed 22T x 7T (= 84" gear), which meant more money for chain ring and cog. Dad was quite happy to oblige. I went through all the training, but with only one meeting in mind, the BSA Works Sports in July. Dad would time Alec and me over the 220 yards. I would sometimes lead out and then Alec would take me. After a few weeks Dad was told by my trainer that I was going to be a good young rider. He told Dad of his vast experience, how he knew the ability of the big men we had been watching, and I felt I would soon be matching them. I found out just how wily this man was later in my life. He was a registered rider, but, with some other good riders from around the country, he would go to unregistered meetings and ride under an assumed name and be paid in cash.

I was very dedicated in preparing for the big day in July and entered all events, a 1-lap handicap, a 4-lap handicap, plus a Devil-take-the-hindmost. I won both the handicaps and was third in the Devil. The experienced riders from the previous year did not even know I had a new bike. I am sure it was quite a surprise for them to see this tall, slim, young lad riding so well. As a result they became very friendly and I enjoyed meeting them at work and chatting about cycling.

I did not ride in any open events that year, but I was still keen about my body being fit and cared for. I read where the famous boxer of that period, Len Harvey, said posture was of great importance. He advised never to slouch, even sitting in a chair. By pushing the small of the back into the chair, a straight back dining chair, and preferably sitting upright, one should never feel any discomfort. Another boxer, Marcel Cerdan from France, in an article about food and eating said clearly, chew your food well, break the food down to minute particles to assist digestion and chew up to thirty times to masticate the food. Don't drink while eating as it reduces the digestive juices.

It was about this time in my life that a rather unexpected offer was made to me. My father had obviously been talking amongst his drinking and gambling friends about how good he thought his offspring was going to fare in the future as a racing cyclist. One day he came to me and said that George Davies (he being the illegal book maker I mentioned earlier) had offered to give me 30/- a week to allow me not to work but to train for my future as a racing cyclist and buy any equipment I needed. It has to be borne in mind that I was only seventeen years old and had only raced in the BSA Works Sports. My reply, much to my father's disgust, was, "I don't want a bookmaker's money." I was quite happy to work for my living, as all young people of that day were expected to do. Thinking back, I wonder just how much more I would have developed and how much more successful I would have been if I had taken the offer. But fate was to prove my decision was a wise one, as the year 1939 would prove.

The rest of 1938 was almost insignificant, other than continued training and looking after myself. However, in September I was riding around one Saturday when I was approached by another cyclist. He said, "Hi ya, kid. Haven't I seen you down at the track?" I replied, "Well, I do go down to train." He then asked if I was a member of a club. My reply was, "No, I'm not." He then started talking to me about the Rover Racing Cyclists Club, of which I had heard, and how it had started in 1908. Their riders had been famous in that year for their success in the Olympics, Vic L Johnson in particular, who had won the sprint. Vic Johnson, Albert Denny, Denis Hodgetts, Ernie Payne and many others used to race at the Aston Lower Grounds on a quarter-mile cement track, now the home of the famous Aston Villa Football Club.

The man who approached me was George Moul, a very useful rider, very strong physically, and very down to earth. He suggested that I go out one Sunday with the Rover boys, but he looked at my old bike and said it would be no good coming out on that. He stated very clearly that all the club came out on their track machines. My reply was that Dad would never allow that. He asked if he could meet Dad to have a chat. The outcome was that the 'Old Man' agreed, but with reservations. He was told that I would not need a brake on the bike as no-one used brakes but just relied on the fixed wheel!

In those days when you went out, some thirty-strong in number, all were on fixed 77" gear with no brakes and rode some fifty miles on a Sunday. A stop for lunch was made at Ma Copley's in Warwick, opposite the Seven Stars pub. Then there was a further ride, going to Aston Cantlow or Fillongley for afternoon tea, with food for 1/- a head, fruit tea 6d extra. There was always a fast line out and a sprint to the tea rooms. Between lunch and tea, riding through the lanes, the big men would tell us to release our straps to get our feet out quickly. Then a session of wheel rubbing in the bunch, senior riders leaning on us trying to ditch us, cutting across front wheels, all to teach us good bike handling.

A good young lad as a time triallist, unusual for the Rover as they were basically a trackman's club, was Wal Hobday, a rider who would have been the Midlands George Fleming if he had not gone into the RAF in the war and been killed on duty as a bomber pilot. Later, there was a trophy in his name for a 25-mile TT, and many illustrious names figured on the winner's list. Wal and I would ride at the front of the Rover Sunday rides for long periods. Some riders would get quite annoyed at the pace we set.

The winter of 1938 was filled with regular riding to and from work, Saturday and Sunday runs, and evenings spent trying to improve my physique. My methods were by regular exercises, evening walks and runs, good food, plenty of sleep and reading books about other sports, trying to learn all the time. Early in the spring the rides with the club and many solo rides got me in good shape. I was then told that there was a club 10-mile time trial on a Sunday morning at 6.30am at Stonebridge, a well-known spot at that time, and we would be changing at The Malt Shovel, a very popular hostelry even now.

I was told I must have black tights, a black alpaca jacket and a dark racing vest. These items I obtained from a local well-equipped cycle shop, Barts of Six Ways, for the princely sum of 27/6d. I also had to have a bike with a brake on, so out came the old Sun Wasp with 26" Endricks, two cantilever brakes, a Lucas Challis bell and a Terry saddle. At the dressing room I saw all new, clean bikes with wood sprints and tubulars. One front brake was sufficient. I hid my old bike out of the way and then went to the start, hiding my bike behind a bush until finally my number was called. It was my first meeting with the very senior, stern officials, timekeepers, recorders and pushers off, all of whom you referred to as 'Mister'.

I got to the line and they looked at my bike. One said, "Name?" I replied, "Tommy Godwin." They all burst out laughing when one of them said, "Well, don't think you are going for the world endurance record." This was the period when Tommy E Godwin of the Potteries was on his record ride, which was finally 100,000 miles in 500 days. I was completely put out by this remark, and as soon as I was released shot down the road as fast as I could to get out of sight. As I rode out to the five mile turn I sensed someone behind me. It was the scratch man, Ernie Bushell. He had caught me by just one minute at the turn. As we turned in the road he immediately passed me without speaking. I panicked, feeling that everyone would catch me. I was riding a 74" gear, and I found later that all the big boys rode 84" on their best bikes.

I kept Ernie well in sight and once went past him. He at once told me I couldn't do that, and I must not take pace, so I dropped back but kept quite close and it was only the in the last quarter of a mile that he rode away from me as he knew the finish point. I crossed the line, eased down some 200 yards past, turned and then I saw Ernie bent over a ditch being physically sick. I asked him if he was all right. He came back with, "What's your handicap?" I said, "One and a half minutes," to which he said, "You've won the handicap, then." I replied, "How do you know? You were being sick in a ditch" He then informed me that he was the scratch man. On returning to the dressing room and everyone in, the officials called out first, second and third and then the handicap winner, T C Godwin. I was overjoyed, ran out and jumped on my old bike and raced fifteen miles home at a faster pace, I'm sure, than in the race. As I turned into the street we lived in I could see Dad in the distance, walking to see his gambling pals. I raced down behind him and as I approached him I began clanging the old Challis bell. I threw the bike into a broadside skid, shouting out that I'd won the handicap and a prize of 10/-.

A few weeks later, after my first club time trial, I was told that there was a track meeting at The Butts, Coventry on a Sunday morning. We all rode over to Coventry, from my home, about twenty-two miles. I was told to ride a gear of about 84", as the big men would be on 88". To go over, I simply used the big sprocket on the double-sided fixed hub that I had, then turned the wheel over for the small sprocket. I still only had one pair of wheels and one pair of tubulars, the heavy-treaded tandem racing pattern, now all smooth in the centre but file pattern on the sides. I used the same wheels for all the road riding. The events held were only Rover Club events. In the quarter-mile handicap, heats and final I finished second and won 7/6d. Next was the quarter-mile scratch heat and final. All the big boys were riding. I was third and won 5/-. Finally, a 3-mile handicap, in which I was given some 180 yards. I rode flat out all the way, was never caught, to win the event and 10/-, with a further 11/- for the lap prize. Later in the season I raced on a grass track at Tipton in a club event and won the 3-mile event, with a 10/- prize plus a medal.

From about May onwards I was riding in open grass track meetings around the Birmingham area. There were many such meetings as most big factories had open sports days. For my first event I had the regulation 42 yards in the quarter-mile handicap, 84 yards in the half-mile and 168 yards in the mile. Apparently I was doing very fast times in the heat and semi-final, but I was always under orders from Dad not to take a prize in the final. As a result, I only had one two yard lift on my handicap mark all season. He wanted me to gain some experience, and he felt I should have the ability to have a double in the handicaps because there was a 10% pull of the yardage of your mark whether you won one event or two on the same day. I was to find out much later in my life why I was being held back.

All of the racing I was doing was in preparation for July 1st. This was the date of the BSA Works Sports, another plan by Dad. He wanted another big day in front of all his work mates. The committee for the day decided on four cycle events: 1-lap scratch, two handicaps of 2 and 4-laps and a Devil-take-the-hindmost. On this occasion, with proper training and more experience, I made a clean sweep of all events. Prizes were a Grandmother clock, an electric standard lamp, a cut glass set on a tray and a gold wrist watch, a total of £10 in one day. Wages in those days were about £3 to £4 a week for an adult male.

All went well until the night of July 17th 1939 when a meeting which should have been held at Villa Park on the 15th was postponed due to rain. It was decided to run the meeting on the Monday at Alexandra Sports Stadium, a banked cinder track where I trained regularly. I rode two handicaps, got to both finals and finished fourth in both as ordered by 'The Boss'. A rider named Roland Rhead won both, having been told by my father that I was not trying. During the meeting Dad had been summoned to the officials, all very strict men. He was told in no uncertain fashion that he must let me win something soon as they had been watching me for some time. Records showed me doing the fastest times in many rides, yet never breaking my novice status. They warned him that unless he let me go my own way and win, I would be suspended for not trying. Dad assured them that I got very nervous in the finals, and that we did want to take some prizes home.

On the Wednesday on the same track in NCU Birmingham and Midland

Centre Track League, I beat the existing track record for the 1,000 metres time trial. On Saturday, July 22nd, once again on my home track, at the famous Waddilove Meeting open to all the top athletes as well as leading cyclists, I competed in 1-lap and 2-lap handicap heats, semi-finals and finals – six races in all and winning all of them. Then there was a 3-mile point to point and I won this event also. One prize was a Waltham Gold pocket watch. The other prizes were a gold wristwatch and a cut glass set. I exchanged these for a double Albert gold watch chain. I had the watch suitably engraved and presented it to my father, with the double chain.

CHAPTER 6

1939
Olympic Trial

However, more important was that during the meeting, after winning my first final, I was handed a note from one of the leading officials:

"YOU ARE INVITED TO COMPETE IN THE MIDLAND CENTRE OLYMPIC TRIALS NEXT SATURDAY JULY 29TH AT COVENTRY BUTTS STADIUM."

The vacancy on the shortlist of riders was due to a very useful local rider named Ralph Digges having to withdraw because his wedding was due to take place on the same day.

Needless to say, the excitement was so great for the next week, not only for me but for my father and the rest of the family. On Saturday July 29th I was told by Dad that we would be going to Coventry by train. I was not to ride the twenty-odd miles from home. Arriving at the track, I found that many other good riders were booked to ride in the 1,000 metres time trial, and I found my name down to ride the 3-mile point to point.

For the kilometre I was advised to ride an 88" gear, which seemed very difficult to get used to in the warm-up, and, of course, I was still riding the only wheels and tubulars I possessed, No 7 file tread tandem tyres. All the other riders had smooth bands, very narrow, and I saw them inflating tyres to very high pressures. I only had my ordinary bicycle pump. The ride for the kilometre was very hard, but I knew I had a track record from ten days previous. I was very fortunate to win with quite a slow time of 1.19, beating Ralph Dougherty by 1/5th of a second. Ralph was the first rider to beat the hour in a 25-mile TT. This he had achieved only two months earlier. In between he had won the Muratti Gold Cup "10" at Fallowfield, beating the famous Denis Horn, thus preventing Denis from winning the second Muratti Cup outright.

I was obviously very thrilled to win, as was my father. I then witnessed Dad in tears for the first time in my life. A man, hard and aggressive, seventeen stone in weight, crying because his young boy had won a gold medal in an Olympic Trial – part of a dream had come true.

Riding in the 3-mile points race was an anti-climax, But as I had won on the previous Saturday I gave it all I had and won in a time of 7 minutes 51 seconds with 27 points. The second placed rider got 14 points. There was a hallmarked silver trophy as the prize. So, one week after breaking my novice status I had a gold medal and a silver cup. Needless to say, our home that evening was one of great happiness. During the next week I received a letter from NCU HQ inviting me to Herne Hill on Sept 9th for Olympic Final Trials for the 1940 Games.

I knew that Reg Harris had qualified in Manchester and Dave Ricketts in London. Dave's ride had been a 1.15, and some of the London riders had assured me that me that on Herne Hill with good wheels and tubs, I could get down to 1-15. Reg and Dave had also already been selected with Bill Maxfield as representatives for GB in the World Track Championships to be held in Italy at the famous Vigorelli Track.

The August Bank Holiday was looming, and I had entered some four or five meetings, as most riders did, commencing on the Saturday, then Bank Holiday Monday, Tuesday, Wednesday and the following Saturday. On receipt of my programmes I found that I had a double pull (that is, a double reduction) in my handicap mark at all of the meetings. Dad agreed that we would go to the meetings, check with the officials and try to get the mark adjusted. At the first meeting there was a point blank refusal. On the Monday there was some sympathy, but I had filled in the forms wrongly and indicated that I had two separate handicap wins instead of a double win on one day. We agreed that if there were no adjustment there would be no handicap ride. That meant I only had the 5-mile event to ride, my first '5' on grass at Oakengates, the home of Ernie Clements. Riding the full distance and with one lap to go, I made an effort. Clements sensed it and, riding in front of me, he jumped and got to the first bend in the last lap. He then ran wide, taking me up to the crowd while other riders went through on the inside. I finally got past Clements, chased hard to get second place to a rider of my own club, Fred Goodall.

Sadly disappointed, I went to get changed and came out to see a miserable looking father. I asked, "Where's the prize?" His reply to me was, "I've given the 'bleeding' thing away. We want firsts only, not seconds and thirds." To be met with this at eighteen years of age, after winning so many events in the few weeks since my first prize ever in open events, was a bit hard to accept. I asked what the prize was. Dad said, "A tea service." He had given it to the wife of George Davies, his bookmaker, who had provided us with transport to the meeting. Fortunately Mr Davies's father-in-law, also a keen sportsman, asked me if he could buy me something for my bike. I immediately asked for a pair of new grass track tyres, Dunlop No 8's, which were duly supplied.

On the Tuesday we attended a grass track meeting at Stockingford. Again, there was no acceptance by officials to adjust my handicap mark. On the Wednesday a close friend who had a retail business and small van offered to take Dad and me to Abertillery in Monmouthshire where there was a quarter-mile cement track. Not the safest track in the world, but a new experience. Arriving at the meeting, we met with the officials, who were very sympathetic and understanding and they amended my handicap mark. I went on to win the half-mile and 1-mile handicap races. In the 1-mile final Dad spoke to Gerry Burgess, who was behind me at the start, asking him to return a favour from May, earlier in the year, when I should have been a danger to him in a final. Dad had assured him that I was not trying and would lead him out. Gerry won the double handicap races.

I was now going for my second double handicap win, and Dad wanted assurance that Gerry would not spoil our day. Gerry said he would have a word with 'THE BOSS', Lew Pond. On his return he told Dad that he would be going flat out to win, as he had already been second to me in the shorter event. Dad told him that I could still lick the pants off him. All this was unknown to me until later. I went after the front markers, caught and passed them in two laps, and got on with the job over the last two laps. Burgess had closed on me, apparently, but in the last lap my 'go all the way' wore him down and I won, with Gerry second. The prize was another Grandmother clock and a pair of pictures, with a total value of £10. I asked if I could change them both for a ladies gold watch and bracelet, which was agreed.

However, a surprise letter came to me only days later from 'THE BOSS', Lew Pond, in which he said he had made a complaint to the Birmingham and Midland Centre officials that I had ridden off a false mark and should be suspended. He also asked me to send the prizes on to the rightful winner, Gerry Burgess. I was called to a meeting with the local big men of the day. My pal, George Moul, came with me. I was asked to give my version of the matter, which after tense deliberation was accepted. I was cleared and could keep the prizes, but was severely reprimanded about my future conduct. My father's ideas were certainly getting me in some hot water. Pond was written to by the NCU Birmingham, telling him that he was out of order for the manner in which he had pursued the case. The watch came to me and I presented it to my Mother on August 26th, suitably engraved.

At this time I became aware of a meeting at Hugglescote, where the Five-Mile National Grass Championship was to be held on August 22nd. I wrote what was considered a 'cheeky' letter according to the Secretary. I had only two 3-mile consolation races and second in one 5-mile race, and I was only eighteen years of age. But to encourage a young lad, he informed me that I would be in the big event.

Came the day and there was a crowd of about 10,000, and all the top men riding: Denis Horn, Ralph Dougherty, George Newberry, the holder of the title, Benny Foster, Tom Blick, winner of the event in 1936, and so many more. Dad had told me to ride in the first four or five places and fight to hold my place. Ralph Dougherty set a terrific pace from the start, pounding away lap after lap. The full distance was twenty laps. The day was hot but the ground was very firm and fast. I held my position in spite of many efforts to get me out of the way. Benny Foster even came up to me and said, "Get out of the way, son." He was at this time the Leicester and Rutland five-mile champion. He kept elbowing and pushing until one lap I heard a crash and next time round I saw Benny being attended to. Someone had got fed up with him making a nuisance of himself and had put him down.

Many top riders pulled out under the pace and pressure, Denis Horn amongst them. It came to the last two laps and Dad shouted, "Up, son!" I immediately reacted and went to the front for two laps. As the bell rang I went as hard as I could into the first bend, then the back straight and final bend, still leading. With twenty yards to go a wheel came up and in the final few yards Bertie Hughes of Ireland came past, bringing George Newberry with him. Thus I came third, a bronze medal in my first National. I was told almost immediately by George that had Bertie not got by me no-one would. He himself certainly could not, but he came by following Hughes.

As I walked outside the crowd to the dressing room I heard a call, "Hey, kid!" I looked round and saw Denis Horn sitting on the top of a car. He beckoned me and when I went over he shook hands and asked me my age. I replied that I was eighteen. He immediately congratulated me on my ride and said, 'You'll win many championships in the future'. Praise from one of the greatest all round trackmen over the last fifteen years prior to that date. His record would stand scrutiny by any researcher.

With September 9th not very far away, I was brimming with confidence, having ordered some new wheels and tubulars. I was living in a very happy, excitable environment, with my family and work mates becoming aware of my success, and building hopes for a promising future. I was on top of the world. I was even stopped one day by someone I didn't know, but he had heard of me. He remarked, "I don't know how you do it at your age, working full-time here at the BSA and still doing 200 miles a day on average." The other Tommy Godwin was getting plenty of publicity at this time about his endurance ride – a case of mistaken identity.

CHAPTER 7

1944
Marriage in
wartime

But also at this time the Prime Minister was still trying to maintain the peace talks of 1939 with that horrible, wicked dictator, Adolf Hitler. A man who had in 1936 shamed the Olympic ideal in Berlin by refusing to acknowledge the famous black athlete Jesse Owens, and did not attend the stadium to witness his superb world beating ability. Now, in 1939, and approaching September, he had already violated international rules and agreements of non-aggression. So, on the day when the world was plunged into what was to become the second Great War, September 3rd, all hopes of peace were brought to an end and Great Britain was again at war with Germany.

All hopes of decent minded people, innocent of any wrong, were shattered. Everyone was made to fear the consequence of a decision in which the British government had had no choice. But to young people like myself, on the brink of adulthood, preparing for out futures in whatever field, the sad news was unbearable. I was at work at the BSA on the morning of the announcement. The firm had gradually been turned into a munitions factory since the 1938 talks in Munich. The government had played for time and some developments had been made towards re-armament.

But almost immediately the press released the news that all international sport would cease and that the 1940 Olympic Games were cancelled. The date at Herne Hill on September 9th would only become a memory. The hopes of young sports people throughout the world had been shattered. Of course, the immediate effect on three British racing cyclists, Reg Harris, Bill Maxfield and Dave Ricketts, was their immediate recall from Milan, which they had travelled out to some days before for the World Championships. They were advised to return by the British Embassy, but there was some thought of them choosing to stay at their own risk. The Championships were to continue, but good sense prevailed and they returned. Jan Derksen of Holland won the depleted Amateur Sprint title.

Disappointment was, to put it mildly, the outcome for our three representatives. Bill Maxfield was a mature, well proved all round trackman, hailing from Sheffield. Very unfortunately, he was to meet his death whilst serving in the RAF during the war. Maxfield was my idol, and in the November of 1939 I wrote to Cycling to ask if possible details of his physical build were available. These came through to me, and in my more mature years (twenty-one plus) my physique measured and coincided in almost every respect to that of Maxfield, something of which I became quite proud. One measurement only showed a quarter of an inch difference, that of the calf size. I was that small amount less. We were both 6' 0¼", 12 stone 7 pounds in weight, 39" chest normal, 3½" expansion, 32" waist, 22" thigh and 11/11¼" calf.

Reg Harris at this time had turned nineteen years of age in March. To be selected for world class competition must have been a terrific confidence booster, and some years after his selection had been justified. He had, of course, proved himself through the season as a budding star, although he had not reached the final of the Sprint Championship, an event where he had been expected to shine. Maxfield had retained the Sprint title. Dave Ricketts,

W. MAXFIELD

Bill Maxfield –
Maxfield was my idol

also only nineteen at the time, had shown wonderful form at Herne Hill, his home track, through the season. A young man full of London confidence, he appeared to be a swaggering extrovert. Yet, as I got to know him after the war, I found him a warm, genial friend. We were to form a very strong friendship, which remained until his death. Yes, the Olympic dream was now over, and the war had taken over as the major concern of my life. I had not yet reached my nineteenth birthday, that being November 5th.

I was, of course, two years into a 5-year apprenticeship in my job as an electrician at BSA. Young men were being called up for military duties. Many others went into jobs connected with the armaments industry, and, once in and qualified, remained in reserved occupations throughout the war. Many young sportsmen, not in reserved occupations, went into the armed forces, never to return to sport through death or because circumstances after the war did not allow them to return.

The sport of cycling did not stop completely during the war, and some organisers tried to keep both the track and time trial disciplines alive, if only on a local basis. Reg Harris even came to ride at Bournville, Cadbury's MC & AC meeting in May 1940. The report in *Cycling* read,

Reg Harris Shines at Bournville Meet

Reg Harris, who is awaiting call up as a dispatch rider, was the only rider to show peace time standards in winning the 500 yards event for the Brooks Bowl, not the usual trophy which has been put away for the duration of the war.

This meet in May, the third Saturday, was a fixed date. I came third in this event, as I had in the 440 yards handicap. But prior to this May meeting I had earlier in the year ridden my first 25-mile TT in the NCU Birmingham and Midland Centre Championship. A good field of local specialists took part, the winner being A Burman, Warwicks RC, with 1.3.25, followed by P Possart with 1.4.6, Wal Hobday with 1.4.6 and T Godwin with 1.4.42, but winner of the handicap with 3 minutes.

The Good Friday meeting in 1940 was held at Paddington. Herne Hill had been taken over as an anti-aircraft and balloon barrage site and was out of use. I entered, and this was my first visit to race in London. Harris and Maxfield, both unfit, raced a sprint series with Ricketts. Dave won all three matches easily. I had entered for the 5-mile points race for the BSA Gold Column. On arriving at the track, I found that there had been a selected number of riders named as starters in the race proper. But I had to ride a qualifying race, regardless of the bronze medal I had won in the 5-Mile National in 1939. I found it very difficult to accept the London attitude to provincial riders on this and many future occasions. I did qualify, but in doing so felt I needed a gear change for the main event. In making the change, somehow I tightened the cones in the rear wheel. I found the big event very hard, eventually finishing third to George Fleming. On stripping my machine down, I was horrified to find that I could not turn the spindle by hand. A very early lesson in taking more care when fitting up your equipment. The Gold Column was then not put up for competition again until 1945.

There was every effort made through 1940 to hang on to some semblance of an ordinary life. Meetings were held at Manchester, Brodsworth, and grass track meetings nearer home, but nothing of any great significance. Most meetings held were to raise money for the War Funds, to supply needs for troops serving overseas.

During 1940 the work intensity at the BSA increased tremendously. All workers on production were being pushed to human limits. Installation and Maintenance crews were needed to develop new areas for increased production and were working seven days a week. The German Luftwaffe was obviously locating the areas where munitions were being made and bombing of the Midlands was quite regular. Eventually the BSA became an important target. Raids on August 26th and November 19th and 22nd created havoc. November 19th was the raid that did the most damage, knocking out some of the most important plant producing weapons. In this very damaging raid two of the four electricians on the night shift became very involved with rescue operations for the hundreds of workers caught in the bombing. Alf Stevens crawled into a demolished building with acetelyne cutting torch, creating an opening for numerous workers to gain safety. He was awarded the George Medal for his wonderful work. Alf Goodwin, who had assisted throughout, was awarded the BEM.

During the November raids some 53 employees were killed and 89 injured, 30 seriously. After each of these raids all staff under the heading of Maintenance were pulled in to search for bodies, get areas cleared as soon as possible and get production back on line. Everyone felt the intense pressure of long hours and hard work. There was continual bombing of the Midlands city centres, particularly Birmingham and Coventry and any other known areas of munitions supplies.

To alleviate some of the pressure from the main works, subsidiary works were being developed to take production of the most important armaments. This meant going to areas up to twenty or thirty miles radius of Birmingham such as Bromsgrove, Dudley, Tipton, Kidderminster and Smethwick. Our job was to lay-on electricity to supply the machines. Some plant being moved over a weekend would require us to disconnect on Friday, move to a new site on Saturday, work through the rest of the weekend both day and night and have the

Don Dearson – my workmate at BSA

plant ready for production on Monday. The one good point was that, if I was able, I could ride to some of these units on my bike. When we were based at a project for a week and sometimes a month creating a whole new work plant I would be riding daily some thirty to forty miles. It was never less than eighteen to twenty miles, so I was keeping as fit as work, limited food and air raids would permit. Sometimes, of course, there would be air raids nightly, and through the hours of supposed rest I would be in a cellar or shelter.

Whilst working at one of the subsidiary units at Smethwick (Hopes Glass Co) I met a young lady who was to become my wife. This was in April 1942. I was surprised to find that she was not a Birmingham girl but her home was in Stourbridge, the then glassware centre of Great Britain. It turned out that she was actually directed to the BSA Main Works from an office job in Stourbridge. Labour could then be forced to move to munitions factories, or wherever needed for the war effort. Her job was in the Wages Office as a comptometer operator. When I invited her out to the pictures in Birmingham it appeared that she knew something about me from a young lady in the same office who I had taken out on odd occasions. As a young man I had no great interest in girls, as I only had thoughts about my future as a racing cyclist. But with a war on, no idea how long it would last and the possibility at any time that I would be called, my ideas changed.

Our first night out was at the pictures, followed by a walk around Birmingham City Centre, somewhere Eileen had never been. I was babbling all the time about my cycling and how it was and always would be my first love. Eileen did not expect to see me again.

We had finished our job at the works in Smethwick on the Friday before going out together on the Saturday.

My new job on the Monday was at Dudley Caves, where an underground works was being created under Dudley Zoo. The idea was that it would become an impregnable safe haven for a munitions factory. My work mate at the time was, Don Dearson, a professional footballer who played for Birmingham City FC. He had come into BSA as a qualified electrician, having served his time before signing pro forms. The idea of getting him into a munitions factory was to keep him from being called up for military service. It worked, but he was an excellent workman.

We had been to the planned site before to do some arranging of temporary lighting for the miners, who were blasting and enlarging the caves. During our earlier visits Don had become friendly with some girls in a confectionery shop, and, as a ladies man, could easily kid them into letting him have supplies of chocolate. I asked him to try to get me a box of chocolates, not easy as rationing was very much in force. However, he did get me a box, and on the Tuesday I raced from Dudley to Smethwick, some five or six miles, to catch Eileen as she went to catch her train home. She was surprised to see me, telling me that after my long talk about what cycling meant to me she thought that would be it, she would never see me again. But to me, and it turned out Eileen felt the same, it seemed that we were very compatible, and we soon developed a great feeling for

Me and Eileen at about the time we met

each other. Although in her home, especially when Grandmother knew, there was the inevitable warning about men from the big city.

I was then twenty-one years of age. I ended my apprenticeship in November 1942. There was, of course, bad news permeating through life about the war, men were still needed and I and another young man, Bill Bonner, went into the city to volunteer for the RAF. Our aim was to get into the air as pilots, observers or whatever we could. Bill, who had been through grammar school, passed with flying colours. I passed the medical A1, of course, but on going back to the works, we had to tell Mr Wallis, the boss, of our actions. He knew Bonner would get into aircrew, but he also knew that I would not get in because of my limited education. He therefore agreed to Bonner going but refused to release me, saying I was important to the Company and the munitions drive. He declared me as being in a reserved occupation, and this was accepted by the military authorities. Bill Bonner went on to serve his country and the cause admirably. He became a Pilot Officer and then Squadron Leader and was decorated with honours by the Polish government.

I still felt strongly about volunteering and went to join the Navy, thinking that as a tradesman I could perhaps become a Petty Officer. Again, Mr Wallis refused to release me. The war continued and there seemed no chance of peace for some considerable time. Even people left behind in their own country began to feel oppressed and morale was low. The idea of ever seeing sport back to its former glory seemed very remote.

Sometime in 1943 there was small grass track meeting to be held in Pontypridd. I entered and Dad and I went by train. On arrival we were well met and I was asked if I would ride in a 5-minute, six-station pursuit as one rider had informed the secretary that he would not be able to attend. I agreed and finished by catching all the other riders with eleven seconds to spare. It was reported as a spectacular ride, and I also won the 5-mile scratch.

But, on the journey home, Dad, feeling so good once again with his 'firsts' only policy, was in for a shock. I had previously asked Eileen and her parents if we could become engaged and it was agreed. I managed to get a nice ring from a work colleague who had friends in the jewellery trade. So, I felt I must tell my parents of our intention. I had proudly taken the ring with me. Telling Dad and producing the ring on a non-corridor train was perhaps not the best thing to do, especially as we were the only two in the compartment.

Dad had always told me not to think of marriage until at least twenty-nine years of age. Then he was confronted with this situation. I tried to explain how we felt, how there seemed to be no future for his and my great ambitions in the sport. There were no signs of the war ending and life becoming normal. On arriving home, the rest of the journey being spent in silence, my Mother, sister and brothers were told. One sister, Irene, worked at the Smethwick Factory where Eileen was in the Wages Office, and their relationship, to say the least, was very frosty. In fact, shortly after Eileen and I got into a continuing friendship, Irene had said, "I don't like you. You have taken my boyfriend away from me." As a young man my sister and I would sometimes go to a cinema together and on one occasion a friend had seen us and remarked to Irene, "I saw you with your boyfriend, but he does look young." I was, of course, three years younger. All of the family gave their opinions but Bob, eight years my junior, said, "I like Eileen." The family was not all that happy, but on Eileen's occasional visits all but Irene were kind enough not to show their feelings, though I had told Eileen of the reaction to our engagement.

We were allowed one week's holiday even in wartime, but there were not many places to go. Eileen and I announced we were going to Blackpool and, all the naughty minds got to work. On the morning, we were to go on holiday we met at New Street Station. On the platform we found my Mother and my youngest sister, some sixteen years younger. Mom said she was coming with us, and this quite amused us as there were no naughty thoughts in either of our minds. Eileen had been confirmed, had a very Victorian upbringing and would never consider any wrongdoing. We had separate rooms at the boarding house and enjoyed ourselves.

Our relationship was very strong and the wedding day was decided for September 23rd 1944. It would take place at Woolaston, Stourbridge, much to the dismay of the Godwin family.

The year of 1944 was rather surprising as sporting bodies, realizing that the war was continuing for longer than had been expected, started to consider that unless something was done there would be almost a complete shut down of sport. Football had created a League North Cup to replace the FA Cup. I cannot tell all the details of the competition but I know that the final was between Aston Villa and Blackpool on a home and away games basis, combined scores to count. Aston Villa won and of this I was to be the eventual victim. My father, totally obsessed with football and on very personal terms with most of the team, arranged a celebration party at our home. He arranged it for the Saturday night of June 10th, little realising that this was on the eve of the first RTTC National 25-Mile Time Trial Championship, scheduled to take place on a course in the Birmingham area. The promoting club was Solihull CC and the secretary was R J (Bob) Maitland.

At the time I had been riding numerous 25-mile TT's. In one, in a battle with George Fleming, I was beaten by 37 seconds, and I had been winning frequently against all the testers (time triallists) in the Midland area. I really fancied getting a medal, and I was almost confident I could win the event if all went well, particularly when I saw the start card. However, all the preparation both physical and mental came to nought on the night of June 10th. The house was filled with a gang of footballers and some of Dad's regular drinking pals. A piano was being bashed by Bob Iverson, a fantastic Villa man. Food had been laid on. Dad had obviously gone Black Market. There was turkey meat and an abundance of whatever it takes to satisfy about thirty men. I went to bed around 9.00 pm, with a promise from Dad that it would all be over around 10.30 pm. My bed was on the top floor in the attic, but the noise was unbearable, sleep impossible, and at about 2.00 am I looked down the stair and screamed, "Tell them to shut up and clear out." The recipient of my complaint went down and told Dad. He came up and we had a few words, me telling him in no uncertain manner that he had ruined my chance of winning.

Usually when I went out to a TT the 'Old Man' would get me up. I had only a small cereal, one round of toast and honey and half a cup of tea. Otherwise, I relied on my Sun Maid raisins and lump sugar with a few drops of peppermint essence just before the start to open up the breathing apparatus. On the morning I didn't even speak to him, just got on my bike to ride to the start some seven or eight miles from home.

The first man was off at 7.01. I was No 90 on the card, but still had not slept much, and was in a wicked mood on arrival. Dad had arranged for a pal to get him down to the start, and even then I refused to speak to them. I found to my dismay that three out of the five riders due to start in front of me had failed to turn up. My 5-minute man was Jack Wainwright of Walsall, who I regularly beat by one and a half minutes. I moved well for about twelve miles, pushing my worries to the back of my mind, and caught one rider. Then I knew there was no-one else to go for and sat up and was riding on the tops when Wainwright, coming the other way, shouted at me to get going. I made an attempt and finished quite well. The result was that Jack Simpson, a superb tester, won with 1.0.55, next A Palmer with 1.1.37 then Cyril Cartwright 1.1.39, Bell 1.2.3 and T Godwin 1.2.6.

I then realised that Dad had really ruined my day. I was pleased for Jack because he was a real Yorkshire lad, the salt of the earth. Jack went on to open a café with his wife, Iris, and in a frame hanging on the wall was the RTTC 25-Mile Championship Medal. It used to upset to see it because I would have been proud to have had it amongst my collection of medals.

So, even in wartime, we see sports organisations realising the need to keep alive the competitive world of sport. Next we found the NCU had agreed to put on a Grass Track Championship. The first National one was the 5-mile event to be held in Birmingham at the Fort Dunlop Sports Ground. On the day I managed to beat Lew Pond in the 500 yards scratch race. This was a feather in my cap as Lew was one of the best short distance men in the country. I went on to win the 5-mile by lapping the field. It seems that at the time I was riding so strongly that the riders would argue among themselves as to who would chase. In the meantime, I went happily on my way. So, after a third in the National '5' in 1939 and now had my first National title at the age of twenty-three. There were regular meetings now at Fallowfield, Brodsworth and Midland venues.

Although I was racing quite regularly, using my bike to and from work and remaining very fit, there was also the date of our wedding, September 23rd, to think of, and Eileen having to do what she could to make it a happy occasion. Near to the day, in fact on the August Bank Holiday Monday, a big meeting was booked at Lichfield, a tricky red cinder track with very little banking and 440 yards to the lap. There was a good entry with riders from London, Manchester and local riders. Lew Pond from the Poly won the quarter-mile handicap and Wilf Waters of South London RC was second. Very unfortunately there were a number of spills in the heats of the 1,000 Yards Coronation Cup, Pond, Jones and Waters suffering. I went on to win the final of the event.

The 5-mile was run at a very fast pace. I was the aggressor, but in the last lap I went flat out in the back straight and into the last bend. I was just entering the home straight when I hit a loose patch of cinders, lost control, hit the deck

Lichfield Sports –
August Bank Holiday
1944

and four other riders hit me. The winner was a rider well behind, who simply rode through the mess to win. Jack Harrison picked up his bike minus a wheel to get second. I picked up my bike, to take third, and went straight to the First Aid tent.

When I got to the Accident Hospital in Birmingham I was told that the wound on my left thigh was a mess and full of the red cinders. I was looked after well, but was in hospital until the early hours. It had been necessary to enlarge the wound to clean it well. With the job finished, I found I had twenty-six stitches and would not be racing again for some time. I was told to go back to hospital some eleven days after to have the switches removed. This I did. The wound was clean and healing well. My mind immediately started to work. Could I possibly go to Manchester on the Saturday where the

Quarter-Mile and 5-Mile Hard Track Titles were to be held? I prepared my bike and was going to sneak out on the Saturday morning to catch the train and go on my own without the 'Old Man' knowing.

Unfortunately, he sensed something was up because I was spending so much time in the attic. I had to leave the house for some reason. He went up and saw the bike all ready, with racing wheels on the wheel carriers and my bag with all my racing gear in it. He then asked my brother, Bob, "What's your big brother up to?" Bob told him, so that idea was lost. Dad called me all sorts of an idiot etc, for Reg Harris, Lew Pond and the Waters brothers were all booked to ride. Harris won both of the two titles, but admitted, as did Lew Pond, that the result of the '5' in particular could have been different as I had won the last twenty-one 5-mile races I had ridden.

With the wedding now only a few weeks away, I thought I would not be riding again that season. However, there was a local grass track meeting early in September for which I had entered. The big draw that day was the first visit to the Midlands of the superb athlete Arthur Went, who was to become one of the all time greats as a 400 metre runner. I knew Dad would go, but I rode to the meeting with my brother Bob. I had put all my racing kit on and put touring shorts and top on. At the meeting I told Bob to get ready to run on the track with my bike just as soon as the starter was about to get the field under way. I would run and jump onto it and ride the five miles, knowing full well that Dad would be upset and try to prevent me from riding. In fact, he attempted to grab me and pull me off the track, but I evaded him. Going the full distance, I felt good and got in a good position at the bell. The attack came early and I rode every one off but little Alan Bannister. He won and I came second. That night the 'Old Man' was mad, claiming I had stopped my run of twenty-one successive 5-mile wins, as the crash at Lichfield could not be considered.

The wedding day was due on Saturday 23rd September 1944. Dad was quite upset at me getting married, but I did go down to his local with him one night to have my customary once a week Guinness, "Good for the blood," according to 'The Boss'. That and sherry and raw egg once a week – how could I still be a virgin at twenty-four? At the pub one of Dad's pals, an athlete many years before, got me on one side to inform me secretly that marriage would finish me. His expression was, "Once you get on the nest it will be all over. You'll never be the same." I felt quite indignant that anyone would even think like that and I responded with, "Oh, we'll see." I told Eileen, my wife to be, and assured her that I would do everything possible to prove this man wrong.

Our wedding day was somewhat laughable, if such occasions were not so serious. Eileen had worked so hard to organise things, but with a war on, rationing, travel uncertain and many other complications it became almost impossible. Eileen was chasing around to get more food supplies to make sandwiches etc for the reception, which was in a hall over the local Co-op shop, and looking for whatever decorations could be found. On the eve of the wedding day, Charlie, the very outraged father, kept me up till 2.00 am, arguing with me and point blank refusing to attend the wedding, saying that we hadn't sent him an invitation. During our argument, in the early hours of the morning, my father lost his cool, called me a little rat, jumped up, white with temper and with fists clenched. I got up to meet him, reminding him that I was very strong and while he might get in one or two in the end there would only be one winner. He backed down.

On the day, my Mother attended, dressed all in black, with looks the same colour, while my sister insisted on being a bridesmaid. All part of a happy day. The marriage ceremony, fortunately, went well. I was pleased because Eileen was a church girl, had been confirmed and was still a believer. From good, old fashioned stock, one of three children, with a father who was truly of the Victorian era and a mother who was one of the nicest ladies a young man could wish to meet. Most of the ladies in both families had been 'in service', as it was known

Our wedding -
September 23, 1944

in the old days, working for various wealthy families in the Stourbridge, Hagley and Lye area – the Black Country, as it is known.

Our honeymoon was spent at Ross-on-Wye, the beautiful little town still visited for its quaintness and beauty. We had a train journey from Stourbridge and arrived about 9.30pm in pouring rain. It was a good walk from the station to the small hotel and we were soaked when we got there. There were no taxis. We were met by the lady of the hotel, who said, "Oh, the honeymoon couple? I've arranged a light supper for you." My reply was, as I told my pals later, "It's okay, we've brought some sandwiches." We were taken to our room and informed at the door, "This is the honeymoon suite." The lady left. I turned to Eileen, gave her a kiss, and then with my wicked sense of humour said, "Which bed are you going to sleep on?" There was a double and a single.

We were quite young, both twenty-three, very much in love, yet haunted by the opposition from my family. Our few days together were quite wonderful, but overshadowed by the war. The period in question was the terrible Battle of Arnhem.

To add to the trauma, one of the guests staying at the hotel was a young widow who had recently lost her husband. She was accompanied by her mother. The sadness affected others staying there at the time and the staff.

On our return to Birmingham, we were due to start our married lives in rooms. We had been fortunate in getting them through a friend. The occupants of the house were a Reverend Dann and his housekeeper, a ravishing, youngish, auburn haired beauty. It was a three bedroomed semi, and the Reverend's son slept in the small bedroom. The obvious explanation was a great shock to Eileen.

On our first visit to my home we found that the Godwin family had arranged a second reception after the wedding, with all the food, drink etc that the Black Market could provide. Dad was never without connections to the 'betting boys', illegal bookmakers, who could get whatever money could buy. No-one was invited from the Jones family (Eileen's family, that is), just Charlie's pals and the friends of the Godwin family.

My winter of 1944-45 was as arduous as any. I was working hard, with plenty of walking, running and ice skating, at which I was very good in the speed skating session. I was still cycling to and from work and there were shortish runs on Saturdays and Sundays until late February or early March. Then the distance and intensity were stepped up, with weight being checked and noted. Normally 5-6lbs increase was allowed over the winter, which had to be removed by March.

CHAPTER 8

1945
Getting back
to normal
– international
call-up

Many decisions had been made by sporting bodies. National Championships were again back on the agenda. Regular track meets, time trials and circuit races were organised. It was feared that sport would go into a decline unless organised events increased. The Good Friday Meeting at Herne Hill was back, and I wanted to go to this. The 5-mile point to point for the BSA Gold Column was my ambition. I was to meet the London boys on their own 'muck heap', and I wanted to show them that there were good 'bikies' north of Watford. I also had a point to prove to my father's friend who had said married life would ruin me.

I had been doing plenty of quality road miles as well as to The Butts at Coventry for track work and was pleased with my preparation. The headline in *Cycling* said:

GODWIN AND FLEMING SHARE HONOURS AT HERNE HILL

The report of the Good Friday event went on to say:

The re-opening of Herne Hill drew some 5,000 spectators and saw some fine riding on the newly re-surfaced track. Oustanding was the riding of Tommy Godwin, Rover RCC, who won the BSA Gold Column 5-mile point to point handsomely from George Fleming, Godwin 21 points, R Waters 15 points. Godwin was also second in the 550 yard invitation sprint to Lew Pond, last 220 yards in 12 3/5th seconds. Pond won by half a length.

The report in *The Bicycle* added:

It should be remembered that Godwin's only training is on the road. If he could have more experience on banked tracks such as Herne Hill, the fastest in the country, he would probably carry all before him.

1945 was a tonic for everyone. The war ended, and the effects of five and a half years of people's lives being controlled and threatened had now come to a conclusion. There was sheer joy in realising that the world could look into

Winning the BSA Gold Column for the first time – 1945

Receiving the BSA
Gold Column from the
President of the SCCU

the future with hope and peace. But for those who lived through that period,
the tragedies that war brings could never be forgotten. People realised that the
recovery would be a long and costly process. The effect on normal life continued while industry got back to making their own products to fill the needs of
various countries. Rationing had to go on for a number of years on food, clothing, furniture, petrol and many other commodities.

But in the sporting world things took off very quickly. Promoters realised
that the public needed something to erase the memories of the last five and a
half years. The pre-war sports associations soon got the ball rolling with all the
known sports of that period. Joint cycling and athletic meetings were quite regular features, held mainly on grass tracks. The response was quite unbelievable.
Athletes and cyclists soon got back into competition and huge crowds, often
8,000-10,000 spectators, turned out to see all the competitors using the same
arena. The runners with their 1"-long spikes tore up the turf and the cyclists
caused furrows in the ground when the track was wet. Prizes were always in
kind, with no money prizes. It was true amateurism, with clocks or canteens of
cutlery, pewter tea services and all sorts of merchandise on show, with tickets
saying for which event the prizes could be won. It was quite fun to see a prize
you fancied and then winning the event.

They were happy days, with refreshment tents for the public and marquees
for the competitors to change in, with baths or buckets of water to wash in.
Many meetings were run as works sports days on recreation grounds owned by
the companies. Others were run in conjunction with gymkhanas, dog shows
and flower shows. Prizes were usually £10, £5 and £3 in the top scratch races
and £4, £3 and £2 in the secondary events. If prizes were not suitable, some
promoters would allow you to go to a store of their recommendation and get a
prize to an agreed value. Cost of admission was usually 2/-.

After the war a tradesman's wage was around £6 -£7 a week. As a competitor, after a good day at a meeting it was quite normal to go home with the equivalent of two to three weeks' wages. Meetings on hard tracks such as Herne Hill, Coventry, Portsmouth, Southampton and Wolverton were few and far between, especially big open meetings. At Herne Hill, the mecca, and Paddington the London boys were always racing mid-week. Coventry had possibly four to five meetings a year. One was promoted by my own club, Rover RCC, on Whit Tuesday, and included athletic events. Otherwise, we were on 'The Meadows' as they were called, except for the meetings held on some of the top county class cricket pitches. The grounds were immaculate, and on a good firm track some of the top boys would ride an 84" gear in the sprint events. The usual grass track gear was 77", or 23T x 8T on a 1" pitch block chain (46T x 16T x ½"). Tyres were always fat, about 1 ¾" diameter with very heavy file tread, or 'bees nest' as they were later called.

I was having great success at all distances from quarter-mile to 25-miles during 1945. I successfully defended my 5-Mile Grass Track Championship, then won the 25-Mile Hard Track title at a big, sprawling cement track at Derby. The track had been used as a motor racing circuit pre-war. The cycle races were run on the flat part but the bends were so far around, you did not need to use the banking. This was just as well as the banking was in the form of a basin with a very rapid change from the flat to almost vertical wall.

Suddenly, out of the blue, from the NCU, the governing body at that time, came an invitation by post:

> You have been selected to race in Paris in June. The other members of the team are
> Reg Harris, Lew Pond and Ian Scott.

I could not believe that I had been so fortunate. Of course, I had to ask for time off work from BSA. It was not easy in those days, but to be selected to ride for the Country so soon after the end of hostilities in France and BSA being a cycle manufacturer, the permission was granted. Little did I know how selection for my Country was going to affect my future.

The trip, of course, was exciting, travelling with the other riders from Victoria Station, crossing the Channel on the boat train to Paris and then being met by promoters' representatives and taken to a hotel. The racing was at the Vincennes Track on June 17th 1945 and it was organised by the Communist Party of the day. There was huge crowd and good racing. The team as a whole committed themselves well. Results were reasonable, but, most importantly, a start had been made in international exchange. It was an honour to be accompanied by Mr E J Southcott, the President of the NCU, a man I learned later in my career to have a great deal of respect for, as well as members of his family. There was also Mr A E Taylor, a well-known Birmingham figure in the sport and president of the Rover RCC, my own club. Mr Southcott gave a very encouraging report to HQ about the riders' performances and their popularity with the spectators.

As a result of our visit to France, a French team came to Herne Hill on June 23rd 1945 for the official opening of the track with its new surface. The stadium had been used as a balloon barrage and ack-ack site during the war and had been badly damaged. The new surface of tarmac by the Resmat Co looked nice, but proved not to be as fast as the old cement surface. In the International Match, England beat France. Reg Harris and Lew Pond were the best sprinters on the day. I had a third in the sprint final and was second in the '5' to Wilf Waters. Herne Hill had meetings prior to this one but this was the 'Official Opening'. Other meetings had been the Good Friday SCCU and a Poly meeting on June 2nd.

Just before the Good Friday meeting I had been called for a medical for the forces. The war had ended and I had been retained at the BSA in a reserved occupation, but it now seemed I would be called up under conscription. My career, I am sure, would have been ended as a racing cyclist. Some time later I was cleared of this call up, but then received a summons to serve as a 'Bevin Boy', which meant going down the coalmines. I had received a travel warrant to the named pit in Nuneaton, a mask and a miner's lamp. I reported this to the BSA and they once again took action and I was given the all clear in respect of becoming a miner. Might I add that many of the pre-1939 and post war cyclists came from the tough school of miners. From that era, the name of Jack Simpson stands out, a wonderful time triallist and pursuit rider. In fact, Jack won the pursuit at the French Match at Herne Hill, beating Rioland and Charlie Marriner.

From my international racing in Paris and London there was a return to the grass tracks, amongst which was the 1-Mile National at the Dunlop Sports Ground, on a very heavy track made soft by rain. I rode very well, as I thought, in the final, but Jerry Waters came up the finishing straight, riding very strongly. We crossed the line together and I had no doubt in my mind that I had just held on to win, and many others thought the same. But Mick McCormack, an official of my own club and held in high esteem in the sport, gave the race to Waters. I questioned the decision and the answer was, "As a National Official I cannot be seen to be favouring members of my own club." My opinion, and that of many others, was that I had been badly treated, but the judge's decision has always been deemed right. Following this, only weeks after, Reg Harris came to Stourbridge on one of his rare grass track appearances. In the final we were having a ding dong when with no hesitation he came across my front wheel as I was passing in the straight and ripped out four spokes. Once again there was no support from the Midland Officials.

I make a point of mentioning Grass Track Championhips because in those days the National Hard Track Championships titles were: the Blue Riband (the 1,000 yards sprint title) and the 25-mile title. The National Grass Track titles were: the half-mile, 1-mile and 5-mile. There were only five National titles for individual riders, so every one counted. In addition there were the tandem sprint and 50-mile tandem paced Hard Track Championship titles. In the year I write about the quarter-mile scratch was added.

My record on grass was three 5-mile Golds, two 5-mile Silvers, one half-mile Silver, one 1-mile Silver and one 5-mile Bronze. On Hard Track my record was:

two 25-mile Golds, one 25-mile Silver, one individual pursuit Gold, one individual pursuit Bronze, one teams pursuit Gold and one teams pursuit Silver.

After the disappointment of the half-mile and 1-mile events I went to Middlesex to defend my 5-mile title, winning from Wilf Waters and Stan Harrison. At the same meeting I had two seconds in sprint events. In the quarter-mile scratch event S Harrison was the winner and in the 880 yards handicap, Don McKellar. On the occasion of the Middlesex event Dad and I were in trouble for getting back to Euston. Our old friend, Gerry Burgess, heard of our problem and came to ask if he could help. He had his arm in a sling from some accident but said he was still able to drive. Gerry had competed in the Monte Carlo Rally, driving a Ford. The one-handed journey to Euston was heart stopping, but he never flinched in getting us to the train on time.

During this period of track racing on the grass I went to Derby Municipal Track to ride in the 25-Mile Hard Track Championship. In the race Jack Simpson and I disputed the half-lap primes. I had some 27, but Jack in the latter part of the race accumulated 79. The primes were for 1/- each. It was a very windy day but the race time was 59.24 4/5th seconds. I won the title, jumping in the back straight and opening a gap which was never closed. On the same day I won the 1-lap scratch and was second in the quarter-mile handicap from virtual scratch. What was coming through loud and clear was my ability to win at all distances from 440 yards to 25 miles on grass, cinder and hard track. My father really enjoyed all of this. His boy was showing the cycling world his capabilities. Never once did he sit me down and suggest that if I specialised, I could become one of the greats. It was a matter of the more we win, the more we want.

At the back end of 1945 there was 'The Meeting of Championship', with a French team again on show. The interchange was becoming quite regular. In

Lap of Honour after winning 5-Mile Championship 1945 at Southall, Middlesex

fact, both Federations accepted the interest Great Britain–France matches were creating, with some 8,000 spectators at Herne Hill and another match at Paddington on the Sunday. Over the two meetings I competed only in a 70-lap Madison, teamed with Cyril Cartwright - how I never knew. He and I were never compatible, and in this event we finished third. On the Sunday the Paddington meeting had all the London stars and the French team. I won the 10-mile scratch.

But the pleasant surprise in September was the selection to ride in Denmark at the wonderful Ordrup track in Copenhagen. I was selected with Lew Pond, Wilf and Jerry Waters and Dave Ricketts – one provincial and four cockneys. However, we knew each other from around the meetings. We got on well together, and the excitement of riding as an international team helped. The journey was very eventful. The only planes available were those used in the war, such as Dakotas and Flying Fortresses with no proper seats, no pressurised cabins, just a fuselage and wooden seats. We got to Copenhagen in the early hours and met Mr Breyerholme , the big cog in the Danish wheel. He took us to his home at 2.00am. His wife gave us bacon and eggs. These were very welcome and we could eat as much as we wanted, very different from England, which was still on rationing. I, in turn, had taken some real coffee, which I gave to the lady of the house. She was in tears. They had been on ersatz coffee, which was made from acorns, bitter and nasty. She thought I was an angel.

We were due to ride on the 16th but some cock up had been made and the meeting could not be run. This meant staying nearly a fortnight to race the next weekend. We were training on the superb Ordrup track, raced in the week with the local lads and had fun. Some days we were taken out by Mr Breyerholme to a trotting track, had a meal and watched racing. Another day we went to a first class Danish restaurant. We couldn't believe the quality of the food after the very basic rations we had had in the war. We had been living on dried egg, toad-in-the-hole and powdered milk. Nearly everything was rationed, and everywhere in England the 'Dig for Victory' slogan had people growing vegetables to fill up on. Here, in a country known for its dairy products, we were having a ball.

On the day of the meeting Jeff Scherens and some of the top pros were competing, in addition to the Great Britain-Denmark amateur match. Distinguished officers of the British Army and Navy were introduced to us in the dressing room suite. We did not perform as well as we expected but the headlines in *Cycling* said,

Britishers at Ordrup, Good Show against Superior Danes.

Outside the match we all showed good form in handicaps and points races. Lew Pond came out as the Best Sprinter, but we all knew this. Lew was a master on the British tracks, even taking Harris and Bannister into the equation. We returned home in a Flying Fortress, with bench seats along the length of the plane. It was bitterly cold and uncomfortable, but who cared? We had represented England.

1946

Racing life and
family life – the
Muratti Cup
– World Cham-
pionships in
Zurich

The 1945 season was over. I was now a recognised international, with invitations to club dinners and meeting new people who were anxious to have a talk.

My dedication to the sport was very unfair to the girl who had become my wife only twelve months ago. All I seemed to do was work, train, check my bike, eat and sleep, even to the extent that I insisted on going to bed at 9.00pm – and that was to sleep. On one occasion a daughter of one of our local officials got friendly with Eileen and said she would like to visit us in our rooms. The arrangement was made for 7.30pm one evening, but the lady did not arrive until 8.15pm. She sat down and started chatting to Eileen. At 8.45pm I suddenly remarked, "You'll have to go now. I go to bed at 9.00pm." Eileen still reminds me of this by saying, "No wonder we never had friends." Why Eileen has made such sacrifices and shown such dedication through more than 56 years of marriage, I will never know. During the winter months there were social events, but I could not dance and got jealous if Eileen danced with anyone else. I always went home early, taking Eileen away from some pleasure she deserved and would have appreciated. But always the dedication and strict routine would take over.

As the1945 season came to an end I was straight into road walking, with special breathing exercises, and road running with some of the famous Birchfield Harriers. There were regular visits to the gym, even working out with a boxer's medicine ball, punch ball and punch bag. The winter became very important in my life as it gave me the chance to get among lots of people who officiated in our sport and attend Club and Division meetings. Attendance at committee meetings was considerable and annual meetings of a division would see 100–150 people in a large room, with keen debating by wonderful speakers. I am sure this led me to take a great interest in later years in the administrative side of the sport.

Always at Christmas and New Year Eileen and I were expected to go to the Godwin household. There was no chance of going to Eileen's family on Christmas Day but we could go on Boxing Day. A Godwin celebration occasion was something to behold, with typical American glitz, everything overdone, food, drink, presents, decorations, surprises etc. Then New Year, with the celebrations lasting into the early hours of the following day, when Charlie, 'The Boss', would lay down what 'WE' would do in the coming year. His ideas were a second share of the BSA Gold Column at Herne Hill on Good Friday, followed by defending our National Championships, plus getting any of the other championships that might come our way. It was all serious stuff, with no concern for our marriage. That was just a hiccup in the overall plans, although by now it had been accepted.

I would be watched carefully from January 2nd onwards for a steady reduction of the 5-6lbs I was allowed to put on over the winter. If I went for a workout to the gym or on the bike, I usually ended up at the family home for a wash down. Then the 'Old Man' would demand admission to the room to poke and pinch at the human machine to test the fat content. Now married and at twenty-five years of age, I was still being tested as trainers would a racehorse.

My usual training programme before Easter was 1,500 miles and two or three 25-mile TT's. I usually rode a low gear of max 65", a medium gear of 72" and one or two on 84" fixed. In March I made a couple of visits to The Butts at Coventry. I went to the SCCU Good Friday meeting in good shape.

In the January edition of *The Bicycle*, a competitor to *Cycling* in those days, a series was started called 'Voice of the Stars'. The first one to appear was about Jock Allinson, Britain's Best All Rounder. I was No 2, which appeared on January 23rd 1946.

THE VOICE OF THE STARS

No 2 – T C GODWIN, Rover RCC

THOMAS GODWIN, Rover RCC, during the past few years has become one of the most formidable of English path riders. He was a member of the first team of English riders to visit the Continent, after the end of hostilities, and throughout his career has proved himself a master of five-mile events. In 84 of these he has been out of the first three on only one occasion. He has contested 18 25-mile TTs on the road, and has secured eight "firsts," three "seconds," one "third," three "fourths" and four fastest handicaps.

At present Godwin is holder of both the NCU's National five-miles grass and National 25-miles championships.

My racing career, which has taken shape in a most inopportune period, I feel, is one which has not altogether been void of its bright and exciting moments. My first ambitions to cycling fame were formed in 1936 as a result of the Olympic Games. I was thrilled at reading of the many great performances put up by the cream of the amateur world. Outstanding in my opinion was Van Vliet, whose performances, especially in 1,000-metre TTs, gave me inspiration and a determination to achieve similar success.

I did not start racing until 1939, and then it was coincident that it was the year when an attempt was made to find potential Olympic hopes – a real attempt, shall we say, to get a strong contingent of good riders. Just prior to the Midlands Olympic Trials, held at the Butts, Coventry, I succeeded in doing the fastest 1,000-metres TT of the season at Alexander Sports Ground. As a result, I received an invitation to compete in trials before I had broken my novice's status, which, by the way, I broke on the day of receiving the invitation with a hard-earned "treble." I rode seven times to secure seven wins!

Then The War
On July 29, I was successful in winning 1,000 metres with a 1-19, but, as the Butts was reputed to be bad for speed, I was very heartened when some prominent London riders informed me that a 1-19 at Coventry was good enough to beat a 1-16 at Herne Hill. Frankly, I never expected to set Herne Hill on fire with my riding on September 9, 1939, but I was bitterly disappointed at the cancellation, due to the outbreak of war. I realised, of course, that war puts a stop to individual happenings, and riders with far brighter chances than mine were subdued as a consequence. During July and September of that momentous year I had a very good run in handicaps and three-mile consolation races; so, with ambition burning high, I appealed to the promoting secretary of the five-mile grass championship to give me a chance.

To my surprise, I was elected and rode into third place, this being only my second race at the distance. I was informed by many that only inexperience lost me the event.

I was very envious at the time over Reg Harris and Dave Ricketts being selected for World's Championship whilst they were so young; not that I had any claim to such honours, but because their good fortune provided them with expert tuition and decent tracks for training. In the Midlands all this seemed far away - and even now, the need is still felt. So, with the end of the 1939 season, little was achieved, and, with the black clouds of war over us, prospects were very dull.

An apprenticeship to a reserved trade provided me with the opportunity to continue with my racing interests during the war. The early days of hostilities were extremely poor for track promotions, and from early 1940 to the end of 1942 I rode at only 13 sports meetings – five of these at Manchester and four at Brodsworth. I got to like Fallowfield very much, and until I rode at Herne Hill, classed it as the best of all tracks. I have always been very lucky at Fallowfield – only once have I come away without a prize.

During this dull period on the track my interest drifted to road racing, and at my first attempt in 1940 I rode a "25" in 1-4-41 in the Birmingham Centre Championship, finishing with fifth fastest and first handicap time - the winning time being 1-3-25. During the period 1941-42 I rode in seven "25's" and managed to get down to a 1-1-47 and a little later a 1-1-35, which stands as a personal best. During 1943 I contested five "25's," won three and was second in two.

Great August Week
The 1943 season saw the revival of many track meetings. It was during this year that I started to attain real success on the track, I was unbeaten in five-mile scratch events, winner of the first Cattlow Trophy at Fallowfield and repeated this performance in 1944 to make the trophy my own property. I have only once ridden in an individual pursuit race in 1943, when, in a five-minute pursuit at Pontypridd, I caught the field with 11 seconds to spare. During August week, 1943, I won six "fives" in eight days, had two "firsts," two "seconds," two "thirds," and raced on cement, cinder and grass to achieve this and in the last "five" suceded in lapping the field.

So much for 1943! In the following April I recorded 1-1-59, 1-2-35 and 1-3-5 for "25s" all winning times, and so entered for the first 25-mile Road Championship. I was very pleased with my 1-2-6 for fifth place, although I would naturally have liked to be in the first three. After riding in the Championship "25" I considered it best to leave road racing alone. Once again I started to prove my ability in five-mile events by winning every one I rode in, including the five-mile grass championship, until the fateful day at Lichfield on August Monday, when, in a serious crash in the five-mile I broke my sequence of 21 five-mile successes without defeat. I walked across the line for third place. The same afternoon L Pond and W Waters crashed, and so ended our chances of competing in Manchester in the two title events, the 1,000 yards and the "five." Reg Harris was successful in both, as we are well aware, and also in the quarter-finals at Slough. The incident at Lichfield caused me to have 24 stitches in my hip, and I did not race again that year.

In 1945, my first success was my greatest, that of winning the "five" for the BSA Gold Column at Herne Hill – the first time I had visited the Mecca of our grand game. The sprint was also very pleasing, for our master tactician, Lew Pond, only beat me by a narrow margin in a last 220 yards time of 12 33-5 sec. This early success created an interest in Herne Hill for me, and I took every opportunity to compete there to get experience.

During my visits to London I obviously must have impressed, for an invitation to ride in Paris came my way. I was very surprised, but, nevertheless, pleased. Being the first international contest after cessation of hostilities, it was indeed a great honour. Although I have never won a sprint final at Herne Hill, I have always given my best, and I tried hard, but racing on a fast track requires special training, which I have lacked in the past. Experience is essential. Nevertheless, after a successful season in longer distance events and thrice selected to race abroad – one offer had to be declined – I feel that I cannot grumble.

I am holder of two national and one Midland title. I was very proud to retain the five-mile grass title, and also to add the 25-mile championship to my string of successes. I am the only rider in the country who has competed in every 1945 track championship, and it was only an unfortunate puncture in the "five" (National Hard Track Championship) at Fallowfield that robbed me of a chance of sharing an honour that our most outstanding sprinter, Reg Harris, holds – that of triple National Champion.

Reg is certainly a grand sprinter and a credit to the game. On our trip to Denmark he was greatly missed, and it is my sincere hope that I shall be fortunate enough to be selected to ride in international events with Reg and the other boys who have proved their worth. In conclusion, I should like to give a word of praise to the NCU officials for their grand efforts in bringing about these trips.

Good Friday 1946 was just that for me. Although I had at times shown good sprinting form, I had no great inspiration in that direction. But Reg Harris and Andre Rivoal, the French champion, rode a special three-ride match. Cor Byster failed to turn up for what was to have been a series. Reg beat Rivoal, and the write up said that the Manchester lad was in brilliant form and won easily. The programme also included a 550 yard invitation sprint. All the top boys were riding, Reg, Alan Bannister, Lew Pond, John Dennis, Rivoal and others, including Tommy Godwin. Heats were run off, then repechage and semi-finals. The line up for the final was Reg Harris, Alan Bannister and Tommy Godwin. I had beaten Rivoal in the heat and two other good sprinters in the semi. Bannister had come through the repechage, beating Pond. 'Banny' went well from the gun, with Reg on his wheel. In the back straight I closed very quickly. Going into the last 220 yards, I closed Reg in on 'Banny's' wheel and went hell bent for home, winning the event. Reg, as I passed him, was seen by Bill Bailey to flick his toe strap and raise his hand to indicate a mechanical fault. The gun was fired but, after some confusion, I was declared the winner.

I was later approached by Bill Bailey, who had in the past been four times World Sprint Champion. He told me he had been to Reg and told him he saw what he did with his toe strap. He then said, "Tommy, come down to London to live and train. You could become a first class sprinter, you have got so much strength." Later in the meeting I went on to win the 5-mile points race for a second share in the BSA Gold Column, beating George Fleming, who was known in those days as 'The Phenomenal Pedaller'. Third was Jerry Waters.

Herne Hill on that day had to close the gates. It was claimed that 10,000 people were in the stadium. There was queue a mile long and thousands were turned away. Police had to be drafted in. It was a wonderful start to a new season and I wondered what else 1946 held in store for me.

Smaller meetings were held during April and May, but at the end of May at the Butts Stadium in Coventry I rode against Pond, Bannister, Meadwell and other top class track men. I had a double win in the quarter-mile handicap and 5-mile scratch and was second to Pond in the 500 yard scratch event, still showing plenty of speed and strength in the distance races.

The last Saturday in May, I was back on the grass. I had my first win for the famous BSA Gold Vase in the 10-mile event, and had previously finished second to Lew Pond in the Brooks Bowl 500 yard scratch. In mid-June I was again at The Butts, Coventry, coming second in the quarter-mile handicap, second in the 500 yards scratch to Bannister and another 5-mile scratch win for the Coventry Evening Telegraph Trophy. J Walters and A Bannister were second and third. I was winning distance races at most meetings.

The Sprint Championship meeting at the end of June was very disappointing from my point of view. I had hoped to finish in the top four. Reg won the title from Lew Pond. In the race for third place it was H Marshall followed by Alan Bannister, myself and L Glover. The final event, a 20-lap Madison, was no better for me. I was continually being given different partners to ride with. Either Ricketts or Fleming I would have chosen for myself, but in this event I was teamed with Ian Scott. We did not perform well and the visiting quartet of French riders took first and second places, both teams lapping the field, while Scott and I finished third, a blow to my morale. It must be said that Reg was now leading the life of a pro and continually racing on the Continent in special sprint matches against all the top riders. English riders were chasing prizes on grass tracks, flat cinder tracks and the very shallow shale track at Fallowfield. Plenty of prizes to be won but not conducive to international competition. The more we raced, the more prizes and occasional expenses for the top men.

On June 3rd in *The Bicycle* there was a report of Harris and Marshall coming first and second in Paris. Dave Ricketts and Lew Pond also rode at this meeting – three London riders, plus Harris. From the provinces you had to do something very special to be selected. A report in *Cycling* from a meeting at Manchester at this time stated:

Harris beaten twice but still the best sprinter. Bannister won with Godwin second. Harris for some reason went up the banking and did not contest the sprint.

I was again beaten by the Frenchman Baldersarrer in the '5' and was not very happy.

The second Saturday in July was a date that had been fixed in the calendar for many, many years, the Manchester Wheelers Meet at Fallowfield. The trophy name of the 32Muratti Gold Cup was synonymous with the success of the meeting. Everyone who attended the meeting referred to it as the 'Muratti Meeting'. On a good day some 14,000 spectators would get in before the gates were closed. Through the years, all the best track riders in the country hoped for an invitation, and many top Continental riders were called upon to spice up the racing interest and enthuse the crowds.

The Wheelers Meet had been held since 1895. Muratti Cups, which every

Beating Reg Harris in
the Muratti Cup – 1946

young rider had dreams of winning, first Silver then Gold, had been raced for
since 1899. The Silver Cup required two wins to keep it as your own. W H Webb
achieved this with wins in 1902 and 1903. However, when the first Gold Vase
was put up in 1904 three wins were needed to win it outright. The first man to
do this was Ernie Payne of Worcester with wins in 1904, 1906 and 1910. Next
came the Muratti Gold Trophy in 1911. Many famous names were added to this
one. In 1912 it was V L Johnson of Rover RCC, a Gold Medal winner in the 1908
Olympics, then H T (Tiny) Johnson in 1913 and Dennis Hodgetts of Rover RCC
in 1914. There was no competition after this until the Great War ended in 1918.

On resumption in 1919 Albert White of Rover RCC from Scunthorpe, an
outstanding rider for many years, was the winner, and had further wins in 1921
and 1922. There was another Muratti Gold Cup in 1923, won by Albert Theaker, of Lincoln, who went on to win again in 1924 and 1927. In between came the
legendary J E Sibbit of Manchester Wheelers and G Owen from Manchester.
The Muratti Gold Cup for 1928 went to an overseas rider, Willy Falk Hansen
from Denmark. He went on to become the Professional World Sprint Champion. In 1929 G Wyld of Derby, one of the famed Wyld family, won, followed by
J E Sibbit again in 1930. Then came the man who was to become one of the all
time greats, Denis Horn, the man from the Fens, winning the Muratti outright
in three successive years 1931, 1932 and 1933.

In 1934 Toni Merkens of Germany, who was to go on to win the Olympic
Sprint Title in Berlin in 1936, put his name on the new trophy, followed by two
more wins by Denis Horn in 1935 and 1936. H Ooms of Holland won in 1937
and E Gorton of Manchester in 1938. 1939 saw an epic race, with Denis Horn
desperately attempting to win a second Muratti outright. The battle was fought
in atrocious conditions with heavy rain all day. Ralph Dougherty of Leamington, who in June had beaten the hour for a 25-mile event for the first time in
England, set a fast pace for the ten miles. Denis Horn and a few more riders

managed to hang on to the relentless pace of Dougherty. He was covered in red mud from the red shale track and Horn was recognisable only from his style not his racing colours, tracking Dougherty all the way. At the bell Dougherty was still leading into the final bend. Horn passed into the straight only to find Dougherty at his side, who with a final kick robbed Horn of his glory.

Earlier in the meeting Reg Harris, as a promising nineteen year-old rider, competed with W W Maxfield, the 1939 British Sprint Champion. Maxfield was also the 1938 Empire Games 10-miles Champion. The sprint final was between Harris and Maxfield for the famous Vitonica Gold Cup. Past winners of this trophy, introduced in 1928, were W Falk Hansen, S Cozens, A Theaker and M Schofield. Denis Horn won the trophy outright with wins in 1932, 1933 and 1935. In 1936 and 1937 H Ooms of Holland, who had won the Muratti in 1937 won. B Loatti won in 1938, who had also won the BSA Gold Column earlier that year at the Good Friday meet in London.

To return to the Harris–Maxfield final in 1939, Harris led out and took Maxfield into the straight. With Maxfield coming up to his shoulder, Harris left his line, running Maxfield right out across the whole width of the track. At the line the decision was given to Harris, with Maxfield appealing against the result. Subsequent photos showed Maxfield's wheel just over in front of Harris. A further appeal in court brought out arguments of camera angle, and shutter speed being used in Harris's defence, claiming that Harris would be stopped dead while Maxfield was still moving! Harris won the case and was declared the legal winner. Then there was no further competition due to the war.

The promoters for the 1946 Wheelers Meet had also decided that the race for the Muratti should be reduced from 10-miles to 5-miles to accommodate Mr Harris. Harris could and did win 5-mile events at Manchester Track Leagues, but there was no way he could last and win a 10-mile event. The tough, gruelling 10-mile race was changed and spoiled by reducing the distance to 5 miles. Some 47 years of tradition and excitement had been forsaken for the whim of some very selfish and devious committee members.

Could Reg win the Muratti race and, as holder of the Vitonica Gold Cup for a 500 metre sprint, which he had held since 1939, have the very great pleasure of emulating Denis Horn, A Theaker and H Ooms of Holland by holding both trophies? Denis Horn had, in fact, won a Vitonica outright in 1932, 1933 and 1935, the same years that he had won the Muratti. The 1946 event saw me taking the challenge of Harris and beating him in the sprint. Reg won the Vitonica with Bannister second and Godwin third.

Headlines in *The Bicycle* for July 17th 1946 said:

GODWIN THRILLS AT MANCHESTER

Continental riders eclipsed on Fallowfield Track
Tommy Godwin the tall Rover RCC rider was the star performer at the 54th Manchester Wheelers Race Meet. His victory was merited in the resumed and revised Muratti Cup Race.

The event, always a feature of the Meet, had been reduced from the traditional 10 miles to 5 miles.

It was a great race from the start, the lead changing continually through the race. There was a very strong English contingent, as well as riders from France and Denmark.

At the bell for the final lap, Lanners of France jumped away, with Godwin up the banking. Harris latched on to Lanners and at the furlong mark, Godwin jumped away in a superb and electrifying burst.

Godwin gained a two-length gap before Harris came off Lanners' wheel and put in a magnificent effort to try and overhaul the Rover man. But Godwin held his lead and, as Harris closed, Godwin found another kick to hold off the challenge."

In winning this famous trophy, one of the most prized in the sport, I found myself in the wonderful situation of having won in this season the BSA Gold Column for the second time at Herne Hill on Good Friday, then the BSA Gold Vase, a 10-mile event on a grass track at Bournville in Birmingham in May and the Muratti Gold Cup at Manchester in July.

Both the Gold Column and the Muratti Cup were hall marked 9 carat, one bearing the date 1928 and the other 1936. The BSA Gold Vase had an 18 carat hall mark and dated from 1908. To gain outright ownership of these wonderful trophies required three wins, not necessarily in successive years.

As the finale to the Manchester Wheelers Meet there was a 40-lap Madison. I was teamed with a little guy from Sheffield, Jerry Watkinson. Points were equally shared with Harris and J Waters. I passed Reg on the final bend and was into the straight when suddenly a pull on my saddle almost stopped me. My friend Harris wanted to win the final sprint in front of his home crowd, which he did. My response was to get to him as soon as possible and physically attack him. He had been summoned to the judges and was making his way to them when, foolishly, in front of thousands of people, I grabbed him with my left hand and drew back my right arm. Suddenly someone held me back, saying, "Tommy, you'll get suspended if you hit him." It was Syd Cozens, a Manchester Wheelers man, who had recently become employed by the BSA Company I worked for. We had become great friends and he was protecting me.

I told Harris I would see him behind the dressing room later. Needless to say, he did not turn up. After waiting some time I was told that I was wanted to go into the city for a radio interview. After making arrangements for getting my bike to the station, I agreed to go, only to find Harris in the car. I first refused to get in but then agreed if I could sit away from him. When we got into the studio we were left for a short while by someone who was unaware of the bitter situation. There was a jug of water and glasses on the table. Reg said weakly, "Would you like a drink of water?" I replied, "Drown yourself with it." I still wanted to physically assault him. The aftermath of it all was that although the judges had witnessed Reg's action of pulling me back, they allowed the result of the final sprint to stand, telling him he was a 'naughty boy'. But it allowed Harris and Waters to get the same points as Watkinson and myself, making the result a tie. But my joy was that I had won the famous Muratti Gold Cup. More will be said about this race later, as I went on to win again in 1947, was second in 1948 and won outright in 1949.

The next week I was back on the grass at Birmingham City Transport Sports Day. There were 15,000 spectators, which was quite the norm on those special days. My results were: winner of the 500 yards scratch, winner of the 5-mile and second in the 500 yards handicap. It was Dad's insistence that I went for the lot. This may have been very appealing to the promoters and spectators but, on reflection, this tremendous effort week by week was not conducive to finding my best discipline.

The report in *The Bicycle* on July 24th shows that I won the 5-Mile Grass Track title for the third time at Ollerton in Nottinghamshire, also winning the 500 yards scratch. On the same page there is: "Harris wins in Zurich." He was now being hailed as the favourite to win the title. Accompanying him was Ken Marshall of Poly CC, who finished third. Harris beat Plattner, the Swiss champion. Both had already been picked for the World's to be held in Zurich, along with Lew Pond.

The road team had also been picked: Maitland, Moreton, Mitchell, and Stanway. Two were from the Midlands and two from the North. There was no Fleming, Waters or Upton. Bill Mills was absolutely shocked. He was always so London biased in his choice and so slighting about the abilities of provincial riders. It was distasteful at times. But there was no mention of a pursuit selection, which was an event being introduced for the first time. The Continental boys knew who had been selected and were being prepared, but not the British boys!

On July 31st 1946 *The Bicycle* announced:

> Tommy Godwin to ride the pursuit for GB in the World's at Zurich, starting on August 24th.

Our preparation for this event was a single trial at Herne Hill, of course, on a cold, windy Monday evening, with no meeting or spectators. Each rider was to ride an individual time trial due to the conditions. The report said: "Godwin clocked the sensational time of 5 minutes 26.4 seconds on an 87" gear. Fleming 5.32.6 on a 92" gear. Fleming had ridden a '50' the day before. He would travel as a reserve for both pursuit and road! Other riders were: Ricketts with 5.40, Scott with 5.43 and Jerry Waters with 5.46. It was reported that club teams were not achieving my time in teams competitions. On August 4th I was second to Bannister in a one-lap sprint, leading out a 12.8 seconds 220 yards. 'Banny' beat me by pushing me out across the track.

There was no NCU direction about riding pursuits even at this time. It was to be a hit-and-miss affair at the World's. Fleming was at the same meeting, winning the points race, but there was no pursuit match between us.

On August 17th at a meeting at The Butts, Coventry, Harris won the 550 yard sprint and I was second. Harris declined to ride the 5-mile, which I won. I had also taken third in the 440 yards handicap off 17 yards.

We left for Zurich on the Wednesday, according to the report in *The Bicycle* dated August 21st. This meant that we got to Zurich by train – boat – train, an arduous journey, to arrive two days before the competition. There were no sleeping berths – just sleep when and where you could. I know that Bill Bailey was the team manager, but I have no recollection of any talk with him or by him at any time during the trip. He was a renowned sprinter and had tried to help me in that direction, but I had no advice, encouragement or help in any way as to my preparation for my rides. It turned out to be a matter of getting to the track, reporting, going to the line and UCI officials taking over.

The track was frightening, with a dirty grey surface and unbelievable banking. Not that I had to worry about that in the ride, but even in a warm up session it was nerve racking.

Remember, this was the first ever individual pursuit championship, amateur or professional. Continental countries had held their own national championships. Rioland was hotly tipped for the amateur title, having shown the equivalent time of 5.10 for 4,000 metres. Piel had won the French pro title at 4,000 metres with a time of 5.11.

So, to the qualifying rides. I was up against Gillen of Luxembourg. He beat me with a 5.24 against my 5.26. I had not improved from my qualifying time at Herne Hill. However, I was brought back into the competition through a repechage. My next ride, all in one day, was against Rioland. He returned a 5.11. I had improved to 5.22. Every heat but mine saw the winners catching their opponents. Rioland had caught his man in 1.28.8. My chance against Rioland was obviously nil, it being my third full distance ride.

Other rides in the quarter-finals were: Gissel caught Le Roy, Pontisso (5.19.8) beat Schar (5.22.6), Janemar (5.22.4) beat Gillen (5.13 .6). My 5.22.6 was creditable. The final for first and second was: Rioland (5.18.2), Gissel (5.18.6). Janemar was third (5.21.6) and Pontisso fourth (5.25.4). By today's standards the times are ridiculously slow, but nothing was then known about pursuit racing. Professional times for 5000 metres individual pursuit were all in the 6.30–6.38 range, even up to 6.43. The track record prior to the World's was 6.34.2. However, the pursuit results - on top of the disappointment of Reg Harris going out in the quarter-finals – just about flattened the British camp, as Pond and Marshall also failed.

A couple of days after my pursuit ride I went to the track to have a few laps, not expecting to see any of our lads. Reg was not staying with the team as was usually the case, but he was at the track and riding around with George Lewis, a close friend of Reg's from the Wheelers. I got on the track, and had ridden a few laps when Reg and George joined me. After a short session Reg suggested having some lead out sprints. My reply was, "I haven't even been up the banking yet." Reg then told me to follow him round, to keep my front wheel pointing up and to push into the bank. After a few shaky laps and a bit of rolling out of the banking Reg said, "Okay, you lead the first one out and then we'll change the order."

A couple of laps at the front and I went wide down the home straight and into the bend, climbing. Half-way round and, swish, Reg dived down the bank and hit the 200 metres entering the back straight. We were on a 330 metre track. I went around the bend at the top of the bank, kicked down, and saw Reg some eight to ten lengths away going like hell. I chased hard but at the line was well down. Tom McDonald, Reg's mentor and Mr Mick McCormack, a grade 'A' timekeeper back home, had timed him. Reg rode around to Tom to be met with, "An 11.8," which pleased him. But a friend of Reg and Tom, a Frenchman, flattened the joy by saying, "Yes, but who was the big guy closing up on him?" The reply was, "Oh, he's our pursuit rider." I then asked Reg if we were going to have another ride. The answer was, "No, I'm quite pleased with what I have done today."

So much for sportsmanship! I was then on my own, except for Mr McCormack, who had gone into the centre of the track to lie in the sun. I approached him, as he was President of my own club back home. "Would you mind timing me, Mr Mac? I'd like to ride a 220 metres on my own." With no other riders, the track to myself and feeling more relaxed, I rode around for a few laps and then nodded to Mr Mac, "Next time." Away I went. The time was 12 seconds dead. I had words with the timekeeper and he remarked, "Tommy, if only you would concentrate on sprinting and ask the BSA to support you, you could become a first class sprinter." But I could never accept just two or three rides a day at a meeting, jockeying for position, stalling, throwing a hook, and being timed for 220 yards or 200 metres. I always enjoyed a battle at whatever distance and in various disciplines.

The amazing thing of the whole Championships was that Oscal Plattner won the Sprint and the next weekend finished 8th in the road race over 117 miles! Our road boys, Stanway, Maitland and Moreton, finished 15th, 21st, and 30th – good placings.

With the pressure off and disappointed, it was still a wonderful experience to be part of a British Team, and to witness all the best riders in the world fighting to prove something to themselves. We knew that on our return we would be slated, and we were, but at the same time we realised how totally inadequate the NCU had been in preparing us for international competition. The analysis in *Cycling* and *The Bicycle* of our shortcomings was embarrassing to say the least, but would the NCU do anything different?

After settling down again there were not many meetings to ride. 'The Meeting of Champions' was a showpiece for sprinters. Harris, Schandorf (second in the World's) and Sansever appeared by special invitation. Harris won against both and then won the three-up. During his rides he was clocked at 11.8 seconds. The headlines said:

HARRIS BACK TO FORM

I was supposed to be matched against Rioland in a revenge pursuit match, according to *The Bicycle,* but I never heard anything about such a match. On the same bill was a 10-minute roadman pursuit, but I was not included.

To wind up the season, I rode the final meeting at Paddington, finishing third to Pond, and Marshall in the sprint and winning the First Class Handicap from Pond and Ricketts.

But the concluding event, a 70-lap Madison, I rode with Dave Ricketts and finished up by winning all seven sprints. The headlines were:

Godwin the Star of the Meeting.

64

CHAPTER 10

1947
The BSA Gold
Column –
changes at home
and work – a
second Muratti
win – World
Championships
in Paris – trouble
at work

Winning the BSA
Gold Column outright
– 1947

The year of 1947 was very eventful. I started the year getting the miles in but, again, as a loner, all my road miles were done solo. I realised later in life that had I trained with and mixed in group riding I might have been a better rider. I always tried to get in 1,500 miles before Good Friday and always got in a couple of sessions on the track with members of the Rover RCC at The Butts, Coventry. Dad would always get some idea of my form.

I always wintered well with road walking, road jogging, gym work and plenty of physical exercises. There was no weight training but a routine using chest expanders, proved invaluable. I worked hard physically and was a bit of a show off with feats of strength amongst my work mates. I was never a drinking man. I had a great respect for my body and never abused it in any way.

For the opening meeting of the season on Good Friday, in anticipation of a super afternoon of racing, Jim Wallace, the promoter, had contracted many of the top Continental professionals, sixteen in all. The two top amateurs, Ray Pauwels of Belgium and Cor Bijster, who had beaten Harris in the quarter-finals of the World's in Zurich the previous August, were to meet Harris in a revenge match. Rik van Kerchove was to meet Charlie Marriner in a pursuit match, which Marriner won.

A large gate of 11,000 on a chilly day were disappointed with the pros but both *The Bicycle* and *Cycling* carried the headline: "Amateurs Save The Day"

Harris won the Good Friday Sprint but in the special three-up races between Harris, Pauwels and Bijster, Pauwels won with 7 points, Harris had 6 and Bijster 5. Marriner won the 10-minute station pursuit, beating van Kerchove, with George Fleming third. Five other good riders were outclassed. The final amateur race of the day, with all the big names riding, was the 5-mile points race for the BSA Gold Column. I already had my name twice on the trophy. In what

was the hardest race by far of the three, I won, scoring 16 points, van Kerch-hove 14 points, W Waters 12 points. I was only second in the last sprint to Wilf Waters, the Belgian boy not scoring. I had won my first Gold trophy outright.

Following the Good Friday SCCU meet was the Coventry CC meeting at The Butts on Easter Monday. There was another big crowd on a very blustery afternoon. I was second to Lew Pond in the sprint, won the 5-mile from George Fleming and Ian Scott, then teamed up with Fleming for the 70-lap Madison. I finished up winning all seven sprints for maximum points, repeating what I had done previously with Dave Ricketts at Paddington. I was finding that Madison racing was my best event for showing off strength combined with speed.

Two weeks after at a NCU meeting at 'the Hill' I met George Fleming in a special pursuit match for the new 'Golden Helmet'. It was a very even race, but at three laps to go I picked up a slow puncture, finishing the distance on a very soft rear tyre. George won. It was intended as a guide to the World's in Paris later in the year. Again George and I teamed up for a 20-mile Madison. It was the race of the day, according to *The Bicycle*. We were close on points with only the last sprint to go. There was some confusion near the end. In the final sprint it was Lane then Marshall, but my third place made our total 16 points. Ricketts and Marshall had 14 points, Scott and Lane 8 points. It was another Madison win. I had also won my 440 yard handicap event, with the fastest time of the series in 28.8 seconds.

Sharing happiness with Eileen, Dad and friends

On the last Saturday in April there was a Kentish Wheelers promotion, again at 'the Hill'. Harris was again matched against Schandorff of Denmark, second in the 1946 World's, and Sensever, the French Sprint Champion. Bijster did not appear. The first event was a 1½ lap International Sprint. Harris won his heat, as expected. Schandorff was expected to win his heat, but in the home straight I very cheekily forced my way past him to win in the fastest 220 yards of the heats. In the final Reg won, Sensever was second and I was third, beating Marshall and Bannister, who had both been to Zurich as sprinters in the World's. Pond was also in the final.

In an England v Rest of Europe Three-Up Italian Pursuit, Harris led out, Pond took the second lap and I took the last lap. "At the bell," according to the report, "England were well in arrears due to a fast start by Schandorff and Sensever and Godwin riding brilliantly turned defeat into victory in 503 yards." In the 5-mile I got caught napping when Ricketts went away with another local rider, 'Digger' Downs, when there were a few laps to go. No-one would work until too late, but Bannister and I closed the gap at the finish. Ricketts had dropped Downs. I finished second and Bannister third.

I had had three meetings at Herne Hill in one month, with a number of successes and the crowds giving me plenty of encouragement. Again I was showing myself as one of the top four sprinters in the country, but still had no desire to specialise. It was now May and there was another meeting at Herne Hill, the Polytechnic CC event. The Victory Cup Sprint 550 Yards and the Alick Bevan Memorial Five-Mile were the main races.

On my arrival at the track around noon I was approached by Syd Cozens, a Manchester Wheelers man, who had once finished second in the World's Sprint Championship. "Tommy, I've got a special favour to ask. Will you ride a tandem race with Jack Lanners of France? Sensever is afraid of the track and the tandem racing was meant to be a guide to the '48 Olympics." I explained that I had never ridden a tandem in my life. "Oh, you'll be okay, you will be on the front." I was kidded into putting my own pedals on the tandem and to ride a few laps just to see how we 'nicked'. Lanners was very pleased, so we decided to give it a go.

In the Harris/Bannister ride against Harrison/Hampshire, the Manchester pair punctured where a re-run was not allowed according to NCU rules. But the object of the exercise was to show Harris and Bannister off to the public as the favoured pair for '48, so a re-run was ordered and they won.

Myself and Lanners, Pond and Burgess (past National Champions) and Scott/Thorpe had a three-up match. It was my first time on a tandem and a win in 12.4 seconds. So we went to the final with Harris and Bannister. Experience saw the Manchester pair riding a very tactical race. My knowledge was nil, and Lanners, only seventeen years of age, could not tell me anything and we were beaten. Lanners thanked me and said he hoped we could ride again some time. In fact, Lanners was given a special souvenir by the promoters in appreciation of his effort and sportsmanship. Other events at this meeting saw me once again in a sprint final with Harris and Pond. They were first and second, in that order, myself third. Sensever and Lanners were eliminated in the heats. Again

Godwin and Lanners

in the 5-Mile event I was caught napping by Lew Pond, who sneaked through on the line inside me. It was most unusual for me to leave room for anyone, never mind Lew, he being one of the finest bike handlers in the game and never missed any opportunity. I had had two defeats at Herne Hill at my favourite distance, and by two Cockneys, to boot. This had to be remedied.

On May 10th I was back at Herne Hill for a special Inter-Centre match: London, Birmingham, Manchester and Leicester. There were to be a series of sprints, a kilometre time trial and team pursuit. I was down to ride the kilo, which I won, with Dave Ricketts second, J Pratt of Leicester third and Cyril Cartright fourth. The final event was a 20-mile medley, in which I won the event as first over the line but Ricketts led me by one point in the race overall.

Around this period I had received an invitation to ride at Aarhus in Denmark in a special pursuit match against Borge Gissel, who had finished second in the World Championships in Zurich the previous year, 1946.

Travel in those days was most arduous. It meant a train to London, crossing from Euston to Waterloo, another train to the coast, ferry to Denmark and then the train to Aarhus. I travelled alone with the bike, spare wheels, a suitcase and a kit bag of cycling clothing. On arrival I had a day to recover, get to the track for a warm-up session, return to the hotel and race the next day at the meeting. The report in *Cycling* said:

> Good Show by Godwin in Denmark. In the 4,000 metres pursuit Godwin led all the way to the half way mark, Gissil pulled ahead in the closing stages to win by one second.
>
> Other events in which the Englishman figured were the handicap when riding from virtual scratch he won in fine style and the six-lap point to point when he finished level on points with Johansen, scoring 10 points each. Godwin was awarded the race by finishing with more points in the last lap.

It was my first trip as an individual and I had had very good results. I came home very happy, knowing I had made many friends in Denmark.

Reg Harris at this time was spending more time abroad than at home, getting the top class racing so important to bring a rider on.

There were continual reports about this time of Ken Marshall, a Poly rider, making attempts at standing records, the half-mile in particular. His aim, obviously, even in 1947, was to establish himself as the top contender for the kilometre time trial in the '48 Olympics. Ken was a very classy rider but could not just find the consistency to prove himself as No 2 in the sprint line up. Pond and Bannister were immediately in line after Harris. Ken and I were in and out as No 4. His attempt at Bill Bailey's half-mile record was 59 seconds against Bill's 57 seconds. It was never in my brief from 'The Boss', my Dad, to attempt these records. Anything from the half-mile to the 1-hour could have been within my reach with preparation. Ken, so it was alleged, was obsessed with the ideas of establishing times to prove his worth. Right up to the Olympics in '48 he would have timekeepers ready at Monday Competition Nights, hoping the ideal night would happen and then, bingo, let's go. It was reported once that had achieved a 1.13.

A new arrival on the pursuit scene was the very shy strong man from the time trial world, Charlie Marriner. Charlie had reached the semi-final stage of the individual championships, as had George Fleming. These qualifications went on for some time around the country. First, by winning through in your own centre, then meeting riders from other centres, then to a semi-final and final at a meeting where the promoter had paid a fee to the NCU. Manchester had won this right, and, at a big meeting due to take place, Marriner and Fleming turned up with me and were supposed to ride with Cartright. He had not ridden his previous round but was to be included in the semi-final irrespective. He did not turn up, so there was much discussion by the knowledgeable officials. I, in the meantime, had won the 500 metres scratch for the Ridings trophy and had been placed third in the handicap final. We were then asked to ride a three-up final. We all agreed, but I had no interest, thinking of the five-mile scratch, the last event of the day. The headline in *Cycling* said:

Marriner Wins But Pursuit 'Final' Nearly a Flop

Another headline was:

Three Sportsmen Made a Race of Pursuit Championship

Marriner was immediately named for the World's in Paris. I was later nominated No 2 when Fleming pulled out. He had decided to concentrate on selection for the road team.

At a meeting on Whit Tuesday at The Butts, Coventry, a very popular day of sport which included athletics as well as cycling and was organised by my club the Rover RCC, I witnessed something which was brought to my attention by a man who acted as a pusher off. Reg Harris, Sensever, Babinet and Lanners (the last three were French riders) were drawing straws or sticks to determine who should be the winner of the 5-mile for the Dunlop Cup, of which I was then the holder. Three riders were to help one rider to get through to win. As events turned out things went awry. Sensever jumped with a block set up against him by other riders. Unfortunately, Sensever (allegedly) punctured and crashed. Harris swung out, hit the concrete wall, snapping his right pedal off. Lanners, Babinet and Lew Pond were involved in another spill and I went merrily on my way to win. It was second claim on the trophy, which I subsequently went on to win outright later in my career.

Other meetings on the grass were taking my time up. I was always looking for trophies to win outright. It became a motivating factor in my life trying to emulate great performers of the past, such as Albert White, Albert Theaker and Denis Horn – all outright winners of the famous Muratti Cup, which I eventually won outright.

My working life was becoming a bit of a problem. I was still working full-time as an electrician at the BSA .The Company were very fair to me, allowing me to take time off when I was selected to race abroad, either as an individual or as a member of a selected team. I had been selected in 1945 and 1946. Now it was 1947 with the World's due to take place at the Parc de Princes in Paris. But I had already been to Denmark, with my wages paid in my absence, which was not acceptable with some of my work mates. There had been pressure put on me to join a union, The Electrical Trades Union. I was not and never have been an enthusiast of this type of thing, choosing to stand on my merit. I felt that if my work was good and I proved myself to be competent, I would be rewarded. I was proud and have always been proud that my ability to work and put the utmost into anything I took on was of paramount importance.

My work mates, not to be outdone, took things further by threatening the boss, Mr Wallis, that if I did not come into line they would strike. The outcome was that Mr Wallis was forced to give me my notice. But, very cannily, he had arranged for the Sales Office to take over the responsibility for paying my wages. This move took me into unexplored territory. I went through various jobs: in the Drawing Office (at which I was a failure), Progress Clerk, Production Control, Viewing, in charge of a Frame Building Section – all out of my calling, but I was fascinated.

During the month of June 1947 on a very pleasant evening and one that I must have been showing some feelings towards Eileen she suddenly said, "I would like to try for a baby." I had never shown any disrespect towards Eileen but was always so dedicated to my training that making love was never my first priority. I was, of course, very thrilled to know that we were hopefully going to start a family. Fortunately, Eileen conceived that night and informed me shortly afterwards when the time of the month passed. A few weeks on it was confirmed by the doctor. We were both very excited and happy. We had been married nearly three years and, God willing, we would hopefully be parents of our first child. We were both then twenty-six years of age. In those days Eileen and I were both very naïve, thinking that sex, as it is now known, was for procreation. So when Eileen suspected then confirmed that she was expecting, the whole idea of lovemaking came to a halt. Every care was to be taken that Eileen should progress through the full time of pregnancy without me making any demands.

Fortunately, my move in my job did not cause any problems domestically because I was still going to be paid the same money that I had been receiving in my normal job. I did find it very frustrating to be directed into a drawing office. I was put onto cycle design. One of the draughtsmen was Bob Maitland, who I knew of in the racing world, having competed against him in time trials, but I had no close relationship with him. He was very surprised when I told him I was starting in the office.

It soon became apparent, and by my own admission, that I was not and could not ever become competent at this kind of work. I was frightened, nervous and embarrassed. I was soon moved but not before I had become very close to Bob and the office. I had been put into an experimental workshop with a first class engineer and tool room man, a Mr Arthur Phillips. Instructions were given from the top brass that I was to help in building my own racing frame. This was very exciting and enjoyable and it was to lead me into my future away from BSA.

From the interest in this venture and the Company now being aware that both Bob and I were international riders, came the idea of building a new range of lightweight cycles. They had always been in the in the consumer market with mass-produced roadsters and sports bikes, but now they wanted something special. This, of course, was early days. On the racing scene there was the World's from July 26th to August 2nd.

The month of July was very important to me. It included the BSA Open Sports Meeting, with both cycling and athletics, a day which attracted many stars of both interests. Crowds of 10,000 would attend meetings of this type. The

T Godwin winning
the BSA Bowl 1947

racing took place on a grass track. The promoters, members of the staff in the Company, went to great lengths to organise the day well. On one occasion, as a child star, Petula Clark came along to present some of the prizes. At that time she would have been perhaps thirteen or fourteen years of age. I was always anxious to do well here because of the huge following from fellow work mates.

Amongst the cycling stars were Lew Pond, Jerry and Wilf Waters and Jack Pratt. Lew Pond won the 500 yard scratch for one BSA trophy and I won the 5-mile BSA Bowl, 43 and 26 beating Jerry and Wilf Waters. I had previously won the 880 yard handicap from the virtual scratch mark of eighteen yards.

In 1947, in anticipation of Harris winning the Vitonica outright, the Wheelers had instituted a Grand Prix of Manchester Sprint Title. Two classic sprint events at one meeting. Harris, having won the Vitonica, the heats and semi-finals of the Grand Prix were held. In spite of Alan Bannister, Lew Pond and many other top class sprinters being present, Harris found himself with T Godwin as his two-up final opponent. This was much to the surprise of riders, officials and spectators, but I had beaten Lew Pond in the semis and Harris had disposed of Bannister.

Then there was an approach from Reg himself, "What could we arrange for the final?" Very casually I said, "What do you mean?" Harris said, "Well I want to win this and you want to win the Muratti, I can help you." My reply was, "I don't need your help to win a 5-mile. You know where I go from in the sprint, the telegraph pole in the back straight, and if you can get by me, you're the better man." There was no reply, he just walked away. The race went as I suggested and Reg did win but by a very small margin. A photo of the finish was later shown by Charlie Fearnley, the fitness expert who used to give training tips

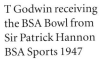

T Godwin receiving the BSA Bowl from Sir Patrick Hannon BSA Sports 1947

in *Cycling,* with the caption, "Two superb athletes, showing determination and style." As it happened, I went on to win the Muratti '5' (or the '10 Mile Invitation Race', as the trophy reads). The report from *The Bicycle* read:

T Godwin with BSA
Bowl 1947

Harris's big haul at Fallowfield Meet

The NCU selectors at Fallowfield, Manchester, last Saturday saw Reg Harris, Alan Bannister, Lew Pond and Tommy Godwin all justify their selection for the forthcoming World Championships.

A magnificent sprint double by Harris, winner outright of the Vitonica Cup and the first winner of the Manchester Grand Prix, and a brilliant triumph by Godwin in winning the Muratti Cup were the outstanding performances in a programme of excellent riding.

In the Manchester Grand Prix over 1,000 yards, the four to qualify for the semi-finals were Harris, Bannister, Pond and Godwin. Harris won one semi-final, Godwin a surprise winner of the other, beating Pond.

A two-up final Harris – Godwin. Godwin met Harris and wasted no time or finesse on tactics. Riding from the front, making his effort at about 300 yards to go, and forged ahead round the bend.

But Harris came round magnificently on the outside and in a neck and neck finish was a wheel in front at the line.

The Muratti, once again a first class field, Godwin, the holder of the trophy, early secured his position in the race and was closely shadowed by Harris for the better part of 16 laps (race distance 17½ laps).

The French riders Babinot and Jeanot both tried to break away, and at one point Jeanot was joined by Worthen (Manchester Clarion) to gain a quarter of a lap. It was not until the 14th lap that Bannister went forward in great style, taking Godwin, Harris and the field up to the break.

Jockeying for the sprint positions, Harris found himself at the rear and at the bell Godwin was still comfortably placed, with Bannister, Jerry Waters of London and the two French riders handy.

From the 220 yards mark, the leaders, Bannister and Godwin, fighting out a great sprint finish. Harris sat up and retired from the race. Godwin came down the straight to cross the line as winner from Bannister by half a wheel, and Waters third.

So, following on from '46, a second win in the Muratti and a surprise finalist in the Grand Prix of Manchester. To beat Lew Pond in the semis gave me as much satisfaction as winning the Muratti for the second time. But, secretly, I would have loved to have beaten Harris in the sprint and rubbed his nose in it.

At this stage in my career I was becoming somewhat disenchanted with the manner in which the sport was being manipulated. Some judging decisions were overlooking the rules, there were arranged rides, with riders being approached to gang up on one rider. I had always ridden with a strong mind, a superb physical condition and a will to win. But I was finding out how some people resorted to fixing races to suit individuals or to suppress ability.

My trophy count was now: the BSA Gold Column, won outright with wins in 1945, 1946 and 1947, the Muratti Cup with two shares in 1946 and 1947 and the BSA Gold Vase with one win in 1946. A number of silver trophies were on hold with a view to winning outright at some future stage, but the beautiful gold ones were always very much in my mind.

With two successful meetings in my pocket, it was now time to think of the forthcoming World's, to be held in Paris. There was only one more big meeting at Herne Hill before my departure on 19th July. Riding a Madison with Ricketts, which we won, I had the misfortune to crash in a change over mix up. I remounted on a borrowed bike, but had picked up some injuries and arrived in Paris with sticking plasters showing.

The arrangements for the World's were not ideal. Believe it or not the notice in the press read:

> The Sprinters will leave Victoria on July 23rd at 9am, the Pursuit riders the next day same time".

The journey was by train – ferry – train, then get to the hotel, settle in, one day on the track and then – "Coureurs, attention!" – racing was underway. Good organisation by the NCU! The road team travelled on July 30th direct to Rheims, both amateur and pro races being on the same day, August 3rd.

We were a little more fortunate as the pursuit started on July 28th. The first day's racing was on the 26th at 3.00pm, with heats, repechage, quarter-finals of pro and amateur sprints, plus heats of the motor paced. One can imagine the time left for pursuit preparation. The second day there were the semi-final and finals of the pro and amateur sprints and the second heat of the motor paced. On the third day there was the third heat of the motor paced and quarter-finals of pursuit pro and amateur, starting at 3.00pm.

The pursuit event, it was decided, would be run over the full 9-laps, 4041 metres. Once more our officials were found wanting. Bill Bailey was again only interested in the sprint racing and old friends, and the other official, H E Miles, the NCU Deputy Secretary, had no racing knowledge but could put his thumb up or down as you went past. Charlie Marriner, the new British Champion, rode well in qualifying. I did not settle well and had chosen to ride 91.8", a bit heavy at first but I did qualify in the last sixteen. Charlie used an 88", the gear usually used at Herne Hill.

In the 1/8th finals we both acquitted ourselves well. Marriner was against Ahlar of Czechoslovakia and won convincingly to go to the quarter-finals. My ride was against Coste, the French champion, and I beat him by some 100 metres, riding just to win. The French crowd booed their man, as he had been tipped in France as well as back home as the favourite. In the quarter-finals Marriner rode against Francois of Uruguay, with Francois going on to win by 45 metres. My quarter-final saw me against Guillmet, a young French rider, in a ride not without incident. I took the lead early, and at four laps we were about level when Guillmet punctured. In the waiting time, I too punctured. Then all hell broke loose. Our officials were not aware of the rule that spare wheels must be on the track. The French boy was soon ready and his handlers knew the score. I was asked where my wheels were. I explained and someone dashed off, coming back with a pair of Reg Harris's wheels. His rear was a 7T x 1" cog, mine was 8T x 1". I had to run the full length of the track centre, grab my wheels, back through the tunnel and across the full length of the track. Someone fitted them and I was ordered immediately back on my bike or be disqualified. I got on all upset to finish the distance. Guillmet's added time, including two standing starts, was the fastest of the series, 5.15. I was out and very demoralised.

Later in the year, at 'The Meeting of Champions,' the French boy came to me and said, "Godwin, Champione du Monde!" I looked at him and he informed me that I should have won as I was in good form to beat Coste. For his own part, he admitted that his trainer had given him a shot whilst I was running for my wheels. He had confessed to using drugs. Incidentally, Francois, who had beaten Marriner, went on to the final and took second place. The winner that year was Benfenati of Italy in 5.20 and 2/5 seconds.

On my return from Paris I was in a trough of misery, disappointed at the outcome of the World's. I was due to return to the hard grind of grass track racing come the August Bank Holiday. On the preceding Wednesday I was at Leicester, defending the 5-Mile Grass Title that I had held 1944, 1945 and 1946, and also third in 1939. In the sprint for the line I just lost to Jerry Waters. A photo showed a very narrow margin. I had finished second to Pond in the sprint earlier.

At the end of that week I decided that I had taken everything out of my body and I needed a rest. I told Eileen that we would take a holiday to Bournemouth and have a week away, Eileen and me and her younger sister, just relaxing. This was very good for Eileen, who was now three months pregnant. No bike, no thoughts about racing, but I still had some commitments on my return.

I had agreed to travel to Southampton to ride a special match against Marriner. The Southern Paragon had organised the meeting to show their appreciation of the honour Charlie had brought to their club as National Pursuit Champion, holder of the British 1-hour record and representative in the World Championships etc. I beat Charlie by a narrow margin of 2/5 second. I had previously finished second in the Sprint final. This event was on September 28th.

The following Sunday I had entered the Wal Hobday '25' time trial. On a cold, misty morning, I surprised a number of people by posting the fastest time of 1-1-32. Second was the holder from the previous year, A W Butler of Woolwich CC, a formidable road man, 4 seconds down, and third Cyril Cartwright, who had been flying in 25's through the year.

I gained so much pleasure from this success. Cartwright was on the road in front of me, and at all the time checks I was up on him. He knew I was moving well when we crossed over. At the finish he stood in the road for some time. He was the scratch man and he did not want me to beat him. But when the shout went up, "Here he comes!" Cartwright went berserk as they stopped the watch and he knew that I had beaten him. I rode back to him, offered my hand and said, "Sorry I didn't wish you good morning on the road." He looked down at my chain, which he said was rusty. I said, "No, that's Fallowfield dust," and every time I looked down at it I thought I must beat him. I then suggested that we go to back to the changing rooms for a cup of tea. Very sarcastically, he refused. I was glad I had no time for him or the Manchester Wheelers. I was also proud when I knew that I had led the Rover team to win the team race. The trophy,

'The Wal Hobday', was in memory of a young Rovers man who had been killed flying bomber planes during the war. My last '25' previous to this was in March on a medium gear of 72", which I won, part of my early season work to get ready for Herne Hill on Good Friday.

The 1947 season ended and I had more thoughts and concerns for Eileen and the new arrival in March. At work I was settling down and facing the fact that although my wages were being paid by the Sales Office, I was simply being accommodated and finding myself being used at whim by various heads of departments.

The first of the new range of lightweight cycles were now being built. The design of which with my practical eye did not seem right. One of the head lugs had been designed wrongly, giving a strange appearance. I mentioned this but it had to be accepted now because supplies had been received from the manufacturer. I also saw ¾" chain stays, which looked fragile against the normal ⅞" diameter. When one of the cycles was completely built I noticed that the bracket seemed very high. I measured from the floor to the centre of the bottom bracket axle and found that it was 12¼". The standard was usually 11" and on a racing machine 10⅞". I mentioned this and it led to some concern. It meant that the top tube height was 1¼" higher than usual, and a person normally using a 22½" frame size would only require a 21" frame with the saddle down on the top tube to facilitate touching the ground.

I was summoned suddenly one day to see the Works Manager, a Mr Albert Woods. He was a strong willed, self opinionated, blasphemous man, who really had no time for me as he and my father had crossed swords on occasion, neither giving an inch. As I opened his office door I was met with, "Godwin, what do you think of this new range of cycles, and I want the truth?" I went on to give my opinion as I saw it and explained what I saw as bad design and inferior to the market. He immediately picked up the phone and asked for Bob Maitland to come down. We waited. There was a knock at the door. I was standing so I backed behind the door. Woods shouted, "Maitland, what do you think of this new range of cycles?" Bob's reply was, "They are very good in my opinion." I pushed the door to and the look of surprise was enough. Bob knew that Woods had been told. I had offered to see Mr Woods and explain the mistake on behalf of the Development Team and this had been agreed. This meeting caused an upset between Bob and me.

Just at that point the phone rang. Woods answered it then said, "Godwin, it's for you." It was from the General Hospital, telling me that Eileen had been in an accident while traveling as a bus passenger. A lorry had backed out of a side road and the bus had collided with it on the side Eileen was sitting. She had been taken into hospital and was under observation because of her condition. I immediately threw the phone down and dashed out of the office, with Woods shouting, "Godwin, come back!" My reply was, "Sod you and the job!" He shouted again and Bob called, "Tom, Mr Woods said that he was phoning to get a car from the Directors Garage." I was driven into town in a large Daimler car, to find Eileen shaken and upset but with no damage to her or the baby.

R Harris and
J Bannister beating
T Godwin and
J Lanners in a special
invitation match in
preparation for the
1948 Olympics

The following day Bob and his wife Muriel came to visit us. We were then living with my parents. I was unable to accept Bob's apologies for the upset caused by our meeting and I was not very polite to him. This passed in due time and we have become very good friends in later life.

Pressure was building up at home with Eileen now very concerned that I should devote as much time as possible to be with her in the later stages of her pregnancy.

On December 3rd in *Cycling* the full team of Olympic Possibles was shown. There were four in the sprint list (Harris, Bannister, Pond and Meadwell), eight in the kilo line up (I Cox, T Godwin, K Marshall, R Meadwell, J Pratt, D Ricketts, I Scott and H Worthen), four in the tandem teams, but Harris and Bannister were obvious favourites, fourteen names for the team pursuits and a long list of road men. In the same issue there was a big story about Marriner being invited to sign the 'Golden Book of Cycling', something which made me very envious.

CHAPTER 11

1948
Touring in
South Africa
– fatherhood
– Manchester
Wheelers meet
and a Muratti
attempt – London
Olympics

Some time in December and invitation came telling me that I had been selected as a member of a six-man team to tour South Africa, leaving England late in January with a total of six weeks away from home. I was sure I would have to refuse as our first child was due to be born on March 18th. The return was not until early March. However, Eileen has never stood in my way, particularly when being invited to represent my country. My family assured me that every care would be taken of Eileen and I was not to worry. Mother, in particular, was most supportive and Eileen was very happy with her promise.

The team selected were Reg Harris, who refused the invitation, which was then offered to Ron Meadwell, Lew Pond (captain), Alan Bannister, Dave Ricketts, Ian Scott and me.

Information given in *The Bicycle* for January 28th 1948 ("Bicycle Interview First Class" by John Dennis) showed that the trip would involve considerable travel as we went to various parts of the Union.

We were due to depart from London on January 29th. The trip included three overnight stops before we arrived in Johannesburg, where we were booked in at the famous and sumptuous Carlton Hotel. The whole atmosphere was bewildering. As we made for our rooms I saw two people that I immediately recognized, Tony Mottram and Kay Stammers, two of our most famous tennis players of that time. I introduced myself after confirming their identity, to find that their itinerary was ahead of ours and that we would not meet again despite an almost identical tour.

The hotel strict dress code gave some embarrassing moments when one of the team strolled in the first evening wearing shorts, sandals, colourful shirt and a Panama hat. Some careful man management was required, which I was chosen to sort out. A coat and tie were supplied by the hotel, the team member did have trousers and shoes. The five star plus menus made choices difficult, but patience and help from the South African officials with the party soon solved any problems. After our first meal we were ushered onto a balcony with local radio people, with crowds of people in the road below, and interviewed. It was a wonderful welcome to a superb country.

We had a local man, Cyril Geoghan as team manager. He was very fair, knowledgeable and a pleasure to travel with. Also at our first meal were Mr Vogt, President of the South African Federation, and Mr Maltz, a wealthy businessman, with whom I struck up an immediate bond. I openly admired his suit, which caught my eye. I told him I thought it was very nice. He smiled and remarked, "Would you like one just like it, Tommy?" I laughed and said, "Yes." The following day he arrived at the hotel with a suit length of this wonderful blue birdseye material, telling me there was enough material to make two pairs of trousers. I could not thank him enough, I was embarrassed, but he simply said, "I think it will suit you very well." We shook hands warmly and parted

Our first match was in Bulawayo, Southern Rhodesia. The headline in *The Bicycle* read:

National Records Broken At Opening Meeting.

Pond took the Rhodesian Record for 440 yards. Bannister broke the 880 yards handicap South African record. In the teams pursuit the national 4,000 metres record was beaten by the British team of Bannister, Scott, Godwin and Ricketts. In the half-mile handicap we all started from scratch. I agreed to take our boys up to the bunch and then get out of the way. The result was Meadwell, Ricketts and Scott in 56.7 seconds. Our next ride was back in Johannesburg at a suburb called Krugersdorp, on a big flat track with a nice surface.

MORE SA RECORDS TO GO – *The Bicycle* headline.

If I had an easy day in Bulawayo, I certainly made up for it at Krugersdorp. In my first ride, 440 yards scratch, Meadwell was first, I was second, with the South Africans third and fourth. In the second match it was Bannister, Pond and then two South Africans. Then there were 1,000 metre scratch races. In the first match it was Meadwell, Pond followed by two South Africans and in the second match it was Bannister, Ricketts again followed by two South Africans. I then rode the kilometre and took the South African Record with 1.13.5, Ricketts 1.15.5, Benvenuti 1.16.3 and Botha 1.17.3.

We then rode the 4,000 metre team pursuit (Bannister, Godwin, Ricketts and Meadwell). Scott was missing from this meeting with gastro-influenza. We won by some 70 yards. I was then asked if I would ride a special individual pursuit against Wally Rivers, who had not ridden in the team. I won this by riding corner to corner and just putting a kick in on the last lap. I asked to be excused from the 5-mile, which was won by Bannister, a very canny 5-mile rider, with Meadwell second and Pond third. The Match result was 32 points to 5.

Our next ride was in Durban, a five hundred mile journey by train. We were greeted with rain, but on the day of the match it dried up after a wet morning. In a series of match sprints, GB v SA, we won 5 out of 6, only Scott, who had recovered from illness, was beaten. Bannister and Pond took the final of the 1,000 yard sprint, with 'Banny' first followed by Pond (220 yards in 12.5 seconds). In the teams pursuit the same riders as in Krugersdorp won in 5.12.5 against 5.24. The 5-mile scratch was won by Bannister, followed by Godwin and Ricketts. The meeting was then rained off. Pond had an attempt at the FSTT 440 yards, which he did in 25.8 seconds, beating the South African Record by 3/5ths of a second.

Our next meeting was at Paarl, thirty-five miles outside Capetown. The track, 1173 yards round, was very difficult to ride. It was roughly rectangular, with bankings no more than five feet high, made of sun baked clay, loose on corners but very fast on the straights! This was our final match before the big 'Test March', South Africa v Great Britain. We had been riding teams from the provinces around the tour but the Test match would bring all the top boys together. Here at Paarl we again won every event, taking more records. I beat the Province kilo record by some 3.8 seconds.

The report from *The Bicycle* read:

Kimberley – the Test Match

South African Tour ends with Test win for England. Every event was won by the
English team, 440 yards, 1,000 metres scratch, 1-mile scratch, 1,000 metre time trial,
4,000 metres team and 5-mile. There were record times in the quarter mile, the kilo
TT and the 4 kilo team, 4.57.7.

Prior to the meeting we became keen on making record attempts. Lew Pond
achieved 29 seconds for the standing start quarter mile (South African Record).
On Wednesday the team achieved 4.58, on Thursday 4.55.6 and on Saturday in
the Test 4.57.7 in the 4,000 metres teams pursuit. On Friday we all agreed to go
for the quarter-mile flying start TT.

Scott went first with 25.3 seconds, then Bannister with 24.7. Pond next equalled this
time and finally Godwin in only his second attempt at the flying quarter achieved
24.5, beating the top two.

Bannister decided to go again with a gear raised from 92" to 96" and equalled
Godwin.

These times beat W J Bailey's record of 24.8 seconds, set up at Herne Hill in
the early 1900's.

We had all trained well, lived well, shared good company, with a fantastic
team spirit and a wonderful manager. We had had perfect hosts to perform for
and great personal satisfaction for every member of the team. The whole tour
could be reported in more detail with regard to experiences away from the racing and the hosting of the team at various stops. There were also our attempts
to assist the local teams in how they should train, race, even to changing their
positions on the bike. There were visits to diamond centres and mines and a
variety of other interests.

Our return home was eagerly awaited, especially by my wife Eileen. I actually arrived ten days before the birth of our daughter, Kay. Her birth was on
March 18th. Eileen had been very well cared for by my family and she went into
hospital for the birth. In those days a mother was kept in for a number of days
to recover fully. In fact, if the birth took place at home with a midwife in attendance, the mother was expected to stay in bed for ten days after giving birth.

On the day Eileen was due home I went to the hospital by bus and a keen
young cycling friend of mine, Teddy Dunne, followed on his bike. When we got
to the hospital I asked Ted to ride to Snow Hill Station, which was not far away,
and to hire a taxi. I went into the hospital to get Eileen and the baby and we then
walked to the gates to find Ted very disconcerted. He met me with, "No-one
would come." Eileen immediately said, "We'll go on the bus," which I refused,
feeling that I had let her down badly. I looked over the road and could just see a
taxi parked in a side street outside a pub. I went into the pub and asked loudly,
"Who is the driver of the taxi?" to be met with, "Me, why?" I said I had a job for
him but he was reluctant to go as he'd just bought a pint. I countered by saying,
"I'll buy you a dozen pints if you'll take my wife and new baby to Perry Barr." A
big swig of about half a pint and we were on our way.

Getting to my parents' home, there was plenty of excitement with Mom, Dad
and my sisters all waiting. Dad had even given up going to the greyhound rac-

ing. Once they saw Kay and laid her on the table with a blanket and pillow, eve-ryone wanted to play with her. Even Dad, who wanted to get her kicking her legs – another sporting hope! Eileen then mentioned that she wanted a few items from the shops, only about quarter of a mile away up the road. I volunteered to go with the shopping list. When I got near the shops I heard the crowds shout-ing at the dog racing track and as I occasionally attended with Dad, I thought I would just pop in for the last three races. At that time 1/- would get you in for the final three races. I was without a programme, but by watching the tote, peering over people's shoulders to read dogs' names and watching the book-makers, I managed to back the last three winners and pick the last three fore-casts for first and seconds. My total winnings were £17-10-0d. I was shocked, thrilled and worried. I would have to tell Eileen and she would be upset at me for even thinking of 'going to the dogs'.

On getting back home, no-one really noticed that I had been away for over an hour. The baby was still being the centre of attention. I made a signal to my Dad and walked out to the back garden. He followed and I told him what I had done. He was more upset that he hadn't been than that I was in trouble. He said, "You'll have to tell Eileen." When we finally got the baby into our own room at the front of the house and Eileen was sitting down, I came out with, "I've got a confession to make." Eileen said, "What do you mean?" I started telling her the story that I had been to the dogs. She was absolutely disgusted. "I'm ashamed of you," she said. "Yes, but I won £17-10-0d," which in those days was equal to three weeks' wages. When I hastily started throwing pound notes and ten shil-ling notes on the table Eileen's face changed and I said, "There, buy yourself a new outfit." I was still considered a naughty husband, but lovely. She did buy a new suit for the christening, which took place a few weeks later.

Herne Hill was only a week away and I was anxious to ride with the form I had, also knowing that BSA had supplied a second Gold Column to replace the one I had won in 1945, 1946 and 1947. But this was not to be. I had picked up an ear infection on the South African trip and a few days after becoming a dad I was suffering the utmost pain. This was diagnosed as an abscess in my ear. I attended the Ear, Nose and Throat Hospital in the week, only a few days before Good Friday.

I was directed to a waiting room for outpatients and waited some time as there was quite a crowd. Three doctors were working. When there was a shout of "Next" I looked round and various people nodded at me. I said, "It's not my turn yet." But they only said, "You can go before me" and, "I don't want that doc-tor." I found out later that he was a Hungarian, nicknamed 'The Butcher.' I soon found out why. He examined my ear very forcefully, then went in with some tool, it certainly did not feel like a surgical instrument, gouged away, twisting and turning, and finally withdrew saying, "That's got it." Obviously, I was in pain for some days and had to notify the promoter of my situation, so missing the opportunity to show my fitness,

The 5-mile point to point was won by Eugene Kamber, a Swiss rider with whom I was to become very friendly later, second was Dave Ricketts and third

Ian Scott. Dave and Ian were two of my team mates, who I would normally expect to beat in points racing. I feel sure from the way the race was reported that I would have been up amongst them. I was subsequently the winner in 1949 and once again later, so proving my ability as No 1 point to point rider in the country.

Reg Harris was also missing at the meeting, having had a road accident on the way to London. First reports suggested that he would be up and racing within a month. On April 14th it was announced that, "Since an earlier report, Harris will not be riding for some time. He has been released from hospital, confined to bed, and medical reports are that he has fractured his spine, definitely no guide is available as to when he will ride his bicycle again." Whenever Reg had a fall or injury it was nearly always life threatening. He was later in his life to become a hypochondriac, always asking how poorly he was and having repeated tests. (From a fractured spine, he did well in the Olympics).

At a meeting on May 1st at Herne Hill, which included an omnium, the South African Touring Team v The Rest, I won the 1-lap scratch from Pond and Meadwell, and then won the kilometre TT and rode in the 4,000 metre winning team. It was very inclement weather and some events were not run. Surprise, surprise, the report of the meeting on May 8th at Herne Hill in *The Bicycle* for May 12th stated:

Harris Still the Master Sprinter.

Amazing how quickly a fractured spine can heal! Further in the report it said:

The NCU have no worry about the sprint in the Olympics if Reg Harris's return to form is anything to go by." The NCU had declared over the winter period, "Not One Olympic Title Must Leave This Country!

On the same day I had chosen to race at Derby, or I may not have been invited to Herne Hill. However, Derby was a happy hunting ground of mine, and not so far to travel. In the 440 yards handicap, I was second to Meadwell (off 23 yards), Godwin (off 16 yards), but went on to win the 1-lap cratch, and also the 10-mile scratch. I was still trying to sweep the board every time I raced. On reflection, once again I realise how I could have been capable of achieving more at international level had I but specialized at one discipline. But the prizes kept coming, so what? Grass track, cinder track, hard track sprint handicap, sprint scratch, 1,000 metre TT, individual pursuit 4,000 metre, 5-mile, 10-mile, 20-mile, 25-mile, tandem paced, Madison, tandem racing – they were all the same to me. In one hill climb I finished second to Bob Maitland.

On May 14th at Coventry, Harris beat Pond and Godwin in the 440 yard scratch. It was the same result in the 880 yard scratch. However, I won a thrilling 5-mile from Bowes and Babinot. The same day the 5-Mile Grass Title was held. It was my first absence from this event since 1939 when I was third. I had followed this by winning the title in 1944, 1945 and 1946 and was second in 1947. On Whit Tuesday May 24th at Coventry the headline was: "Harris – Godwin

Retain Trophies. The Dawes Cup 500 Yards finished Harris, Pond, Godwin and the Dunlop Trophy finished Godwin, Ricketts, Babinot."

On June 2nd there was a very interesting preview by John Dennis in *The Bicycle* of all riders in contention for Olympic places. This was a very sincere and knowledgeable assessment, and one which largely came to fruition. His choice of riders in each event proved to be very close to the final selection.

The National Sprint Championship on June 5th at Herne Hill produced the headline in *Cycling*:

> Bannister Dethrones Harris, New National Sprint Champion.

This was the surprise of the year. I was beaten in the quarter-finals by Ken Marshall. In the semis Harris beat Pond, and Bannister beat Marshall. In the final Pond was third and Marshall fourth.

Cycling reported that:

> An Olympic teams pursuit trial became a farce. Godwin, Ricketts, W Waters and J Love beat Geldard, Meadwell, Fellows and Keeler. Ricketts and Keeler punctured, Meadwell sold out with two to go, nothing proved.

At Manchester on June 19th I received a good press for a win in a 5-mile, beating four Belgian riders. They were taking the lap prizes and attempting to control the race to provide a winner. At the bell Casein jumped, there was an attempt to block me, but I chased and caught Casein and passed him, going on to win by five lengths from van Brabant. Earlier I had finished third in the invitation 500 metre sprint to Harris and Geldard.

Around this time at an evening meeting at Fallowfield Reg Harris rode a 1,000 metre TT in 1 minute 18.2 seconds and Bannister 1 minute 21.8 seconds, both obviously still interested in being the selection for the kilometre in the Games. At the Butts, Coventry at an evening meeting, I rode 1 minute 14 4/5 seconds for the kilometre, establishing a new record for the track under by no means favourable conditions. The previous record was 1.16.

The Muratti would be mine with one more win, to add to the BSA Gold Column already mine after three successive wins. But what would be the outcome? Would fate be against me, or would some other reason unfold to prevent me winning? The result was that I did not win. Bannister did and I was second. Remember, the previous year Harris wanted an arranged final to the Grand Prix of Manchester and I would not agree. He had offered his help to me in the Muratti if I agreed to help him win the Grand Prix. As has been previously described, the Muratti had been reduced to a 5-mile from a 10-mile race to suit Reg, who was competing in this, the '48 race. I did not know until 1982 when Schandorf, a regular competitor in England, came to me at Leicester World Championships, patted me on the back, and said, "Tommy, you win the Muratti in the end, eh?" I said, "What do you mean?" He then explained that his two countrymen, Benny Schnoor and Andersen, had been paid by the Wheelers to stop me from winning the Cup outright.

On reflection, I remembered that in the final lap, and, by the way, after Reg had crashed out with Geldard and Nihant of Belgium, I was following Benny Schnoor into the back straight. My favourite place was the telegraph pole in the back straight. I made my effort, got up to Schnoor and was passing as we went into the bend. Schnoor never attempted to get around the bend but took me right up to the fence. I forced myself past him but 'Banny' had gone through the big open spaces. I chased hard but could not just get up to 'Banny'. I felt that the Danes, coming from the steep, banked cement track at Ordrup, were not used to the flattish shale track and could not handle it. I blamed myself for the mistake of not taking the lead earlier. Needless to say, Bannister was happy, a local boy winning. The Wheelers officials, not very nice people, were gloating over a well-organized 'fix'. I was very disappointed, knowing that I would have to make another bid in 1949.

On July 18th, a Monday evening, at Herne Hill the SCCU staged a 1,000 metre TT under Olympic conditions as one of the main events of the evening. Reg Harris was absent as a result of his crash at Manchester on July 9th and thus delayed his showing at the distance still further.

> Tommy Godwin showed terrific form with 1 minute 14 seconds to beat Ken Marshall by 1.2 seconds (*Cycling* report).

But Schandorf, riding later, bettered my time by 2/5th seconds. Marshall was fourth. Nihant of Belgium was third with 1.15.2.

Things were now going my way in respect of selection for the Games, so I thought.

A special report in *The Bicycle* for July 28th said:

> Marshall dropped from Olympic team, the NCU removed his name from the list, his nomination in the 1,000 metre TT to be taken by Reg Harris.

The Olympics were due to start on Saturday August 7th with the sprint and team pursuits up to the quarter-finals. On Monday 9th August the schedule was sprint and teams pursuit up to and including the finals, tandem prelims and repechage. Then on Wednesday 11th August there were the tandem sprints up to and including the final and the 1,000 metre time trial. On August 13th there was a 121 mile road race in Windsor Park. It then seemed clear that Harris could not ride both tandem and kilo, but no decision was taken. In trials in this country we had not broken the 5 minute barrier for 4,000 metres with differing combinations, the best was 5 minutes 2 seconds.

What may surprise readers now was that for the Olympics there was no village as such. Teams for all sports were placed all around the London area in schools, hostels and so on, 20with transport arranged to the stadiums. The track cycle team stayed at the private home of W Mills, Bill, as he was known, who was the Editor of *The Bicycle*. Rationing was still in force, though the war had ended in 1945. Food parcels and supplies were sent from all over the world to help the Olympic cause. To look after the needs of the team with regard to feeding them, my mother, Dora Godwin, volunteered, and was well received. An extremely capable woman in the culinary arts, she soon made her mark with the boys. Needless to say, there were times when 'Toad-in-the-hole' made its way onto the menu, it being a large Yorkshire pudding with sausage in the mix, baked with vegetables and gravy. Dried egg and spam were also included. It was very basic food, with plenty of fruit, milk, cereals, bread etc. There were plenty of home made cakes etc. We were most grateful to Bill Mills.

The team was happy with Bill Bailey, the Team Manager, until the Reg Harris fiasco, after which Bill resigned from the job, saying he wanted no more to do with the Olympics, the NCU, nor racing of any kind and he would never visit Herne Hill track again. The Reg Harris episode was once again Reg choosing to cock a snook at anyone who ordered him to do something, and his own selfish attitude of never wanting to join in with a team. In 1945 he refused to visit Copenhagen with a team, and early in 1948 he would not accept spending six weeks in South Africa with people he considered below his standard.

Reg was possibly the most hated and disliked member of the track racing fraternity, and yet immensely popular with the public and the media. The latter went along with all his phoney excuses, and time after time, after crying off through ill health or a minor crash, he would return so quickly he would be considered Superman with his powers of recovery.

When directed to join the team for the Games he came up with a broken wrist bone and, under medical advice, was to stay at home to complete his preparation. He was also due to have trials with Bannister to decide who would be the sprint choice. Remember, Bannister had beaten Reg in the National Sprint Championship only weeks before. 'Banny' was training well, and in lead out sprints with a tandem he was getting inside 12 seconds for the last 220 yards. When Reg refused to comply with orders he was dropped from the team. This was big news, only for the NCU, weak kneed again, to reverse the decision when Harris said he would come down two days before the Games started for sprint trials. He was also expected to ride a kilo against me to decide who would

Track Team fooling at
HQ Half Moon Lane
1948 Olympics

1948 Olympic track
team exhausted by
antics on lawn at HQ

ride, or hope that the officials would let him ride if the programme could be changed. Bill Bailey, incensed by all this, stated that Harris should be with the team. Failing which, either Harris should be dropped or he would resign. The NCU accepted Bill Bailey's resignation.

Harris did come down, when it suited him. Bannister, meantime, was a nervous wreck. He was always a very edgy guy, but a super little bike rider, with a tremendous burst of speed. The tandem pairing was also in his mind. If Harris was not chosen for the sprint, would he ride tandem? No chance! (My interpolation). Or, what about the Manchester Wheelers officials after the Vitonica and the Muratti race decisions, paying riders to stop someone winning? Did they get to Bannister, or is that too sinister? We were then without a Team Manager. Bill Bailey was perhaps not too suited to advise teams pursuiters, but he did arrange trials and timekeepers and he was a gentleman in every respect. As a four times World Sprint Champion and record holder at various distances, he was very popular in this country and respected abroad. His replacement was Harry Ryan, a past gold medallist on tandem, but he could hardly inspire us at the last moment and our morale was not at its highest when we had our first ride.

However, Harris did finally show his ability by winning the best of three against Bannister. But Alan was nowhere near the lad we had been watching for the last couple of weeks. Whatever took place in his mind will never be known, but in my opinion he would have finished at least as well as Harris. In the final, who knows, 'Banny' at his cheeky best may have found a way to beat the man who won, Ghella of Italy. Again, no questions asked, but it appeared and was alleged that Ghella did not win unaided. In fact, for each ride he was physically carried to his bike on the start line by two beefy Italians. When he finished each ride he was carried from the track to a seat in the Italian camp.

Harris, as it is well known, was beaten in the final by an eighteen-year old Italian especially prepared for the occasion. A very fast, smooth riding Italian sprinter is a pleasure to witness. Ghella's times through the series were outstanding, and the 11.8 seconds 220 yards against Schandorf in the semi-finals was something special, particularly at Herne Hill, a track known for its lack of speed potential. The Resmat asphalt surface was always suspect from the first day it was laid. Very often on getting to your mark when the weather was hot you could see the surface moving into a rut, consequently the track was very rough in places. So, in two straight rides, Ghella became the new Olympic Champion. Harris, sadly, took Silver, a blow to British pride, so much had been made of Harris's superiority, and the public expected victory.

On the same day as the Sprint heats and quarter-finals the first round heats and the quarter-finals of the teams pursuits took place. The GB team of Ricketts, Geldard, Godwin and Waters went to the start to ride against Canada. We were not brimming over with confidence because of all the upset in the camp, and the knowledge that we had not really ridden as a team regularly before the final selection. A lot of rides had been done with different combinations and finally we were the four selected. By whom I never knew, certainly not by Bill Bailey, the original Team Manager. He was probably down in Brighton relaxing after his resignation. I am sure Harry Ryan would not have been called upon due to his lack of experience and understanding, and certainly he did not impose himself on the team.

However, ride we did, but certainly no fireworks. Our winning time was 5.12. France qualified with 5.3, Denmark 5.4, Belgium 5.5 and Italy 5.10. No doubt we felt relieved at qualifying for the quarter-finals and relaxed a little. The sheer terror of riding with the responsibility of representing your country in the Olympics is an awesome thought. The uncertainty throughout the season as to whether you would finally make the team and how the selection would be made was frightening. All other teams had been selected well before to allow them to travel with confidence, and their minds were settled. Every team selection was in jeopardy until the last moment so far as we were concerned.

The quarter-finals saw GB v Denmark, France v Switzerland, Italy v Belgium and Uraguay v Australia.

Our ride against Denmark got the crowd going as we matched them throughout, riding with style and feeling good. We finished with a 5.2 ride against Denmark's 5.5. We had made a 10 seconds improvement in one ride. France showed 5.05, Italy 4.59, the fastest so far, and Uraguay 5.3. From this our confidence grew. We were now in the semis and very much in touch, and competitive. One can imagine the feeling. We were now relieved of the pressure, proud of our position in the last four and a happy that the partisan crowd was behind us.

A journalist's report in *Cycling* read:

> Britain is not a demonstrative nation, but when the national team beat Denmark, people went mad with excitement. Herne Hill echoed and re-echoed to the surging roars of encouragement and congratulations, many handkerchiefs were in evidence to wipe away the tears of joy, and we must admit we had unusual lumps in our throats as the British team rode around, waving their crash helmets to acknowledge the cheers.

In the Denmark team, the rider who cracked under pressure was Benny Schnoor, my adversary in the Muratti Cup Race, who had seen to me in the final sprint, thus preventing me from having a chance of winning. So to the semis, with a draw against France. What a ride they put up to win in 4 minutes 54.4 seconds! We led early on, in a very fast start to the race, and until about half-way were up by about three lengths. Then, suddenly in one lap, they pulled us back and took a two-length lead. I responded by taking a hard, fast turn to close the deficit. As I swung up the banking Wilf Waters kicked through instead of just maintaining the increased speed. I came down to drop on the back and there was a gap I could not close, try as I may. Our remaining three went on losing distance all the time, finishing with 4.59. The report read that even the French were 'hanging on' for the last one and a half laps, feeling the effects of a superb ride, the fastest ever at Herne Hill.

In the dressing room after our defeat by the French, I was distraught, throwing my crash hat across the room and declaring, "You'll never drop me again." I blamed Waters for kicking through, a tactic which has ruined many good teams and prevented classy bike riders from being included in team squads. In a previous round Dave Ricketts had gone off the back, looking lethargic and very uncomfortable. I could not be accused of either. I was proud of my strength, my ability and consideration for other team members. I felt I was in disgrace, and not justifiably, a team mate had worked me over.

In the other semi-final, Italy v Uruguay, the Italians were well up at the half-way point. The Uruguay team realised they had little chance, and both teams finished the distance with no great effort, the Italians winning by 6 seconds. By now we had realised that our best hope was to finish in Bronze Medal position, as GB teams had done in 1932 and 1936.

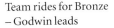
Team rides for Bronze – Godwin leads

We now had the final for third place to ride. We had sorted ourselves out and so many people had told me not to take it personally. I had respect from the team, officials and the public and we all felt good for the ride against Uruguay.

Team crossing
finishing line to take
Bronze

We started fast, as we had done against France, only to find the South Americans up on us in the first lap. In the second lap we were still down by 3 seconds.

> The Englishmen seemed tired, but then Godwin put in a steaming half-lap, then
> Waters another flier, and the margin was reduced. The 'home' riders were now riding
> like demons, a remarkable recovery, and in lap six, a one second lead, then a gain of
> three seconds, when the opposition cracked, lap eight another 2.5 seconds. The bell
> and the four Englishmen went on to finish in grand formation, 49winning by half the
> length of the straight in 4.55.8, the second fastest of the series. France's time in the
> final was 4.57.8. (*Cycling* report.)

The final for first and second was a farce. France was never in command
from the start, as Benfenati had taken the first one and a half laps on the front,
giving the Italians the lead, which they held for some time. Then a big effort
by the French put them into the lead, which they never lost. Benfenati made
a big attempt to get the boys in blue going again, which led to Citterio being
dropped. Now three against four, the Italians were still holding on, when suddenly Decanali went off the back of the French squad.

Two laps to go, France 3.48.6, Italy 3.49.8, a superb finish was expected. Coste
worked hard and at the bell the French lead had increased. Benfenati responded
with a tremendous kick. That one sudden effort was the Italians' downfall. They
opened out like a concertina. The crowd shouted but to no avail. Benefenati was
miles in front, his team mates, shattered, sat up. In fact, one rider nearly stopped
and one of their officials ran across, took hold of the saddle and bars, and proceeded to push the rider around the track to the finish line, a time of 5.36.6.

As I had assumed the role of Captain of the GB Team, I made a protest about
the rider being assisted across the line. The Italians should have been disqualified and GB placed second as Silver Medallists. I was over ruled, but many years
later a German team was disqualified for pushing a team mate in the home

straight to cross the line in Gold Medal position. The Danish team was then declared the winner. Our placing, and the very much improved times from first round to the finals, only confirmed to me the need for a settled team, selected early, with constant practice as the only way to success.

So at twenty-seven years of age, my father's dream had come true, an Olympic Medal. The seed sown some seventeen years before had flowered. Emotions were very high when I finally got to Dad in the crowd and other members of my family and supporters from the Midlands. The team were obviously happy, and the officials of the NCU very proud of what we had achieved. But there was yet more to come. It had finally been agreed on Monday night, after Harris had ridden in the sprint final, that Tommy Godwin would ride the 1,000 metres TT in place of the last minute nomination of Harris.

The kilometre was held on the Wednesday evening and not without some unfortunate incidents. I was happy to be representing GB in the event, but again without any precise preparation. All through the year it was in my mind that Harris or Marshall would be selected. I had beaten Marshall just prior to the Games, and he was informed that he would not be riding. But Ken, a London rider and member of the Polytechnic CC, had been preparing specifically for two years with the kilo in mind. It must have been devastating to him not to get the ride, to come up against a mixer, someone who was just strong, fast and very enthusiastic, competing in all disciplines, being asked to ride the 1,000 metre TT when called upon. In those days I was always said that a good kilo rider or teams pursuit man must come from the tough, hard riding school of grass tracks. It sorted the men out from the boys. But the truth is that without the speed work of the faster hard track surfaces, there is just that little bit missing.

On the night I had a good warm-up, at the right time according to the programme schedule, returning to the dressing room to towel down and have a light massage. By this time in the proceedings Syd Cozens, a famous name of the Thirties, once second in the World's Professional Sprint Championship and a Manchester Wheelers man to boot, came into the picture. Syd and I were good friends, and he had recently moved to Birmingham to take up a job at BSA Cycles as a salesman representative. On entering the dressing room, Syd introduced me to a Belgian soigneur, Louis Guerlache, who had been asked at a late date to assist the GB team – NCU at work again! I was asked if I wanted a rub and, on Syd's recommendation, accepted. During the light, very professional massage, Louis Guerlache remarked, "Godwin FORMIDABLE." I understood this, but the rest of the talk between Syd and Louis I did not understand as it was in Flemish. Syd looked at me as I lay on the table and said, "Louis has remarked that you are in wonderful condition, and he thinks you could win the Gold. I must ask you this, would you like a little help?" The inference of this I understood. I immediately said, "No, if I can't do it with what I have been gifted with then I don't want it." But at the mention of "No" Louis had picked up all the things laid out for the massage, threw them into his suitcase, which was packed with about half a chemist's shop, and stormed away. Syd's remark was, "I think you have upset Louis."

Syd Cozens

While this was happening the tandem racing had been going on between Harris, Bannister and the Italians. It was then the time for the kilo. Dupont, the eventual winner, was in the first group of six riders. Suddenly, the kilo was stopped and the tandems had to continue. The light was fading and there were no floodlights for evening racing. Some three-quarters of an hour later the rest of the kilo riders were summoned to the line. There was no further warm-up, even the use of rollers had never been considered in those days.

When I was called to the line I knew Dupont had ridden 1.13.5, well below what was expected. I also knew that Nihant, the Belgian rider, who had not been in the start list the night before, had ridden 1.14.5. On the start line the track was now in darkness, apart from lights around the outside of the track from building and the officials enclosure. As I started the crowd was unbelievable. I had chosen to ride a 92.5" gear, very heavy at the start. I was always in contention with Dupont and Nihant on the split times, always within 1/10th or 2/10th of a second up to the last 220 yards. At that point I was dead level with Dupont. But over the last 220 yards I lost one and a half seconds to finish 1.15. It was reported in *The Bicycle* that:

Dupont had perfectly still conditions, the flags hanging down the poles. When Godwin rode the air had chilled, the flags were blowing and waving in the strong breeze, and Godwin riding three times into the wind just could not find any more, but finished third in the event that it had always been his ambition to win. He was given a wonderful ovation, truly merited."

So Dad now had a double Bronze Olympic Medallist. Tears of joy flowed that evening.

But I realized that I had not emulated the wonderful Arie van Vliet, whose picture at the Berlin Olympics of 1936 had inspired me. At eighty years of age as I write of these unforgettable moments, the tears flow once more. How near, yet so far. Memories of a sporting career can be very moving and emotional, so much happiness, some sorrow and disappointment, but always that wonderful feeling of achievement and pleasure you have given to so many people. There is also the pride you share with those near and dear to you, your family, who have made sacrifices, encouraged and believed in you.

Harris and Bannister had been beaten by a superb Italian pair, Perona and Terrazi, but Silvers were ours, which meant that every member of the track team had won medals and taken their place on the rostrum. The British crowd had been superb. They had not witnessed what they expected, a Gold Medal or two, but their support was incredible. We had made them happy. Our team had not had the preparation of the Continental teams, there had been numerous upsets, but in the end we could hold our heads up high.

The road team, inspired by the trackies, rode as a team and, for their efforts, took Silver in the team race. Bob Maitland was 6th, Gordon Thomas 8th, and Ian Scott 16th. Clements had retired with a mechanical fault. Thus we added to our medal haul. Every member of the cycle team was proud to be a medal winner.

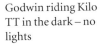

Godwin riding Kilo TT in the dark – no lights

Dupont – Nihant – Godwin – medal winners in the Kilo TT

During the Games I had been approached by the USA officials, who had found out that I was American by birth, asking if I would swop my allegiance and ride for the USA. My answer was that I could not possibly consider such a move as I owed so much to the National Cyclists Union and all the cycling enthusiasts who followed me.

The closing ceremony was not in the order of modern glitz. It was a very revered occasion, with the massed bands of the Brigade of Guards and a brief but moving Closing Ceremony of the Games of the XIV Olympiad. 82,000 people took part in the colourful yet simple atmosphere of pageantry at Wembley that ended the greatest sporting festival in the world and had lasted sixteen days.

An interesting observation from the Official Report of the Organising Committee was that the total expenditure for the Games was £732,000, receipts were £762,000 approximately, with roughly £29,000 profit, subject to tax. The Games are not promoted as a commercial venture, but in the best interests of sport. For this reason many means of raising money are not permissible, for example, the inclusion of advertisements in the programmes or brochures. To read the restraints and conditions is mind boggling today. The mere thought of a coldly calculated business proposition, of which the principal motive was to make a profit, was taboo.

The team broke up with a few handshakes after some six weeks together, Reg Harris not included and who had never shared our makeshift accommodation.

CHAPTER 12

1949
Domestic
upheaval
– the Muratti
again – World
Championships in
Denmark

It was back to our families and home comforts, to the warmth and love that had been sacrificed. In my case, a return to Eileen and Kay, our new born daughter, of whom I had seen little since her birth some five months ago. I wanted to spend some time them in private and bond with our daughter. We were, of course, living with my parents and family, so there was not much chance of privacy. However, we coped, and I found a great deal of happiness. Needless to say, the interest from my friends and work mates was overwhelming. I, of course, had to return almost immediately to my job.

Not long afterwards Eileen and I had to return to London to attend a dinner organized by the NCU to mark the success of the team. This was her moment. She had been unable to attend the Games because of the baby. Eileen was still breast feeding and also no-one was at home to allow her to leave the baby in safe hands. At the function Eileen was asked to say a few words. The Report read, "Mrs 'Tommy' Godwin remarked that it was worth all the sacrifice and loneliness to see the boys happy with the success of the team."

The *Cycling* report read:

NCU Quarrels at Dinner to British Riders!
Olympic Team Forgotten as Officials Clash
A dinner in honour of the team disintegrates into something approaching an open quarrel etc

Regardless of all this, some nice things were said and we knew we had been appreciated and respected for our efforts.

The final sentence in *Cycling* was:

It was a sorry ending to a great week of cycle racing.

Although now back in our respective homes, the riders had further racing commitments, so we were soon at each other's throats again. But our few weeks together as a team had made us very respectful of each other.

The first Saturday after the Games a meeting was held at The Butts, Coventry, including the 25-mile Hard Track Championship. Quite a good field was assembled and this was a title I had held twice, in 1945 and 1946. I missed the 1947 event. The result of the race was a win for Alan Geldard, one of the Olympic teams pursuits riders. He broke away in the latter stages, opened up a good lead, with the viewing public and other riders shouting at me to chase. My reply was, "He's one of my team mates. If you want him, you chase, I'm not going to." The result was a race spoiled for the crowd, Alan winning comfortably. I won the sprint from the bunch for second place. Scott, who had ridden in the Olympic road race Silver Medal team, was third.

There was one more meeting at Herne Hill in September, 'The Meeting of Champions.' We were expected to ride in that, obviously. I won the only event I competed in, the 3-mile points race for the Cooper Cup. Dave Ricketts, another Olympic teams pursuit man, finished second, with the Australian, Russell Mockridge, third.

There was no more racing for 1948. I even declined from riding the Wal Hobday '25' promoted by my own club, the Rover RCC. I had been the winner in 1947 and normally would have defended my title. The year had been a long one. South Africa in January and February and then almost continual training and racing for eight months and more. I was also now the father of a six month-old baby daughter. The autumn and winter were more relaxed, but my mind was then on 1949, so my usual strict routine of general fitness training was soon in action. Obviously there were demands in the social season to attend cycling club dinners, which were very popular in those days.

The usual Christmas and New Year with the Godwin family was very enjoyable with plenty of good food well prepared by Mom, the wonderful lady who had kept the GB Olympic Track Team happy and satisfied with her culinary arts. New Year's Eve with Dad was something special, every detail was discussed about what 'WE' would do in the coming season. The first item on the agenda was to put a share on the new BSA Gold Column on Good Friday. Remember, we had missed the 1948 race as I had picked up an ear infection during or immediately after my return from South Africa. Then we had to get back on the trail of the BSA Gold Vase, 10-miles on grass at Bournville. I had won this event in 1946. In the meantime Jerry Waters had won it in 1947 and Wilf Waters in 1948. I did not compete in the latter. We then had the Muratti Gold Cup, in which I had two shares already and was only beaten in the 1948 race by the Wheelers 'fix', Bannister winning.

The dedicated preparation went on. The same physical and psychological build up from 'the old man', 'THE MOTIVATOR.' But the best of plans can be brought down to naught when fate rears its ugly head.

I was in wonderful condition in January and February 1949, but towards the end of February there was a domestic upheaval. My wife, Eileen, was a very quiet almost timid individual compared with the Godwin family. In particular, my eldest sister, Irene, had openly told Eileen in the past that she disliked her. But, through the years, both had compromised for the sake of family unity. A storm blew up over some small amount of money which had been borrowed from me by my youngest sister, Shirley. Irene took up the defence of her sibling, causing a very unpleasant argument with Eileen. The outcome was that Eileen immediately left the Godwin residence to return with Kay to her family in Stourbridge some sixteen miles away. Communication was very difficult between us.

After being parted for some two weeks I received a letter from Eileen asking me to meet with her in Dudley, just a few miles from he home, and to bring along her ration book and various other personal things. At our meeting in a small café Eileen told me she could see no way out of our problem, and that she felt our marriage was over. I returned home and for a period of fourteen weeks lived in a very hostile atmosphere, staying in my own rooms, only sharing the kitchen and bathroom and fending for myself. On odd occasions when my big sister was out Mom would sympathise with me and continue to be kind. My sister's influence over my parents was frightening. Dad and I, of course, continued our close relationship in the quest for honours in the sport.

Good Friday was very late in 1949, at the back end of April. Regardless of all the upset, I was in good form for Herne Hill and, after missing the 1948 event, proceeded to put my name on the new BSA Gold Column, winning from Ricketts and Scott. This meeting was advertised with the pros being the star act. Harris was making his professional debut in England against A van Vliet and Gosselin. Although Reg won the match, the report read, "Amateurs steal show with spirited racing." I was happy once again to have proved my ability to be well prepared for the season's opening track meeting. I was now four times winner of the Gold Column.

Getting over to see Eileen and Kay as often as possible, kept my hopes alive of keeping us together as a family in the future. At this time it was almost impossible to find houses to rent, and the idea of purchasing could not even be considered as we had no money. Prizes were plentiful, canteens of cutlery, clocks, watches, Grandmother clocks, all sorts of household goods, and an occasional £10 for expenses to a meeting. Some prizes were sold to personal friends. This helped but did not bring in a great amount of money. Eileen did manage to convince an old club mate of mine now retired from racing of her need to get back near to me. He and his wife had a large house and three children. They agreed that another two in the house would make little difference. So Eileen and Kay came to live within a mile of my home.

The meeting at Cadbury's, where the BSA Gold Vase was the main interest, was always held on the last Saturday in May. I had put my name on this famous old trophy in 1946 and, needless to say, I was pleased to put a second share on the trophy at this point in my career.

Just prior to the meeting a young man, a friend of the Godwin family, came along with an offer of a small house to rent. To get the house it meant £25 key money, as it was called in those days, the rent being 12/- a week. Was I interested? Of course, I was interested, but on going to the address, 67 Moseley Street, I found that it was a really depressed area of Birmingham, very close to the well-known market and Bull Ring. The house was a filthy, neglected hovel. The lady who had lived there was obviously poverty stricken, although the number of empty bottles suggested a heavy drinker with no pride or respect.

It was a small terraced house, two rooms downstairs, a minute kitchen about six feet by four feet, a small brown sink and the smallest gas stove imaginable. The outside toilet was to be shared with neighbours, they none too proud but sociable. A brew house with a boiler and another brown sink was in the very, very small blue brindle back yard. My immediate reaction was to refuse, but I held out hope that I might be able to get back with Eileen and Kay. I went to see Eileen and asked if she would come and see it. I could just about manage the £25 key money. Eileen's response was shock and horror. No, she could not live in such a house. I informed her that I was going to take it on and do it up as best I could and live there. I had to get away from the unpleasant family home.

I started by taking out all the old rubbish that remained in the house. I then swept through and set about scrubbing it from top to bottom. The upstairs consisted of two small bedrooms and an attic. Thinking about it now, I can just imagine the thoughts of all the 'bikies' if they could have seen me on hands and knees scrubbing for hours on end to clean a house out. I was still working 47 hours a week at BSA, still training on Tuesday and Thursday evenings on the road and racing when I could.

After the clean out I started the painting and decorating. Eileen called in one day and saw what I was trying to achieve and the place now clean and smelling fresh. She immediately said, "I'll come and give you a hand when I can." She then had to rely on our friends to care for Kay. Eventually we moved in, Eileen remarking, "To think I've been used to seeing cows and sheep, open fields and leading a quiet life, and now here I am in the centre of Birmingham." We worked hard getting rooms set up with linoleum on the floors and making the place look like a home and then went off to bed. Kay was already asleep in the blue room at the back of the house. Our room at the front looked out straight over the roadway, there was no front garden. Off to sleep, very tired.

Around 5.30 in the morning, there was one hell of a noise going on, with lots of shouting. On opening the curtain, I gave one look and shouted to Eileen, "You wanted cows, you've got cows!" The whole road was blocked with what looked like hundreds of cows being taken from the railway depot at the top of the hill to the abattoir by the meat market in town. It became a regular feature of our lives, cows, sheep and pigs all going to slaughter.

Eileen tells me that we moved in during May, so I must have been working on the house just prior to winning the BSA Gold Vase.

June passed and, from memory and also checking through bound volumes of *Cycling* for that year, I appear to have decided that getting my family together was a priority.

There were meetings at Herne Hill and also the opening of the new Fallow-field track around Whitsun. The old red shale track which had existed since the 1800's had been demolished and a new pink cement track built with the same lap size of 503 yards and 30 degree banking. It was a dream come true. For the Manchester boys, the North had the finest track in the country. I did not neglect myself and had been training well, and was very contented with my life back on the track and with my wife and baby.

Looming up was the Wheelers Meet, always held on the second Saturday in July and the Muratti Gold Cup. Come the big day, I travelled up with Dad on the train, riding from the station to the track on my bike, with my racing wheels on wheel carriers. Dad came on the bus. Eileen was coming to a meeting, a big meeting, something she rarely did, with Kay by car with an old friend, Alec Tennant. He had helped me in my first year of racing and he wanted to see the Muratti race. When they arrived at around 1.30 pm they were told that the track was packed out, gates closed and a reported crowd of 15,000. Fortunately, a local man said, "You can't turn her away, she's Tommy Godwin's wife." The security people agreed to let her go in, but she said, "I'm not going in without my friends," whereupon the gateman gave the nod. When they got near the crowd some official not known by Eileen invited her and our friend and his wife to follow him to the track centre where they were given seats.

Dad and I, of course, were already at the venue. When I saw the track and

Finish of Muratti 1949
– Godwin second from
left

knew the field I remarked, "I'm not going to win here today. The continentals will murder me." So much was in favour of riders who competed on such tracks and trained all the time on similar tracks.

The usual preparation was done. Warm-up, usually quite hard, with groups of riders raising quite a sweat on a very fine day, then into the dressing room, strip off, rub down and fresh clothes. I competed in a sprint event but was not very bothered as the 5-Mile was the event I was after. Suddenly, there was a visit from Syd Cozens, the only Wheelers man I had any time for. "Tommy, I have to tell you, Eugene Kamber has told me he has been offered big money to stop you winning." I knew I could not converse with Kamber because of the language difficulty, but Syd was capable. But Kamber and I were good friends. We had for some time been dealing in racing clothing and nylon stockings from Switzerland in exchange for BSA cranks, chain wheels and pedals and also Brooks saddles, also Continental gear mechanisms and multi-freewheels. We were both doing very well out of it. His message was that he would like to help me and not prevent me from winning. He would lead me out for the last lap. Jack Heid had also been approached. We too were friends from the Olympics and both Americans, at that. He came to me and said, "The f...... b......s won't get me working for them against a fellow Yank."

My decision then was to gear up, something I would not normally consider. I put a 92" gear on. Usually I would ride an 88" and keep kicking away from the bunch, riding in the first three or four, ride a fast lap, ease, kick again and get rid of the wheel suckers. Now I was going to be a wheel follower. I had been worked over in '48. What was in store for me now? It was something outside my experience to be riding a race in a completely different manner to what was my usual practice. I normally controlled a race. Here I was waiting for other riders to attack or chase if a break went away.

T Godwin, Dad and
Jack Murfin, pusher
off

I felt almost detached from the action for some fourteen to fifteen laps, simply following Kamber, who was riding a very smooth and relaxed race, staying with the pace but in about 12th place. This continued until about two laps to go. Patterson punctured, the field was still compact, a bunched finish was inevitable. At the bell Jerry and Wilf Waters were leading and moving well. Still back in the bunch, I felt certain I had been conned into believing in an arrangement with someone I could not even talk to. Suddenly a gap opened in the field, Kamber reacted immediately. His pick up of pace was fantastic and he went through like a hot knife going through butter with me on his wheel. We were into the last 200 metres, going like a train, and into the straight. I was giving it all I'd got, moving up fast. As we got to within a yard of the line I gave one desperate lunge, threw the bike forward and crossed the line. As I did so another rider came through on the inside. With me throwing the bike over the line, the immediate reaction is to pull the bike back under you. In doing this and one yard over the line, the rider inside was in front of me. It was Alan Geldard and he threw his arm up really thinking he had won. The crowd was going mad.

One report said,

> Never since the inception in 1899 has the famous Muratti Cup race witnessed such a close finish when Tommy Godwin, Rover RCC won the Gold Trophy for the third time and made it his own property.

The judging at the finish was unanimous: Godwin, Kamber, Geldard, Heid. Jackie had been covering me all the way. Kamber's lead out was actually superb, and I often wondered if he felt he should have been the winner. I did not pick up the result until the announcement on the public address: "The winner Tommy

Running to Dad
– shadow can be seen

Godwin." I jumped off the bike in the home straight, ran over to my old Dad, who hugged me very tight indeed

We were still on track for yet another milestone. We now had a BSA Gold Column, plus one share on the new one, a Muratti Cup, in spite of Manchester Wheelers 'Mafia', and two shares in a BSA Gold Vase.

The outcome of the Muratti win was totally unexpected. I was summoned to the man acting as commentator for the day, Tom McDonald, Reg Harris's personal mentor. He switched off the mike and said, "We will give you £350 for the Cup." My reply was, "My name is not Reg Harris. I do not sell my prizes." His reply was, "You will never ride at a Wheelers Meet again." I responded with, "I don't bloody well want to ride here again. I've got what I want." Needless to say, I was never invited to a Wheelers Meet again, yet it was some four years later that I retired from racing.

My celebration of this event was to travel with my wife and daughter, along with Alec and Dorothy Tennant, in the car to Blackpool and to spend a weekend in a hotel. We were, of course, overjoyed, and, on booking into the hotel, I asked if they could put this wooden case into the safe overnight, which was agreed. We had our evening meal, no mad drinking, none of us were interested, just a warm feeling amongst friends and then to bed.

Next morning I got up to go for a walk alone, as is my wont when staying in hotels, when from behind the reception desk the manager or owner said, "Excuse me, is this you?" He showed me the sports page of the Sunday Empire News and a report from Jim McDermott, a sports journalist who always covered cycle racing. He was always very complimentary to me when I won and for the way I raced, hard and with determination, a fine sportsman etc. Here was an outstanding picture, on the back page, banner headlines and a glowing report. My reply to the question was, of course, "Yes." The next question was, "Can I see the Trophy?" to which I agreed. A quick move to the safe, and I opened the case, which was locked. He was absolutely 'gob smacked,' but very pleased that he had us in his hotel.

The terribly vindictive thing about the embittered Manchester Wheelers was that the race had not been ridden from 1939 to 1946 because of the war. But on the wooden plinth or base were beautiful gold shields bearing the names of previous winners. All the space on these had been taken up, three names to a shield. My first two wins in 1946 and 1947 and Alan Bannister in 1948 would have taken up another shield, and my 1949 calling for another shield.

After my victory and now the owner of the Trophy I wrote to the Wheelers asking if I would be getting the shields. Their reply was, "If you want them, you get them." To this day the base is void of four winning names. The Manchester Wheelers connection goes on! I must add that the reports and write ups in national papers, Sundays and dailies as well as cycle journals, did justice to my success.

The next item of interest was, of course, the World Championships, to be held in Denmark. I had a letter from the NCU informing six selected riders to attend at Herne Hill on the last Monday in July for selection trials in the individual pursuit at the forthcoming World's. The riders in alphabetical order were: Cartwright, Fell, Fellows, Godwin, Marriner and Simpson. Trials would take place in the evening.

On arrival, we were informed that there would be time trials over the distance not match races. This method was criticized in *The Bicycle* when reporting the results:

First, it appears unfair that 'shortlist' riders are gathered together to ride a time trial

Celebrating Muratti with the crowd – the trophy had been filled, passed among the crowd and returned safely

Happy after winning – Eileen and Kay, Dad and Jack Murfin and two officials

for final selection when the very races that gave them their position were completely ignored at the last minute.

All named plus others had been competing in a season-long competition run through the Centres throughout the country on a knock out basis. The semi-finals and finals were due to take place on August 4th at the Coventry Butts Track.

Secondly, it is quite possible the winner of the National Title would not be selected. Sprint nominations made Alan Bannister as National Champion an automatic selection. Why could not the pursuit title have been decided before nominations had to be finalised?"

The result of the time trial that evening was: G Fell 5.23.6, C Cartwright 5.25.6, E Fellows 5.28.0, Godwin 5.28.2, Marriner 5.28.8 and Simpson 5.32.0.

A report of the National Pursuit Championship by *The Bicycle* reads:

GODWIN – AT HOME – WINS NATIONAL PURSUIT TITLE
Semi-final results, Marriner 5.23.4 beats Simpson 5.26.2, Godwin 5.22.6 beats Fell 5.34.8. Final, Godwin 5.22.6 beats Mariner 5.26.8.

Cartwright had not ridden any rounds of the competition but was No 1 selection. Fell had been given the No 2 slot. I, the National Champion, stayed at home. Fortunately, Cyril Cartwright went on to take the Silver and Knud Andersen took Gold. There was to be a sequel to all this in the 1950 season, but first I must conclude the year 1949.

The report of the World Championship Pursuit was very interesting. In the qualifying heat Cartwright clocked 5.24, Fell 5.31. The Ordrup track was one of the finest venues on the Continent at that time. This was my winning time at

Winning National
Teams Pursuit
Championship at
Herne Hill
1949 – Rover RCC:
Godwin, Bridgewater,
Bell and Otley

The Butts, a track called a 'Mickey Mouse' track both for its shape and surface. Even Herne Hill was always quoted as 3.4 seconds faster for a kilo, so over 4 kms one would expect an 8 seconds faster time, and Ordrup was always a much better track than 'the Hill'. Cartwright followed with 5.14.5 in the 1/8th finals. There was no time for quarter-finals due to punctures and restarts. The semi-final time was 5.15.9 and the final time 5.21. Fell 5.31 failed to qualify. Our amateur sprinters were eliminated in the 1/8th finals, Patterson winning, beating Bellinger. Harris won the pro sprint from Derksen, the first Englishman to win the World's Pro Title.

Riding the Catford CC promotion on the first Saturday in September, I pleased the journalist reporting the meeting, Peter Bryan of the *News Chronicle*, who wrote:

> **Catford meeting thrilled best Saturday crowd of the year**
> Godwin's fine form in the tandem paced.
> The high class international field makes it difficult to pinpoint one event or any one rider as outstanding. If it were possible, my own choice would be an Englishman, Tommy Godwin, as the provider of the biggest thrill of the afternoon.

The audacity of the ride was when my pacing tandem was too slow. I jumped in behind another rider, following his tandem for one lap until a faster team came on and in the final lap, although leading, I actually jumped past my own pacing tandem in the last 220 yards.

Another point was made about my late season fitness and that I obviously had in mind the Empire Games selection soon to be made. Bryan wrote:

> Godwin's form shot him to the top of my list of Probables.

'The Meeting of Champions', a regular feature in those days, was held on the second Saturday in September. Harris and Patterson were both on the card, also all the National Champions of the year. I was there as National Pursuit Champion, but my club, the Rover RCC, had qualified for the final against Willesden CC. A knock out competition throughout the whole country during the season sorted the men out from the boys. More than a hundred clubs would ride in their Centres, then in the Area and finally to Herne Hill. The Rover Club were the winners by a very slender margin But during the ride a very cunning and experienced man, Eddie Bridgwater, rode on my wheel. If he felt he could not go as fast as me, and he sensed that I was riding well, he would shout, "Stay down, Tom" as we approached the changeover point. As a result of this, I calculated that I did 5 ½ laps of the 8 ¾ laps ridden. We were delighted, of course, and my club mates, Eddie, Frank Bell and Pip Ottley were very proud and complimentary.

I later rode in what was billed as a World Championship 9-Lap Pursuit, with four riders: myself, Jack Simpson, George Fell and Eric Fellows. The result was Godwin and Simpson tied for first place, G Fell third and E Fellows fourth – no Cyril Cartwright! On the day, Harris broke the 440 yards flying start TT record. Harris was timed at 24.3 and Van Vliet 24.4. This meeting was usually the last big promotion of the season.

1950

Empire Games
in Auckland
– goodbye BSA
– on the retail
side – World
Championships in
Ghent

In the September 14th issue of *The Bicycle* a shortlist of riders for the 1950 Empire Games to be held in Auckland, New Zealand was presented: Cartwright, Geldard, Godwin, Alf Newman (Road Race Champion), R Waters and Dave Ricketts. The events were: 1,000 metre sprint, 1,000 metre TT, 4,000 metres individual pursuit, 10-mile scratch and 100 kilometre road race.

In the October 12th edition of *The Bicycle* a novel idea was put forward:

Empire Games: Do You Agree With The Selectors? A question mark about the team selected the previous Friday.

While no definite policy has been laid down, it is assumed that Godwin will ride sprint, kilo and 10-mile, Cartwright the pursuit and probably road race. Geldard is likely to be No 1 sprinter and also figure in the 10-mile. Newman, as Road Champion, automatic for leader of the road team.

The article then goes down to name ten other riders who could have been selected for their all round ability. We were named, "THE AUSTERITY TEAM".

It then goes on to invite readers to give their selections, and these selections to be given at a later date. On Nov 2nd the Poll Result read: Tommy Godwin, Cyril Cartwright, Jack Simpson, Alf Newman, A W Butler, R Waters, D Ricketts then Scott, Bannister and Geldard. So three of the selections were confirmed but Geldard was in tenth place. Financial difficulties had forced the team to be cut to four, with a fifth rider, Eric Holroyd, nominated as a team member. He had emigrated to New Zealand only a month before. (There would have been four more who would have emigrated had they known).

The travel arrangements were not too popular in the Godwin household. I would be away for Christmas and the New Year, leaving a wife not too happy with a baby less than two years old. We were to leave England from Southampton Docks on December 16th and arrive in Auckland five weeks and one day later on January 21st. Racing was to take place on February 7th, 9th and 11th.

Getting time off work in those days from your employers was not easy, even if you were representing the country. But to think of five weeks to New Zealand, three weeks there and then presumably five weeks to return, a total of thirteen weeks, was of. However, BSA was very understanding and agreed to let me go. In fact, they arranged for Eileen to receive my basic wages, about £7 a week, while I was away.

Once the news got out that Birmingham had two riders selected for the Empire Games cycling events there was obviously a great deal of interest from the media. Alf Newman had been selected as the current National Road Race champion. I had been selected for being a National Champion over various distances and also the current National Pursuit Champion. I was entered in the sprint, kilometre, and 10-mile race, also as second string to Cartwright in the individual pursuit. He had gained Silver in the World Championships.

I was extremely surprised when a local manager of a city centre Stork Hotel, a Mr Jack Warner, organized a farewell party for me. He had invited Vic Johnson, a gold medallist sprint cyclist from the1908 Olympics, a local man and past member of Rover RCC, Jack Hood, a very good past champion professional boxer. From athletics there was Joe Blewitt, a very distinguished Birchfield

Harrier and a very strong distance runner and Jim Murphy, a sporting entrepreneur who ran the Farcroft Hotel, noted for its bowling greens, in Handsworth, who organized many sports. In the boxing world, Jim had presented the Turpin brothers, Randy, Dick and Jackie. Randy, of course, went on to win the World Title from Sugar Ray Robinson. There was also Vince Hawkins, a British, European and Empire Champion, and many more.

Dad was a close friend of all those named, and he was very proud that such a gathering, and many more, was being held for me. He suggested that I took the four gold trophies with me that I had in my possession, two of which were my own property. The evening was a tremendous success, and at the conclusion I was presented with £100, which had been collected from the various people present. Best wishes from all, "BON VOYAGE AND A SAFE RETURN HOME." What a wonderful farewell, and what a wonderful way to set off to the other side of the world.

Before leaving there was a farewell reception held in London. It was very exciting to join up with competitors from other sports. Then there was the train journey to Southampton to get on the boat, wondering what was in store for us.

On arrival at the docks we saw many large ships, and as we were directed along the dockside there was speculation as to which of these wonderful ocean going craft would be ours. We were in for a shock. Suddenly, the *SS Tamaroa* was spotted by one of the huge party. Tucked in amongst ships of 30,000 tonnes and more was this almost miniature, dismal-looking thing of 14,000 tonnes, a semi-cargo ship, due to cater for the bulk of the English, Scottish and Welsh teams. Some fortunate chosen ones were flying out some time nearer to the dates of the Games.

How was this diminutive little boat going too satisfy the needs of so many bodies? We all had to try to keep fit, eat and drink, apart from possibly having to cope with boredom, sea sickness and fear of going into the unknown. We were going to be travelling so far and arriving to find that the locals, Australians and New Zealanders etc were already fully acclimatised – it was mind blowing. But we were on our way. We, the cycle team, had Mr and Mrs Southcott and their daughters Pam and Daphne, as travelling companions. Mr Southcott was the President of the NCU, a very wealthy and distinguished man, who had married a lady who looked to have foreign blood, almost gypsy-like, and with a bit of an unusual personality. The girls were very prim and proper ladies, at first almost snobby.

However, food was more than adequate for our needs, yet our first port of call was not until Curacao, before Panama.

Trying to keep fit was difficult. It was only possible to do simple exercises or walk the deck following athletes etc. The wrestlers had mats to do their work on. One of them was Ken Richmond, the guy who used to be seen as the gong striker for Rank Films. Swimmers had a tiny swimming bath, a three strokes to a length job. There was lots of fun in the pool, with water games and a Crossing the Line ceremony.

Leaving from home on December 16th, it was obvious that we were to celebrate Christmas Day and New Year's Eve on the high seas. We were in the Caribbean Sea on Christmas Day. In the evening there was to be a celebration meal. On a lovely warm evening and the ship decorated, the girls' teams were all excited about getting dressed up for the event. They came into the dining room looking wonderful. The table settings were beautiful, the portholes open to cool the air, everything was set fair for a wonderful night.

Everyone sat down at the tables, music flowing through the air when suddenly there was a terrific roar, the boat started swaying and, whoosh, through the port holes water cascaded into the room. Tables were cleared of cutlery and plates etc, girls and lads were soaked to the skin. A freak wave had caused havoc, which no-one could do anything about. The meal was postponed for the crew to clear up. The girls, crying and upset, returned to their cabins to try to re-arrange in some form or other, drying clothes out and re-styling hairdos. The lads were in fits of laughter. Needless to say, sports people being very resilient made light of it, and at the second attempt all went well.

On News Year's Eve we were docked at Curacao. After a meal on board at the usual time, thoughts turned to going ashore to join the locals and experience their celebrations. As we, the cycling team, were leaving ship, I noticed Mr Southcott and his family. On approaching them, I asked, "Are you going ashore?" He answered, "I don't want to go, but the girls, I feel, would not be safe alone." Immediately the gentleman in me took over, saying, "If they care to join us, they would be most welcome." Both Pam and Daphne had been very isolated until then as Mum and Dad were always very protective.

The outcome was that they really enjoyed themselves, no naughty goings on because in those days even sports people were very controlled – yes, even bike riders.

Our next part of the journey was for the ship to go through the Panama Canal. I thought it would be nice if we could ride through by road and meet up at the other end, some fifty-six miles, if I remember. Permission was granted and four English, one Scot and one Welshman set off. All the other sports teams waved us off, wishing us well and a safe journey. The sheer pleasure of getting on the bikes to get some miles in was exhilarating. The local people were very excited to see us riding past. There were stops for drinks etc and all in all it was a very pleasing break from shipboard.

All went well and as we approached the outskirts of the big town at the end of the ride toe straps were being tightened and chains whirring onto different sprockets in readiness for some obvious sign for the usual sprint to prove who was king of the road. Suddenly a big strong looking black guy coming in the other direction waved and shouted, "Hi, guys. Hold on," and turned to ride with us. We continued riding with the big man and he told us that there was a reception at the US Military Base for us, He suddenly said, "Okay, boys, turn in here." So there was no sprint, which was disappointing, but what fun we had at the base. There was plenty of food, wonderful facilities and everything arranged to get us to the ship in time, quite an experience.

On the high seas again, we were in for a long, long journey. The Christmas and New Year celebrations had got people together. Girls and boys made up as couples and during the day there were some exercises and workouts, some leisure deck games, card playing and board games. Edna Child, a diving competitor, befriended me in the nicest way, knowing that I was a married man with a child and had been teased by some of the young girls about being a loner. But the interesting thing that developed, and word got around, was that what was called the 'SUN DECK' during the day became the 'SIN DECK' at night. So it is now obvious that young people of the early Fifties had similar ideas to those of the Nineties and the new Millenium.

Our arrival in Auckland was an amazing sight. The wonderful Maoris gave their superb welcome, the docks were lined with people, bands, flags, bunting etc. We had arrived and were welcomed by people who we found later to be extremely warm and friendly, very royalist, who talked of the home country and their desire to visit. The teams were split up, and the cyclists' base was at Ardmore, an air base some twenty-five miles outside Auckland, not far from the famous Rotarua Hot Springs. Our main thought, of course, was to get on our bikes as soon as possible. The road bikes had been stored complete and used on the journey, so we soon got our first ride in.

We were told we must attend a large Civic Reception in the Town Hall in Auckland. On the day there was a massive turn out, with food and drinks, welcoming addresses and the usual formalities. Suddenly, I looked up and above the main room was a seating area. Looking over the balcony was a most attractive young lady. I caught her eye, waved and beckoned to her to come down. She waved for me to go up, which I did. On meeting her we exchanged names and I said, "Would you like to join us downstairs?" I also asked, "How did you get in?" She replied, "I work here, I'm the Mayor's secretary." She then asked if I would like a tour of the building.

The outcome of my sudden interest in ladies brought some rather caustic remarks from some of the boys who had been kidding on the trip. Upon joining the others in the main area, I introduced my new friend, Fay, also explaining her job and the reason for my delay in returning. Just as an aside, I asked Fay for her telephone number, just to keep in touch. Little did I know how all this would kick back on me in due time.

As a follow-up to this new friendship, I contacted Fay by telephone and was asked if I would like to bring a friend along one Sunday. She would bring another young lady for a foursome to visit a small offshore island easily approached in a small boat and with a very relaxing picnic area. I chose an athlete who I had met on the boat to accompany me. He agreed and the trip was made. Just a friendly day out with pleasant company and good food supplied by the girls. There was lots of talk about our respective lives and a dip in the sea. No attempts or hints of romance and on our return to the mainland we went back to our various dwellings.

One day after training at the track I came outside to get our transport home to find Fay waiting. The coach was not due for some forty minutes or so. I suggested that we go for a cup of tea at a nearby café. Once again a very pleasant half-hour and a suggestion of going to the cinema one day, to which I agreed. This was done one afternoon, ensuring I would be in time to get the last bus back to Ardmore.

Then one day, out of the blue, Fay asked if I would like to visit her home and meet her parents. Again I agreed. Meeting the family was very pleasant. They were nice people with a comfortable home who made me very welcome. On leaving to catch the bus once again, Fay remarked, "My parents feel that you are a married man." To which I replied, "Yes, but I have never attempted to romance you, I have made no move to gain your affections, I have just accepted you as a friend." Once I had explained things did not change. She seemed happy to meet occasionally, so long as it did not interfere with my preparation and that I always got back to camp by the official transport. When the racing programme commenced I was completely involved and no thoughts of meeting Fay entered my mind.

It was obvious once the racing began that in the sprints we were outclassed by Russell Mockridge and Sid Patterson, who had won many international titles, including World Championships. Fortunately, we had Cyril Cartwright, who had won a Silver Medal in the World's in Copenhagen in August 1949. Albeit, I was the British National Champion of 1949 but had not been selected for the World's. My selection for the Empire Games had been made on my all round ability and not as a specialist, also as captain because of my vast experience. The events I had been entered for were: sprint, kilometre and 10-mile. I was also listed as reserve pursuit rider, if required.

The sprint, of course, requires superb fitness and confidence, which did not add up after five weeks on a boat and ten days in Auckland. I was eliminated in the quarter-finals. I felt quite good about the time trial and felt sure I would get a medal. It was run in the evening. A number of riders went before me, among them Russell Mockridge, who was to be the sprint winner. Mockridge returned a time of 1.13.4. I was quite happy I could match that time but finished with 1.13.6, very disappointed, but thought a Silver medal would do. Sid Patterson was the last man to ride. The watches all showed him matching our times but as he came along the home straight and just before the line an overhead light blew out with a bang. Patterson reacted by throwing his bike forward. His time was 1.13.5. So, Gold was gone, Silver was gone, only a Bronze left for me, with one tenth of a second separating each rider. There was no disgrace. I had been beaten by two men who were at peak fitness. Cartwright meantime had been successful in the pursuit and taken Gold.

The final event on the track was the 10-mile and both Alan Geldard and I were renowned for this type of event. I was the 'gaffer' back in England, regularly winning 5's and 10's against all opposition and on all surfaces, so I was the fancied 'Brit'. In a team talk it was suggested that Cartwright would work for Alan and me, chasing any break that went, and in the final four laps would lead me out for the finishing sprint. Cartwright was never a team man, did not understand the ideas put forward and never spoke to me for advice. We had never been close friends and I found him a difficult person to have a conversation with.

In the race itself, with a big bunch of riders and 40-laps of the track, I did expect to see Cyril, but not once did he pass me. I always rode in the first few riders to control the race. A few attempts were made to get a break but were always pulled back in. Getting towards the end of the race, with the pace moving up, tension increased and, with adrenalin flowing, there was a sudden sound of desperate moving behind me. With three laps to go Cartwright came screaming past, bringing a crowd of riders with him, shouting at the top of his voice, "TOMMY!" I just could not respond quickly enough. With about six riders sweeping past and two or three to get around, I was lost. I chased frantically and passed some riders, but the Aussies were dominant, working together to take Gold and Silver, with the Bronze going to a New Zealander. My dream was shattered. My hope had been to emulate the great W W Maxfield, who had won the Empire Games '10' in 1938 at Fallowfield, Manchester.

The road race was the final event. The British boys (English, Scottish and Welsh) were never a force and Australia again took first and third, the Silver going to a New Zealand boy.

So, with the cycling programme concluded, there was little time left before being on the move for home. It was, however, announced by the administration of the team that there were tickets available by air. The athletes who had come out by air expressed a wish to return by sea, for the experience and as a period of relaxation. A draw would be made of any names submitted. I in particular wanted to return as soon as possible. Firstly, because of my job situation and secondly, because I would be able to compete at Herne Hill on Good Friday.

I had already won the BSA Gold Column in 1945, 1946 and 1947 but, as described previously, had missed the 1948 event due to an ear infection on my return from South Africa which required specialist attention. In 1949 I had again put my name on the Column, BSA having decided to continue to support the event, which was one of the most popular races in the calendar. With the thought of adding perhaps to my BSA Column and the Muratti won in 1949, I was still seeking as many gold trophies as possible.

In the draw for the air tickets I was not successful, but word had got around of my reasons for applying. Fortunately, one of the lucky winners came to me and said he was prepared to let me have the ticket as his return was not imperative, which made me very happy. I travelled back with other competitors, one in particular that I remember was Roy Romain of the swimming team. In 1950 planes made the journey with some five or six overnight stops. It was quite arduous but was another dimension in travel and we called at some very interesting locations.

On my return I set to in my training to prepare for the Easter racing programme. But immediately after my return I received a letter from a Sunday newspaper telling me they were happy I had returned as previous to my departure I had qualified for the finals of a roller racing competition, which was due to take place at the Royal Albert Hall. In my absence a young up and coming rider called Billy Jones, who I had nurtured from his early interest in racing, had been chosen in my place as he was runner-up to me in the Midlands final. Obviously he was most disappointed to lose his place on my return, as was his family, and it caused a rift in our relationship, which had previously been quite strong. The competition had caused a great deal of interest but I was beaten by another Australian, Keith Reynolds.

Come the Good Friday meeting and before the 5-mile point to point race for the BSA Gold Column, I was approached by Sid Patterson, my adversary in the1000 metres TT in Auckland and the silver medallist. He remarked, "I see you're the holder of the trophy. If I can help you to win, I will." During our time together in New Zeeland I had struck up quite a good friendship with him, to the extent that he had made a suggestion to me that we should consider turning pro and ride the Six Day Circus. He was convinced that two big guys, both with broad smiles and friendly characters, would be a big success. He said, "With your experience and my youth…" He was at that time twenty-one years old and I was twenty-nine. But even at the suggestion, I declined. I was married, with a wonderful wife and two-year old daughter. The Six Day events were all held on the Continent, which would have meant living abroad and almost certainly meeting attractive young ladies. I thought it was almost inevitable that there would be a break up in our marriage.

Reg Harris and many other sportsmen had succumbed to such temptation.

Back to the race and I, as usual, had totalled up a fair number of points throughout the race. But as the final lap approached Sid Patterson knew that I had to finish first or second to be sure of winning. He rode up to me saying, "I'll lead you out for the last lap." I was glued to his wheel into the back straight, moving very fast indeed, feeling confident I could win the last lap and get six points, ensuring a win. A sudden clattering ended my chances. Ian Scott had fallen across my back wheel. Fortunately, I did not crash, but it finished my challenge. A sad disappointment as it would have been nice to have won the BSA Gold Column again.

It was now back to the usual programme, which in the1950's was quite hectic. I knew I was riding well, but my situation at the BSA was becoming more difficult. I had been moved around in so many different jobs, with no security in any of them. I was riding a BSA-made frame, but other than showing the name on the transfers, the Company could do little more. They had always paid my wages when I was racing abroad, the princely sum of £6-10-0d, which my wife received weekly.

As the year progressed, about May time, I received a rather large envelope from New Zealand. I had always had post delivered to my parents' home, as during our married life we had had a number of address changes. Young couples were lucky to get rooms to live in, flats or houses were impossible, although in 1949 we had moved into our first rented home. The envelope contained a mounted picture of a very attractive young lady, my friend Fay from New Zealand. I looked at the picture in amazement, then I read the accompanying letter, in which Fay asked when I was getting my divorce and returning to her. I was flabbergasted, but foolishly I kept the picture and letter, placing them in a shoulder bag I used daily to carry things to and from work. I had been doing this for some time, not thinking much about it, until one day Eileen was looking for something which I had mislaid and, quite innocently, went to my bag.

Needless to say, all my explanations and assurances that there was nothing in it from my point of view, only the romantic mind of a young lady running amok. The whole thing took a lot of resolving. Many times since Eileen has pointed out that on my return home after a long absence I seemed to have changed and been very quiet. I could not and never have convinced her that life at the BSA was not very comfortable.

The job I had been detailed to do by Sir James Leek, the Managing Director of the Company, was to act as his eyes and ears at the cycle works, and to give weekly reports on what I saw happening, good or bad. I tried to do this in a constructive manner, and I did not want to make enemies. But one day I witnessed a bicycle, complete, being wheeled along to the packing bay. The wheels were out of track. I checked back through all the stages of building and found the fault in the frame shop. The rear ends were being stamped out carelessly, a fault which could not be detected at this stage. I immediately stopped the operator and reported back to the MD. This caused a very unpleasant situation with managers and supervisors of the works. I was called into the office and told in no uncertain terms what the y thought of me.

This observation of mine obviously made a mark. I was told one day that two of the top Directors were coming down to Waverley Road Works and wanted me to conduct them around the works. There was no more explanation. On their arrival, I took them from the basic frame building through all sections, right through to the final assembly and viewing. Very fortunately for me I got on well with all the workers. They were proud of my achievements and I was well met by all. On completion of the tour, which took some hours, Mr Wood and Mr Dickenson returned to the main works with no more than a, "Thank you, Godwin."

I was almost immediately approached by Len Hughes, who at that time was the Chief Inspector and responsible for all the viewers, as they were called. He had befriended me and knew of my unhappiness at work. I had confided in him that I was looking to find something else for the future. By coincidence, his seventy-four year-old father was considering selling his old established cycle retail shop. I expressed an interest, and he asked if I would like to come and see it that night. I was quite happy to do so and agreed to meet him at the shop that evening.

On arriving at 10-12 Silver Street, Kings Heath, Birmingham, I saw this very big shop, double fronted, two large glass doors and a raised platform show area. It was all very impressive but sadly neglected and very much in need of a lot of hard work cleaning and a clear out of junk. Mr Hughes senior was a very nice man, and obviously very experienced in cycles, motor cycles, radios, gramophones etc. He was obviously tired after many years of work, but very astute. Through his career he had managed to purchase his own shop plus three adjacent premises and his own detached house about a mile from his business.

I was immediately impressed by his friendly manner and his genuine approach to everything. On talking figures – laughable today – he said he wanted £1,000 for the business, stock included. The main stock was fifty-two new cycles, fifty-one of them all black wartime models. The other one was a ladies sports cycle with blue enamel, white mudguards and chrome rims, handlebars etc – a BSA Golden Wings. Otherwise the stock consisted of tyres, tubes and most components for old fashioned cycles. I had £247 to my name, but I agreed to buy, subject to raising a loan somehow. His son, Len, then came into the picture by saying he wanted to be a partner, which reduced my obligation somewhat and was more practical. Hughes senior was not happy with this arrangement, I sensed, but he agreed. He realised that his son was protecting his own future regarding his father's estate, but an agreement was made.

Upon my return home to Eileen I told her what I had done, using up our £247 to buy a run down business with a partner. I had still not been accepted as an honest husband regarding the Fay debacle. However, I was determined to proceed. My mind was clear, irrespective of Eileen's wishes, I had to get away from the job I was in.

I went into work as usual the next morning, Friday. Shortly after 9.00am I was called to the office of Mr Taylor, the Cycle Works Manager to be told that I was wanted at Mr Dickenson's office at the main office in Armoury Road. Presenting myself to his secretary, I was immediately directed to his rather palatial office.

"Sit down, Godwin, I want to have a talk with you. We were very pleased with the manner in which you conducted us around the works. You appear to be very observant and seem to get on well with the employees. Mr Woods and I had a chat on our return yesterday and we would like to offer you a promotion to Chief Inspector of the Cycle Works." My reply was a complete shock to him when I said, "I'm sorry but I bought a cycle business last evening and I'm giving my notice."

"What do you mean, Godwin? We spent nearly all day with you, trying to evaluate your ability, and now I find you were wasting our time."

"No, I had no idea why you ordered me to take you around the works, There has never been any suggestion I was being offered a job of responsibility."

When we had both cleared the air he asked, "Where is the shop?" I told him the name and address. He said, "I know the man, he is a BSA agent," which, of course, he was. Mr Dickenson then said, "Well, Godwin, I know your mind is made up, so perhaps you can give feedback as a retailer and help us in that way." We shook hands, and I realised I was on my own, there was no turning back. But the dreadful thought struck me almost before I left that I had been conned by Len Hughes. It was obvious to me that he was aware of the situation. He knew that his job was on the line and that I was unhappy and he had quickly got me out. Then, of course, I was in his hands. He as a partner and I with no experience of running a cycle shop. He was an unscrupulous man, who would twist me round his little finger given the opportunity.

I then, of course, had to arrange a £250 loan. It was fast track to Dad to ask if he could persuade George Davies, a back street bookie, to act as guarantor at the bank for a loan. The answer came back "Yes." I was on my way.

Having given my notice on the Friday, I had one week to tie things up. I went to see Mr Hughes on the Monday. He was most kind to me, but soon told me that he feared for me with his son as a partner. He knew him to be a scrounger, unreliable and a gambler, who wasted his money at the dog track and drinking. Very promising!

At this point I feel that I should make it clear to the reader that I am now in my eighties. The last twelve pages were written before retiring for the night. Getting into bed and almost immediately going to sleep, has never been a difficulty for me. Tonight the pattern remained the same, but during the night, most unusual for me, I woke up. My mind was in complete turmoil. The memories of 1950 and having taken the decision to change the course of my future came flooding back to me. To relive those days and the hardship that ensued was not easy. Remembering the pain and suffering I imposed on my wonderful wife Eileen over the next few years was unbearable. I lay awake for some considerable time, and a feeling of shame enveloped me. I realised more than at any time in my life the debt of gratitude I owed to her. She has been firmly behind me in everything I have done, sometimes critical, but always with words of wisdom and suggestions about how I should conduct myself in various situations.

From the first day at the shop, I had the very kind Mr Hughes attempting to give me confidence and telling me to relax. Finally, to cap it all, he said, "I know it's going to be difficult for you, so instead of £3 a week rent I shall only have £2 a week for the first year."

It is difficult to describe the premises but think of the set for 'Steptoe ands Son' on TV but related to cycles, motor cycles, radios and gramophones and you've got it. Behind the shop was a large workshop, which was the area of the backyard of two terrace houses and an entry, which had been covered with asbestos sheeting. The floor was earth, no concrete, no wood – just compacted dirt. The contents were some hundred or more old bicycles, stacked in rows, then more bicycles laid on top up to the roof.

There were at least ten old motor cycles: a BSA Square Tank, a BSA Sloper, a New Imperial, a Triumph etc. The prize one, which was not visible, was a magnificent Indian Twin, with a basketwork sidecar. Mr Hughes knew about it as he was the owner. With only 800 miles on it, he had turned it over on one run and never used it again. Even in those days he had been offered £100 for it by the Wall of Death riders, who used them at fair grounds, but Mr Hughes had told them it was not worth the trouble getting it out.

My first job was to clear the shop out and clean, paint, re-stock or whatever, to try and get some business through the door. All the old bikes were readily taken off my hands by old pals from the BSA. They came from some two to three miles away with flat hand carts, piled bikes on six or seven high, tied them with rope and pushed them back to Sparkbrook, Small Heath and surrounding areas. Cleaned up and renovated, the bikes were sold to friends. The motor cycle stock was taken away in a big truck and dumped (I think). I paid the driver £1 a load. However, all except two went: the Indian with sidecar and the BSA Sloper, a young man paying me £10 for the latter.

Table and cabinet gramophones were sold or given to interested parties. There were stand up speakers and earphones used in the days of crystal sets and even an Edison Bell Cylinder record player with eighty new cylinders, eventually to become a collector's item.

After the junk disposal an attempt was made at cleaning the place, illuminating and stocking it. A painful task, which took long hours and many sacrifices, but I was still conscientiously training. I was still only twenty-nine years old, full of running, and hoping to achieve further noted success. In my mind, although I had already won two gold trophies, the BSA Gold Vase was unfinished business – only two shares.

Apart from the Good Friday meeting, I have overlooked the racing season so far since returning from the Empire Games in New Zealand. A promoter in Coventry, Charlie Viner, always had an eye to a spectacular event. He was an exceptional man for the sport. His events for both road and track were always a great success. The public followed him and he did the business. He remembered that I had won the 1949 National Individual Pursuit Championship at Coventry, but had not been selected for the World's in Copenhagen, This had been against the NCU ruling on selection. Cyril Cartwright had been selected, although he had not competed in the National Championships. He had won Silver in the World's. He decided to give me a chance of revenge. He invited Cyril Cartwright to one meeting to meet me at 4,000 metres, £15 to the winner, £10 to the loser. This was quite good money in those days, even workers from the BSA arranged charabanc trips to witness this event.

In the match I rode Cyril corner to corner, just holding level throughout the ride until the bell went and I proceeded to take 4 seconds out of him to win comfortably. Reg Harris, who was riding as a pro at the same meeting and a club mate of Cyril's, had been at the trackside giving instructions. After his defeat there was no handshake from Cartwright. He went straight to Harris and was met by, "Why the hell did you let him do that to you?" Cyril, throwing his bike and helmet on the floor, replied something like, "If you want him beaten, get on the bike and do it" – but the language was a bit stronger. I was overjoyed. A terrific crowd, my favourite track and I had proved a point.

Much to my surprise, I was asked by Charlie Viner if I would take on Knud Anderson of Denmark, the current World Champion, if he could get him over, in two weeks' time. The match was arranged. It was a wonderful evening weatherwise and there was a big crowd. Anderson, used to the super tracks on the Continent, was not very impressed with the saucer shaped, tarmac surfaced, bumpy Butts track. Yes, it was another win. This time I was actually in the same straight at the finish, a resounding victory. I had beaten the Gold and Silver Medallists at the 1949 World Championships. My confidence was high and I was still enjoying the racing. These events both took place in late May or early June, before I had been drawn into my departure from BSA.

Gradually, as the shop was cleared, I started to make it look as if we were interested in the public and doing business. The first few weeks takings were meagre crumbs. Figures like £29 a week were usual, with around £14 a week payable on hire purchase payments to Cycle and General Finance Co, which I found later to be a subsidiary of BSA.

After some six weeks one Saturday morning I was endeavouring to put on a window display using some crepe paper – all the fashion in those days – for some of the old black bikes now sporting chrome rims and handlebars and the one blue ladies bike. I was also cleaning the windows and floor. As I was doing this who should turn up in a nice white raincoat, or mack as they were called, but my supposed business partner, Len Hughes. He had to date served no useful purpose in clearing the shop.

His question was, "What are you doing?" I replied, "Putting a show on," to which he replied, "One day I'll come and show you how it should be done." I exploded at this and told him in no uncertain terms, "It's either you or me. This thing is never going to work. I'm working my guts out and you come and sneer at me. I will speak to your father on Monday for his opinion." As a result of this he suggested that he was prepared to get out, but he wanted the £500.

On speaking to Mr Hughes, he agreed it was the best thing to happen. But the idea of £500 to Len was not on, I must pay the money direct to Mr Hughes. Upon telling his son I was met with, "I want £100 goodwill," to which I agreed, but to be paid over a period of time. This was also agreed. I was then to be completely on my own. Now I had to arrange finance. I had a word with my father, who approached George Davies, the only man I knew who would help, saying that I needed a guarantor for a further £500. Then there was a visit to a branch of Barclays, Mr Davis telling the manager to set up the loan with an agreement of £4 a week until settled.

It was obvious that there was going to be no income from the shop, so prizes I had won were sold to friends, vouchers redeemed and my usual £10 expenses from promoters of the track sport used to pay our way. As the season went on until September, I had to keep leaving Eileen in charge of the shop. A very close friend who worked on cycle assembly, Charlie Price, would come and help on Saturdays – no wages, just as a friend, invaluable!

Gradually people realised the shop was functioning and cycle repairs were being done expertly, either by myself or Charlie, both experienced in every way.

I was pleasantly surprised to be informed that I had been selected to ride in the World Championship individual pursuit at the Rocourt track in Ghent, Belgium, the other selection being Cyril Cartwright. Eileen agreed to try to hold things together at the shop. I then employed a young boy just to help out in any way possible. Little did Eileen or I foresee what was going to happen in respect of my selection to represent the country over the years. I hoped my experience of two previous Worlds, Zurich and Paris in 1946 and 1947, would see me through. My father had agreed to accompany me, but not officially with the team. It was his first and only trip.

In the qualifying series I returned the second fastest time. Messina of Italy was first. This usually ensured a pretty safe run through to the semi-final, at least. But in the meantime, Sid Patterson, the big Australian and holder of the World Sprint crown of 1949, had been beaten in the quarter-finals by Verdeun of France. Fortunately, Sid had entered for the individual pursuit in case of emergency. He was not a renowned pursuit rider, but an Australian, tough, full of guts and the need to get something out of the Championships to ensure staying on the Continent to earn a living in the bike game.

Sid, immediately after failing in the sprint, went into the pursuit. His time in qualifying was the second slowest, 5 minutes and 26 seconds. But this by the ruling put us together in the quarter-finals, second fastest against second slowest. Big Sid went for the jugular using a very big gear of 94". I chose a gear of 90". Sid worked very hard early on to get a lead. I gradually came back smoothly and with just over a kilometre to go we were level on our respective stations. At this point I punctured The ruling was a restart from the point of trouble.

At the restart I was informed that I was 55 metres behind 'Patto'. Two people, Ron White, a Daily Express journalist, and Ken Mitchell, reserve for the pursuit, had been standing back to back, touching each other as we crossed the line. Both were very firm that we were level. An appeal to the judges was in order, but the team manager of the day had not got the bottle to argue for me. I sat down on the track in protest, no support,

no-one could speak French, the communicating language of the UCI, but very firmly I was told to get on and ride or be disqualified. To try and pull back 55 metres in just over 1,000 metres was impossible. I was shattered. Big Sid went on to win the title from Gardini of Italy. Seeing Sid after the ride in the track centre, there was every indication of drugs, but there was no testing in those days.

The next morning at the track other Aussie riders were laughing in their cocky manner, boasting that Sid on winning with 'something' had taken a young lady to his hotel and indulged in a sex spree of thirteen times. Over the years there has been little doubt that Belgian trainers or soigneurs were the people with the medicine.

Cartwright also failed to get through to the final stages, a sad day for the British interest.

Harris won the pro sprint. His trainer was Louis Guerlache, a Belgian. On Harris's success, the Raleigh publicity team went to work with posters and picture cards of Harris which had already been prepared:

HARRIS RIDES A RALEIGH. WORLD CHAMPION 1950.

Returning to England, I found Eileen very worried but assuring me that all was well. Only 'The Meeting of Champions' at Herne Hill in September remained, the final meet of the season.

About this time in my life I had quite a surprise when one evening a visitor called at the house. "Does a Mr Tom Godwin live here?" He was uniformed chauffeur. On finding that he was at the correct address, he announced that his boss, a Mr Phillips, a wealthy man and a Councillor from Coventry, would like to speak to me. Our very small terrace house was almost an embarrassment.

Mr Phillips informed me that part of his council work was to visit a home for children who had been adopted from broken homes or just abandoned. The home was in Spencer Road, Coventry. On a recent visit he had seen pictures all around the room all of the same person. He questioned, "Who is this man?" The answer was, "Tommy Godwin." The youngsters always visited the Butts Stadium when big cycle meetings were promoted. They had made me their special pin up. Without me knowing any of them, they always came onto the track centre, asking if they could push my bike, carry my helmet and my holdall. I had always fooled around and had a chat with them and I had become the special sportsman in their young lives.

The request from Mr Phillips was for me to visit the home one evening when there was a special drama event with the young people involved. At one point the room would be in total darkness. I was to be ushered into the room at this point. On cue this happened. The light went on and very excited youngsters recognised the surprise guest. This led to a long and continued period of visits by Eileen and me with our daughter Kay, enjoying all the company of the children.

On one occasion I took along a very dear friend, Eric Thornton, a member of the Rover RCC with me, who was very impressed by my sincerity and concern. Later on in my life, Eric invited Eileen and me to a Masonic Ladies Evening. He invited us again for the next two years. The third time I asked, "How do you get into Freemasonry?" His reply was, "It's about time you asked that, you've cost me a b----- fortune." He had seen that I was suitable for Freemasonry by my concern for other people and he envisaged a charitable character. I was accepted into a Lodge at thirty-six years of age. From this point on in my life, I realised I enjoyed caring for others and I had a natural ability to communicate. As the years rolled by I became very involved with work in the community.

I was now involving myself more with the business and feeling that I could concentrate through the winter to build a foundation. This was not to be. There was another invitation to represent the country, this time at Christchurch in New Zealand for the Centennial Games.

CHAPTER 14

1951

The Centennial
Games in
Christchurch,
New Zealand
– breaking point

Christchurch had applied for the 1950 Empire Games and lost out to Auckland, so they had decided on their own spectacular. The only trouble was that it was over the Christmas and New Year period. Once again my wife was left to make a decision, to allow me to represent the country once more or to say firmly, "Enough is enough, your place is at home with your family." Very reluctantly, I'm sure, she said, "I know how proud you are and what it means to you. We'll manage somehow."

The trip was by air, a rather lengthy affair in those days. But accompanying us were Roger Bannister, Arthur Wint, McDonald Bailey, all representing England in the athletics events. These famous names were to be joined by Mal Whitfield of the USA, Olympic Gold Medallist in the 1948 Games in London.

Willi Slykhuis of Holland competed in the 1-mile event, Bannister winning from MacMillan of Australia. Slykhuis won the 5,000 metres. In the women's events, Shirley Strickland, a superb athlete, won five events and Marjorie Jackson two events.

Other sports were swimming, boxing, rowing, with top internationals in each, quite a fantastic promotion following Auckland in 1950.

In the cycling events, both pro and amateur, we had the world renowned Arie van Vliet, a Gold Medallist in the Berlin Games of 1936, at the kilometre distance and Jan Derksen, World Amateur Sprint Champion in 1939 at the famous Vigorelli track. This was at the very start of the Second World War when the British team of Maxfield, Harris and Ricketts was recalled by the British governing body. Both van Vliet and Derksen were representing Holland.

Alan Bannister from Manchester travelled with me. He was a superb sprint-

Centennial Games in
Christchurch, New
Zealand 1951 –
A Bannister,
T Godwin, Arie
van Vliet and Jan
Derksen

er and Silver Medallist in 1948 when he was the stoker to Reg Harris in the tandem event. Amongst the amateurs were riders from the USA, Denmark and Australia and a strong team of New Zealand lads. The southern hemisphere riders were right in the middle of their track season.

Alan Bannister acquitted himself well in the shorter distance races, winning the quarter-mile, half-mile and 1,000 metres. I, on the other hand, won the 5-Mile Centennial Championship and the Canterbury Championship at the same distance. I was also third in the quarter-mile, third in the 1,000 metres and second in the half-mile handicap. I was very happy with the results in view of my pressure back home.

I rather surprised the athletes one morning before breakfast at the college we were staying at by joining them as they were lapping round the track. In the pack were Roger Bannister, Slykhuis, Mal Whitfield, Arthur Wint and others. "A cyclist running?" "Yes," I said, "I do quite a bit of road running with the Birchfield Harriers in the winter." I quite enjoyed it and they were amused.

I did have the pleasure of sharing a room with Roger Bannister. I think there was a slight mistake with there being two Bannisters in the team, and I had been inadvertently paired with the great man. Our stay in Christchurch was very pleasant indeed, with Christmas Day spent with sports people from around the world.

As the Games finished and everyone was thinking of home, I was approached and asked if I would like to return to Auckland with the Danish rider, Claus Hansen, for a final meeting. I answered, "Yes." Arriving in Auckland, I met up with people who had befriended me only twelve months before and received a warm welcome.

The headline in the local paper after the meeting was:

Godwin stars at cycle meeting.

I had had a wonderful meeting. The report went on:

Normally a middle distance man, Godwin excelled in the sprints.

In one race from the scratch mark in a half-mile handicap I was timed at 57 seconds, which transpired to be a New Zealand record. I later received an official certificate for this ride.

The last race was a 20-minute team event. I was paired with Claus Hansen, and rode in Danish colours, but throughout the race I found Claus was not going too well. I was doing the chasing in the bunch and still coming in for the sprints, winning four out of five of them and just getting pipped by inches in the final one. The race was hard for me having to work hard throughout but the ovation from the crowd was music to my ears. The report stated:

England's broad-smiling thirty-year old Tommy Godwin triumphed over New Zealand riders last night fresh from one his success at the Centennial Games. Godwin gave the spectators a taste of international cycling at its best.

During the meeting I saw in the crowd Fay, the young lady who had caused

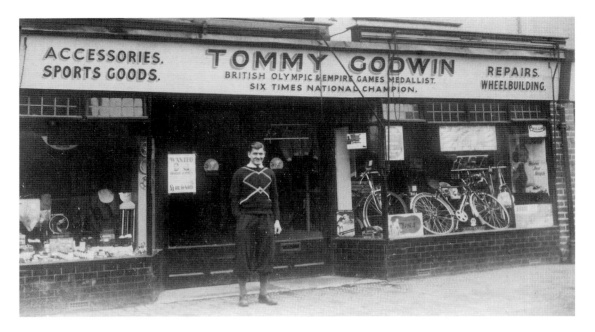

The shop in 1951
– Gold Vase year

some distress in my family life. I moved into the crowd to speak with her and her mother and father, who were all very polite, and then I was introduced to her husband, a sailor from Scotland. So, since my refusal to divorce Eileen and rush back to New Zealand she had found another Brit and tied the knot.

Returning home, I realised how unfair I was being in continuing with my travels to the other side of the world. Eileen was in a terrible state and in my absence a representative of one of the cycle firms, Phillips, a local manufacturer, had called at the shop, demanding immediate payment or he would have the stock removed from our premises. He did, in fact, arrange this, with no feeling for our situation. The man was named Les Lee and I never spoke to him again.

Added to all the pressure in the shop, caring for a three-year old child, and taking little money, my wife was very depressed. The shop was very sparse, there was very little heating and it was a severe winter. At home there was a more desperate situation. We were short of money, with very little fuel for the open fire in our small terraced house and deliveries were poor, even if you had money. Eileen mentioned to the young fifteen-year old lad who worked for us that she would have to go to the gasworks in Saltley to get some coke. Between them, on a Wednesday, they trekked through snow and slush pushing a pram with Kay in it some four or five miles each way to get one small bag of fuel. When I was told I was so ashamed of myself and was determined to improve matters. As the spring approached business started to improve. I was working hard on repairs, sometimes working until 11.00 o'clock at night.

Still in my mind was the BSA Gold Vase, to be run at the Cadbury's Ground in Bournville on the last Saturday in May. I still carried on doing short hard training rides on the road – high quality but not endurance miles.

Getting close to the day of the meeting, I asked a friend who had a motor

Start of BSA Gold
Vase 10-Mile 1949
at Bourneville
– Godwin
front right hand

cycle to take me for a ten mile paced ride on the road. I put a fixed gear of
92" on. I usually pedalled on a 77". On the evening of the ride along the main
Stratford Road on a measured course used for club time trials, I followed the
motorbike, with a pillion passenger sitting high. I was riding my track machine,
with no brakes. Approaching Hockley Heath, we were catching a Midland Red
bus. Suddenly the brake lights went on. The motorbike stopped but I couldn't
and shot past both, just missing the dog that had caused the trouble. I got to the
turn at the Royal Oak, put my hand (in a leather track mitt) on the front wheel
and turned in the road just as the motorbike came up behind me again. I picked
up the pace again and returned to the start point in just under twenty minutes
(19.54). I felt good and had been well looked after with food. Eileen has always
been wonderful in that field. I had been resting a little more in recent weeks.

Come the day, I worked in the shop until 1.00pm, then jumped on the bike,
carrying my racing wheels in special wheel carriers, and rode down to Bournville only about two miles away. There was a wonderful crowd, a grass track, and,
as I circled the track for a warm-up, there were shouts from spectators wishing
me well. I had two shares on the trophy. Wilf Waters also had two shares and
his brother, Jerry, one share. Since 1926 five other top class riders had gained
two shares, but could not get the third to win it outright – a real bogey event.
My Dad was there, of course, and he had brought with him an old friend from
our American days, Jack Ellam originally from Yorkshire, who was visiting the
country. Dad's question as usual was, "What do you think, Big Boy, can you win
it?" My reply was, "Not if it's in a sprint. If I can get a break, I might."

46Very early in the race I had a dig, soon to be followed by the bunch. Then
after 4½ miles (18 laps) I made a big effort and opened a gap. There was a shout
from Dad, "Ride a pursuit." There were twenty-two laps to go. Behind there was

Godwin leads after breaking away – W Jones and J Pottier chasing

apparently a hesitation, then an argument as to who should chase. I kept going on my way when two local lads, Billy Jones, an up and coming rider, and John Pottier, a member of the MC&AC, the organising club for this meeting, took up the chase. Suddenly there was a shout, "They're after you!" Within two laps they had joined up with me. My first question was, "Are you going to work?" There was no reply. I opened up once or twice. There was very little effort by either of them. I knew if the pace slowed the field would get up, so I was forced to keep the pace going. About four laps to go, I felt rain, which pleased me as the track was already soft. I knew immediately that I must have the lead at the bell.

Both Jones and Pottier were happy following me. I knew the track well. The bend out of the back straight, about 200 yards from the finish, had a tricky camber running out of it. In the home straight, approaching the bell, I raced hard. Then the bell, the first corner roll and into the back straight. I kicked hard and, as I guessed, they both challenged. I took a bit of width from the line, forcing them wide into the last corner and onto the camber. As I approached the corner I got back on the line that was so important. They were both wide on the corner, having to ease to get around safely, while I got into a three-length lead. Coming into the straight, the crowd was screaming, my head was down, making every effort. Pottier and Jones closed a little but I crossed the line to win the race and my third gold trophy.

There was a lap of honour and the crowd was wonderful. But I was emotional and got off my bike in a terrible state. My old pal, Benny Foster, was up for it. He dashed over to me with a towel in his hand and put it over my head, then, "Here, have a good whiff of this." It was a big bottle of smelling salts. A brisk rub of the towel by Ben and his next order was, "Now go and get that trophy." In the meantime, our next door neighbour in business, who had come to witness

Crossing the line –
winner for third time
of BSA Gold Vase

the race, ran out of the grounds, jumped into his car and dashed back to collect Eileen from the shop. One of my old BSA pals agreed to look after the business and Eileen was able to get in to see me surrounded by crowds of people wanting a piece of the action.

That evening Dad and Mum had one of their celebration parties, of which there had been many. This one was a double header. Firstly, for the BSA Gold Vase win, which was the third gold trophy in the collection. No other rider in history had ever won three gold trophies outright. Secondly, for the visitor from the USA, an old friend who had known my parents since 1920, the year I was born. Needless to say, the trophy was filled and all present shared in my wonderful day. But being so joyous and feeling on top of the world, I had no idea what was going to happen in the very near future.

We continued to struggle in the business, but there was a huge press about my past and present successes and people started to visit us to purchase bikes for their kids, simply to boast that their bike was from 'TOMMY GODWIN'.

Following the local success, I was invited to race in Darlington at a very big promotion on the Feetham's Cricket Ground, a grass track. The programme included world class athletes such as Shirley Strickland, Arthur Wint, McDonald Bailey, Bob Richards, a pole vaulter from the USA and their national champion, and many others. The was a big foreword in the programme, showing the highlights of all the above named and then finally, "but Darlington's favourite is Tommy Godwin, always popular with the crowd for his determination and class." I felt so proud and confident even before racing.

I won my first event, a 1,000 metre scratch race heat, but immediately I had got off my bike and put on my track suit I was summoned to the dressing room by the promoter of the meeting, Bert Goodwin. Upon arriving in the room I

Receiving Gold Vase
from Mr Brearley of
BSA

was introduced to one of Bert's friends. "Tom this is Dr ......, a friend of mine.
His immediate question to me was, "Do you mind if I examine you?" My reply
was, "What for?"

I think you are on the verge of a nervous breakdown.

I was stunned but agreed to his request. Going into a quiet room, he proceeded to carry out his examination. He then shocked me more by saying, "I
don't want you to race again this evening." My reaction was, "I'm sorry, but
Bert pays me to ride. I have first class hotel accommodation and travel and I an
expected to perform for the public." A rather heated exchange took place, with
Bert saying that I need not ride, me saying I would, and the doctor adamant that
I would not. I went back to the track, having promised that I would not ride
hard but just to show myself to the crowd.

In the final event, a 5-mile points race and a very hard test of endurance, I sat
in for a few laps and carefully told Les Wilson my plight and that I would not
be trying. He scoffed at me. Very early a young local lad raced hard away from
the main bunch. I nodded to Les. There was no response. The crowd started
shouting, "Come on, Tommy, have a go," to which I immediately reacted. At
that point I was told later the doctor left the ground, leaving a message: "Tell
that young fool to go and see his own doctor for a second opinion." I won the
race and was severely castigated by my friend Bert, and had to promise I would
see my doctor as ordered.

On my return to Birmingham the next day, I told Eileen, booked and
appointment and visited the doctor that same evening. Dr Thompson was man
very interested in sport, as I was to discover later in my life. After his exami-

Riding lap of honour
– very emotional

nation, which confirmed what had been said, I was told in no uncertain terms that I must not race, I must have as much rest as possible and it would take some time to recover. A course of medicine was prescribed and I was under close observation.

I was due to ride the next week at the Halesowen track, another big meeting, with Harris, A van Vliet, Derksen and Patterson as the pro riders and many top amateurs. I attended the meeting, having previously notified the promoter. During the racing there was an announcement that Tommy Godwin was not riding due to a warning about a nervous breakdown. Many people stopped me, offering best wishes etc, but one man, unknown to me, approached and said, "Excuse me, I am Chief Inspector ……….. I heard the announcement and if you take my advice, do exactly what you have been told by the doctor. I have been away from my job for nearly a year and I'm just getting right." I realised that this could be the end of the season and perhaps the end of my career.

It was now June. I obviously had to continue in the business as it was our only means of income. Contrary to recent times, an amateur in the old days received prizes 'to the value of …', but there was no cash. If a top star was riding, promoters would agree to £10 for expenses. In the year 2002, nearly 2003 as I write, top sports men and women are very wealthy, have no financial worries and do not compete as often as the sports stars of yesteryear.

After some weeks of very special care I was told that I could ride the bike gently, that I was more under control and the business was improving.

There was no thought of any serious racing again that year until a sudden press release stating that Olympic Trials for 1952 would take place at Cannock track, a newly developed stadium. Riders would also be selected for a trip to South Africa to take place in early 1952. My name was included in the list of possibles.

As we got nearer to the day my doctor agreed that I was progressing well and allowed me to train, but only over short distances, no long endurance rides. On the day I rode a 1,000 metres time trial and a couple of teams pursuit rides over 4,000 metres and did myself justice in all rides. Shortly after, I was notified that I had been selected for South Africa as team captain. Yet another shock for my invaluable partner, Eileen, and once again she conceded. "I know what it means to you." So, once again there was a serious autumn and winter programme, with long road walks, road running, gym work and roller training. I was getting plenty of rest, good food and had a loving wife and a very interesting little daughter. In the old days bikes were a number one on Santa's list, so we had a reasonable demand. The stock room was full and we were settling down in our family life.

CHAPTER 15

1952

Touring in South Africa – no more racing

With Christmas over and New Year celebrated, there were travel arrangements to be made for the trip. Two weeks by boat to Cape Town, six weeks touring and two weeks to return. The ships we travelled on were the *Arundel Castle* and the *Edinburgh Castle*. Ten weeks away, with Eileen once again taking all the responsibility. Needless to say, the voyage was superb, but I had as a team four young, untried prospects, Lloyd Binch, Don Burgess, Ken Mitchell and Wally Box. There was also Alan Geldard, who had ridden with me in the 1948 Olympics and the 1950 Empire Games.

Throughout my life I have been a very strict disciplinarian. It was going to be put to the test on this trip. I laid down a strict programme of physical exercise to be carried out each morning on the deck. The action started at 7.00am when the crew would be washing down and checking all facilities for the passengers. I controlled the meals, something I felt very serious about. I also ensured that the team had adequate rest periods, not too much sun, and roller training. There was a strict 10.00 o'clock curfew to be in your cabin, anyone late would be locked out.

The Purser of the ship gave us a storeroom for our bikes and rollers. This was upon deck, so there was no manhandling. By good fortune, our activities soon became noticed and passengers were very inquisitive. One man came and made himself known. He was a qualified masseur from Derby, where he worked with athletes. He offered to massage us every day after a workout on the rollers. His intentions were good, but after a couple of days he found massaging six was too much and he arranged a four a day rota, which we accepted. We took part in daytime activities, deck games etc, and enjoyed the company of other passengers. After about four days we called in at Madeira, a lovely island and a leisurely day.

Soon after leaving Madeira I was approached by a Cockney lad who was going to Rhodesia to work in the copper mines. He had made up with a fantastic German lady and every male passenger on board was envious. For the evening meal, entertainment and dancing she would turn out in the most attractive dresses and gowns. I was told by this young man that he was looking after her needs, up to three times a day. But during their moments of love making, she was telling him, "I want that tall cyclist, the one who seems to be in charge." I laughed and tried to pass it over, whereupon he said, "Well, look around, wherever you are, playing, training or sunbathing, you'll find her very close." He proved right, she was always very near to me. It was embarrassing to realise one was being stalked. Fortunately, I only got in her company one evening when was having a drink with another party and she came and asked if she could join us.

I had to leave before 10.00 o'clock because of the curfew I had set. Erica, the German lady, said, "I think I will walk with you, I want an early night." Getting down to the cabin level, she suddenly said, "My cabin is along this passage," to which I replied, "I am one level lower down." She kept me talking for a short time, then I excused myself and got down to my cabin to find the door locked. I banged on the door and there was much laughter from Lloyd Binch, who I had locked out on the second night of our trip. He had had to sleep in Ken and Don's cabin. I had set out the rules and I meant business, extreme discipline - and I had been caught out. After some threats on my part I was allowed in, but only after making apologies.

Upon arrival in Capetown on a Thursday we were met by numerous people of the organising party, to be told that our first meeting was at Paarl on Saturday. Five of the team rode on our cycles the thirty-eight miles to the track, the exception was Binch. Accommodation at the hotel was almost immediately adjacent to the track. I had, of course, raced on it in 1948, but the team were surprised at what they saw, a big, flat asphalt track with very little banking. In 1948 the surface had been dirt, watered and rolled to give a fast but bumpy track.

Our programme for the tour was eleven meetings in seven weeks, including two test matches. Quite a hectic schedule, taking into account the amount of travelling involved.

The first meeting and the results prompted the Following headlines from one of the South African papers:

> ROUSING RECEPTION - INITIAL SUCCESS FOR SOUTH AFRICAN TOURISTS
>
> Only two days after arrival the British Team on a difficult track, and under windy conditions, won every event, Binch winning the quarter and 1-mile scratch events, with the captain, Godwin, showing his usual expected performance in winning the 1,000 metres time trial and the 10-mile scratch. In the latter event Don Burgess, who celebrated his eighteenth birthday on the trip, came second. Burgess, Mitchell, Geldard and Box formed the winning team in the 4,000 metres pursuit.

We were off to a good start, with our next match in one week's time in Kimberley. Yet again there were very convincing performances at various distances. The team was being changed around in different events to get some idea of the most suited discipline according to ability. The team of six had never trained together prior to leaving England. Only Burgess and Mitchell, both of Willesden CC, worked together regularly at home. These early matches were against local area South Africans.

Meanwhile reports were coming through of the improvement of the South African team riders in their final trials for selection to meet the English squad. The top sprinter, Tom Shardelow, had shown 11.7 seconds in the last 220 metres twice in the trials. At the 1,000 metre time trial distance he had rides of 1.11.1, 1.11.2 and 1.11.4, all of world class standard. More frightening, was the teams pursuit time of 4.50.7, the fastest ever recorded time in South Africa. These trials were held at the Malvern Track in Johnnanesburg, with 30 degree banking and a lap size of 483 yards. After this news we had a ride at Port Elizabeth, winning 5 out of 6 events.

We had just arrived in Johannesburg for the first test match when news of the death of King George VI was received. Our hosts were very concerned and hoped it would not affect the racing. Something upset us, that is certain, for the track was excellent, our training had gone well and we knew the South African team were in good form.

The headlines reported:

South Africans take first test 5 – 2, every race a thriller.

The first paragraph read:

Inspired riding by team captain Tommy Godwin failed to prevent a defeat for the
NCU team in the first test against South Africa.

Godwin gained the first win by a brilliant ride in the kilometre, finishing with a
1.11.5 ride, the best ride of his long career.

Our other win was by Lloyd Binch, who won the 440 yards event, with Shardelow
second, Godwin third. Binch had failed to master Shardelow in the match sprint of
three rides, he only won one heat, Shardelow was really in form.

I was next on a tandem with Geldard against Ramsey and Vorster. We won
the first ride with 11.1 seconds for 200 metres, but lost the other two rides with
11.4 and 11.5 seconds, the latter by a wheel.

Still the match was wide open, now a 4000 metres teams pursuit, Godwin, Mitchell,
Box and Burgess, but the local boys very confident won in 4.50.1 seconds to the NCU
team's 4.51.8 seconds, the winners in a new South African record.

The report goes on,

Although the match was lost, Godwin was desperate to keep the result as close as
possible by scoring in the final event, the 5-mile.

Twelve riders, all keen, all capable of winning, Godwin riding near the front
hoping to control the race, watching Fowler, the home rider, closely, which suited
Jimmy Swift, a canny rider with a fast finish. In the final lap, Swift found his way
through the pack with a terrific sprint to win from Godwin, with Vorster third.

So, in one evening I had competed in a quarter-mile sprint, a 1,000 metre
TT, a three race tandem series, a 4,000 metres team pursuit and 5-mile. Other
riders, in some cases, had had one or two rides only.

Our next rides were in Pietermaritzburg and Durban. At both these venues
the NCU team showed good form, Ken Mitchell winning an individual pursuit
in a new South African record time. I was beaten in the 1,000 metres by Jimmy
Swift. I had obviously not recovered from the previous energy-sapping meeting
in Johannesburg. Only four days had elapsed, plus travelling.

The teams pursuit race was another thriller. With me resting, Geldard,
Mitchell, Box and Burgess beat the Natal team in a nail-biting finish. In the final
event, the 5-mile, as we started the rain began to fall but the track was safe to
ride. After six laps Swift broke away and only I could close the gap. We worked
together at a very fast pace. We were half a lap up on the bunch with four laps to
go. Geldard, who was lapped, was joined by Burgess. They were called out by the
judges and appeared to be ganging up on Swift, but he broke away again and I
was the only one to go with him again.

The report reads:

…round the last bend the two fought wheel to wheel, and as they raced to the line
Godwin just got his wheel in front. It was a fitting conclusion to a fine meeting that
this event should bring a new National Record of 10 minutes 44.3 seconds.

So, Jimmy had turned me over in the kilo and I had reversed the placings in the 5-mile from the Test Match the previous Saturday.

The next stop was Durban as arranged, with a two-part meeting, both afternoon and evening. The early programme was badly organised, only the tandem race prevented a fiasco. To quote the report:

> Ken Mitchell won another individual event, riding a nice kilometre time trial to beat local favourite Swift. Binch beat Vorster in a 500 metre sprint.

The team for the 4,000 metre of Box, Geldard, Burgess and Mitchell, was beaten. I had declined up to this point from being involved as I was suffering from enteritis and did not want to compete. The promoters were very firm about having a tandem race. I was forced into riding as no-one else had experience as a steersman. There was only one ride over four laps, which the Natal riders won. I had not much interest at the time. The evening meeting saw the local team showing good form, winning three events. I reluctantly rode the final event as a token gesture, but could not add another victory at the distance, finishing a close second to Vorster and just beating Swift again who was third.

We then travelled back to Kimberley in comfort and had a full week to help our recuperation from the continuous pressure of travel and racing, including the very hard first test.

Local headlines said:

> Godwin scores over new South African 'TEST' choice, beats Robinson in 1,000 metre TT in 1.12.6
>
> Final result, the tourists beat Griqualand by four events to one, the only home win was by Robinson, not a local, who was allowed to join the home team with Godwin's permission and who rode to victory in the 5-mile event.

A lovely compliment added:

> Team Captain Tommy Godwin, whose riding never fails to impress the South Africans.

Our boys won the 4,000 metres team event once again, and Lloyd Binch was superb in the 440 yards sprint and the 1-mile, winning both. The last sentence read, "interest in the big match next week is high."

Moving down towards our departure from Capetown, there was a meeting at Worcester and then the final test at Paarl, the track we raced on first after our arrival. Riding at Worcester, with myself absent still suffering from a bowel complaint, the young team under my care rode with a lot of confidence. Having broken into international racing, three of them at least, on this trip, they had learned very quickly how to handle the pressure and the need to be versatile. My report to *The Bicycle* said:

> Here Don Burgess put in a fine 4,000 metre individual ride. This young man, now eighteen, showed so much promise, smooth style, powerful bursts, very controlled in his feelings, eager to learn a pleasure to work with.

Lloyd Binch won the 440 yards again but has not been inspirational at any point, so much talent, but his judgement at times is found wanting. Easily out manoeuvred mentally, any tactical rider can upset him.

Wally Box had his second win of the tour in a 5-mile event, beating Geldard, a time of 13 minutes 3.3 seconds, rather pedestrian.

Alan Geldard has not shown all the ability he has, and as a member of the 1948 Bronze Medal winning team has not shone on this trip."

So, we went to the final test. I had already stated that we would not be riding a tandem match. This event had put so much pressure on the team. Binch would have been superb with me as steersman, but he refused point blank even to consider it. He was and only wanted to be a sprinter, very individual, no real team spirit about him. This was rather disappointing as I had great confidence in him as a personal friend. Sad to report, after losing the first test 5 – 2 we lost the second 5 – 1, with tandem omitted. I was very, very upset with our failure to handle the big occasions.

The South African boys were in very good form. Shardelow immediately stamped his authority over Binch in the sprints. I was beaten in the kilometre by Robinson, whom I had won against the previous week. Binch was beaten in the 440 yards, having lost the sprint match 2 – 0. In the 1-mile and the 5-mile it was South Africa 1, 2 and 3 – unbelievable.

I was still suffering with a bowel problem and was sent straight from this match to Capetown where I had been booked in to see a specialist. The boys were transported to Belleville for the last meeting of the tour, a very low-key event but, I understand, very friendly. The lads were well looked after, had some fun and a wind-down before joining me in Capetown for departure. The specialist, after many tests, assured me that I was in a very low, weak state and that the two-week sea trip was just what I needed. With some medication and a careful diet, I was getting back to a reasonable state by the time my team mates joined me.

However, sitting in the hotel restaurant one evening with a light meal in front of me, I was approached by the waiter, who informed me that a lady was asking for me, "May I bring her to you?" "Yes," I replied, "by all means." Who should it be but the beautiful German lady from the ship we had travelled in. She was stunning, with a lovely dress, a wide brimmed hat, very elegant. I stood up and said, "This is a surprise." Erica then told me that she had read in the paper that I had been to a specialist, and in the report it named the hotel where I was resident. She, by coincidence, was staying with her sister only a short distance away in a suburb of Capetown.

I was flattered by her interest but also knew from what I had been told that she was rather a passionate lady. After the meal we retired to the lounge. She had already eaten. Chatting for some considerable time, I found out so much about her life. She even got to intimate details of her fraternisation with both sides during the war, German, American and British officers. It was an incredible story. Looking at her as she spoke, it was difficult to believe. She was such a charming lady, immaculate in every way, speaking wonderful English and living in London for some time.

The next day my team mates arrived after having a wonderful time at the last venue, Belleville. They had experienced a light hearted meeting with no-one treating the racing too seriously, but enjoying the social side of the event. We only had a couple of days before our departure, enjoying the wonderful city of Capetown and the surrounding tourist attractions.

All transport was laid on to get us to the boat we would be travelling on. To our surprise, there was a huge party on the quay to see us off. There were some of the South African racing boys, loads of officials, local inhabitants and, surprise, surprise, Erica the German lady. Once again looking stunning, she made her way through the crowd, aimed straight for me and, to the bewilderment of all the officials, gave me a kiss and said, "Tommy, I am sorry we did not get to know each other better." As we boarded the ship some of the locals came on with us, Erica included. We were led to our cabins, to find them filled with boxes and boxes of tinned fruit, wine and other gifts, and enough fresh for the journey home.

For the two-week return trip I did not insist on a curfew or early morning exercises. Having controlled the eating on the way out, the lads could eat what they wanted. I had some fun giving the head steward a tip, then telling him to give Wally Box anything he wanted, including any seconds or thirds from the desserts. As a result, Wally rolled down the gangway some one and a half stone heavier.

We were well received in London by NCU officials, and had to leave some of our goodies to follow. The cycling press had covered the trip well. We had not covered ourselves in glory, but some of the younger riders had established themselves by recording some good results and creditable times in certain events.

On my return home, having been away for over seven weeks, I was met by a very tired wife. Eileen had carried the business and the responsibilities once again. I realised that I must start to put some more time and effort into our livelihood. This became a strain, and my form soon started to deteriorate. At the first Olympic trials, where Benny Foster expected so much of me, the sparkle had gone. As the season progressed, I found myself struggling. In the kilometre trials big Don McKellow, a London boy, showed good form continually and eventually was the selection.

In the teams pursuit, my favourite discipline, I was tried with many different combinations, sometimes showing some very quick times but my contribution was no more than other riders. I could not lift the pace, as was my norm, or think of taking an extra half lap at the front. As the season went on Benny had to come to me, very emotionally, to say he could not recommend me for selection. He always had in mind that I was the man he would build the team around. At the Olympics in Helsinki the British team once again had Bronze medals. This continued the run of 1932, 1936 and 1948 – all Bronze. In 1956 at Melbourne there was Bronze again, no medals in 1960 or 1964 and Bronze again in 1972 and 1976.

I continued riding at meetings around the country but only in a limited way. The business was now moving along, my family life more settled and our daughter now four-years old.

My enthusiasm for cycling kept me in good shape. I was always very disciplined and had no trouble in keeping fit enough to continue racing. However, all thoughts of championships or international selection had gone. This pattern continued until mid-1953. I went to race in Darlington at an evening meeting mid-week, staying overnight with my dear friend Bert Goodwin. Wishing him and his wife goodbye, I had no thoughts in my mind as to what I was going to decide on the way home by train.

Arriving in Birmingham, I rode the three miles from the station to the shop. We had by now moved into the six roomed flat on the premises. On my arrival, the shop was closed as it was Coronation Day for Queen Elizabeth. Eileen opened the door. I kissed her, then said, "That's it, I am finished. I've decided to retire." I was still only thirty-two years of age. Eileen said, "What's the matter, did you lose?" I replied, "No, I won the 5-mile and the 1,000 yards events, but I've had enough." We then agreed to reassess our lives, planned how to come to terms with me being ever present and taking on all the pressures of business life. Eileen had been through a rough time, and it had taken all the vitality out of her. But little did we realise exactly how much harm it had done to her physically and mentally.

We got through the rest of the busy summer period. The shop was becoming a haven for young cyclists. Mums and Dads were bringing young children to see Tommy and to buy juvenile bikes with the transfer on. In the old days in the 1950's and 1960's, no sooner had the autumn arrived and people would come in paying in on a Christmas Club card and ordering bikes to be stored. By December a shop could be holding sixty, eighty or a hundred bikes until the week prior to Christmas.

But, come October, Eileen started to complain of not feeling well. She was making regular calls to our GP and being told that there was nothing wrong, it was all in the mind and a tonic would get her back to normal. She was losing weight, feeling cold and not sleeping well. Finally, in February 1954, she told the doctor that she was not satisfied and wanted a note to attend the Chest Clinic. On her visit, a chest x-ray was taken and she was informed that if she didn't hear from them by Thursday she was in the clear. But on Wednesday a notice came for her to attend the clinic again. Eileen made arrangements for her sister-in-law to go with her as Joan was a matron in a hospital in Stourbridge.

Eileen was asked to sit at the desk, with Joan accompanying her. Looking across the desk, Eileen could see, "WEST HEATH HOSPITAL 9–12 MONTHS." The x-ray had shown that she was suffering from Tuberculosis. The outcome was fifty-three weeks in hospital with various forms of treatment, some very unpleasant, some painful, and ending with an operation to have part of her lung taken away. We had been through a very telling time for some three or four years, with my job, the business, lack of money, me being away for weeks at a time and now a twelve month separation.

Tests had shown that Kay, just coming up to six years and having started school, had a shadow on her lung. She then had to go and live with her grandparents, Eileen's mother and father, in Stourbridge some 14 miles away.

In one fell swoop, we were all separated. Eileen could not come to terms with being away from Kay, although she knew her Mum would care for her in every way. We had hoped that if her health had not failed we would pick up the pieces of our marriage and enjoy some time together. We had paid a huge price for my devotion to sport.

The twelve months were an ordeal for us all. I visited as regularly as was allowed, but only three times a week for one hour only. Bed rest and peace and quiet were essential for a successful recovery. The 1950's were a time when a big effort was being made to find a way of arresting the disease, although they never claimed a cure was possible. The doctors at that time in West Heath, Doctors Thomas and Lee, were absolutely dedicated to ensuring the well-being of the numerous patients. Sadly, there were many deaths, but the success rate was wonderful. As it happened, amongst others in the same ward were young girls of seventeen, twenty-one and twenty-three, who showed such spirit that they made the older women feel better. There was a lot of humour in spite of the seriousness of the complaint. Visiting days for the youngsters were the day for goodies, always welcome.

Having been cared for all my life by a woman, for twenty-three years by my Mom, and for ten years by a loving, devoted wife, it was a case of get on with it and fend for yourself.

My family had decided about this time to leave England and go to Canada, to return to the life they had left behind in 1932. Dad had already left in 1953 and after a few months Mother followed. One of my sisters had moved some years before and my younger brother Bobby had gone to the States in 1946 at eighteen years of age to do military service there instead of being conscripted into the British Army. This was on Dad's advice as he saw better prospects for young people in North America. It only left my older sister Irene in England. She was married but was determined to follow the other members of the family. There was no thought of her helping me through this difficult period of my life, and she never visited Eileen in hospital.

After some months our daughter Kay was allowed to come home and to go back to school. A number of people and families rallied round to give support because of Kay, some caring for her during business hours, some providing meals etc, for which I was most grateful. Kay was never allowed to visit her mother, so there was a complete absence for twelve months of the motherly love Eileen had given her. A father at that age was a poor replacement. When Eileen came home on February 25th 1955 it was on the understanding that bed rest and care were essential, with four hours a day up, increasing gradually to eight hours and so on.

It was so difficult to accept what had happened. A wonderful young lady had gone down with a life threatening disease at thirty-four years of age and a strong, healthy, fit man of the same age, just retired from a sporting career that had been very successful and taken him around the world, were now facing a life of seemingly little future. But Eileen proved to be a tremendous fighter. She immediately started to put things into perspective. We had to clear the air of any negative thoughts. We would get back to a sound, happy life and build for the future. I expect that I was being selfish thinking of how I would not be able to lead the life I had in mind after retiring from the sport.

Eileen had progressed admirably in spite of the worries I was causing and she gradually took on the household duties, cooking, which she was always wonderful at, light cleaning duties etc, and even getting back to doing the bookwork of the business. She had only just got up to eight hours a day when I was rushed into hospital with renal colic. A kidney stone was diagnosed. There was no treatment at that time, only care and more liquids. My mistake was that I never did take enough water or other liquids, which was based on my father's advice to have a drying out from Thursday to Saturday, as practised by the boxing boys.

As our lives began to get back to normal and we both accepted what had happened in our relatively short married life of some ten years we found the importance of a relationship, and certainly "for better or worse."

CHAPTER 16

1956
A National
Training Scheme?

During 1956 I felt the urge to put something back into my sport. I realised that cyclists made so many mistakes. They had no direction. It was a matter of buying a bike, joining a club, getting into time trialling, following all the older men and just hopefully improving and, if not, just enjoying riding a bike. I soon realised that, knowing of coaching in America, I had prepared myself somewhat differently from the average cyclist. Physical and mental preparation was so important. Discipline and respect were essential. Programmes and schedules had to be laid down and adhered to. Recording progress and referring to this had to be carried out.

We had a track in Birmingham, Salford Park, built in 1951 with a very nice 440 yard asphalt track. This had been laid down as a training track after much pressure for many years by dedicated officials. It had a dressing room with showers, but no other facilities.

As I write this at eighty-three years of age I think back and realise that I never imagined what I was getting involved in, and that my enthusiasm for cycling, cycle racing and coaching were going to last through my life. No regrets!

I also developed an interest in the admin side of the sport, and soon found myself in the Birmingham Division Committee. Taking on various duties and being very firm in the ways I thought the sport should be taking, I advanced quickly and was soon Chairman of the Committee. Some of the older officials, W E McCormack, Tim Field, Alan Tomkins etc, gave me every support as I formed groups to carry out various duties. I started encouraging young riders to attend evening classes of PE, as it was called in those days, before circuit training, weight lifting, scientific readings, heart monitors etc were thought of. For winter training, I had walking, jogging, special breathing exercises, chest expanders, chin-up bars, all very basic but effective.

In my late thirties I was asked by John Perks (Porky) to go out for a training ride with some lads from the Earlswood Road and Path Club. He felt that they were not getting enough speed training. I had obviously kept myself in good shape, and found out where they were failing. The ride was on a Tuesday evening in the dark. There was not too much traffic in those days. Taking them on controlled gears with short turns leading, I could get them practising smooth changes and sitting close on a wheel. It was all very enjoyable. The lads were full of enthusiasm and asked if we could make it again on Thursday. I agreed and this time the speed was much higher, and on one turn on the front I upped the speed as John tried to come through. Up again with the pace, and John finally admitted he had never ridden so fast.

The word got round about March that I was taking a few riders of my own club down to Salford Park for controlled training. This began with warm-up sessions, riding to schedules, teams pursuit riding on moderate gears to timed laps, and then progressing on gears and distance to achieve targets. To help developing sprinters, there were lead out sprints, timing over 200 metres and two-up, three-up and four-up racing with suggested tactics. The improvement in young track riders was very encouraging. My work over the next few years with an enthusiastic group saw the local track league being more popular than ever.

During 1958 I became aware that many other Divisions were working to the same ends. Training schools, with people keen to progress, wanted to be recognised nationally, and noises were being made in the right direction. In September 1958 a meeting of all interested parties was held at Herne Hill Track. The attendance was very encouraging. Most people agreed to an idea of forming a common coaching scheme. The principle was agreed and, after many recognised experts spoke on their special subjects, it was agreed to start drawing up a basic plan.

Directly after this meeting I drove to Southampton to meet my father, who had decided to return from Canada and was travelling by boat. I had received a letter from the Cunard Shipping Co that I would be allowed on board ship to meet my father and accompany him ashore. I did not know at this time that he was in fact in very poor health. On arrival at the docks I showed my letter of authority and was directed to the berth. Having got on board, I went to the arranged deck and asked a few questions, only to be told that 'Charlie' went off with the first class passengers. Typical of the 'Old Man,' he could talk the hind leg off an iron pot.

I went to Customs, straining to look over a crowded room, hoping to get a sight of him. Suddenly, I saw an arm-waving smallish man, shouting, "Tommy!" I could not believe it was my father. From a seventeen and a half stone man he had shrunk to a wizened nine and a half stone, facially different also. I saw a man who had come to his homeland to die. When I finally got to him, I was met with, "Where the bloody hell have you been? Here's my case, come on, let's get the hell out of here and get to Brum." I phoned Eileen before leaving the docks and told her how poorly he was. I said, "Dad's come home to die."

At the time I was driving a Morris Minor 1000. The drive was all on old roads, narrow and twisting, which were strange to me. All I got was, "Can't you get this goddam car to go any faster?" (It had a top speed of 74 mph). We finally arrived home in the early hours around 2.00am. We were at the time living in the flat above the shop.

Eileen was shocked but handled it well. She has this wonderful, calm way about her. After a cup of tea we fell to talking. Within half an hour of arrival, Charlie pulled out of his pocket the gold Waltham watch and double gold Albert watch chain and said, "I'm returning this to the rightful owner." It was a combination of my first three cycle races in open competition. The watch was shown in the programme but prizes from two other events were changed for the double Albert. I had an inscription put in the case of the watch showing the date, 22 July 1939, and the venue.

I was quite emotional at this gesture as it confirmed my own thoughts about my father's reasons for returning home. But from this tense moment came a revelation which absolutely astounded me. Dad said, "Well, Big Boy, I've got a confession to make. Do you remember when you asked me in 1951 if I could get George Davies to buy the three gold trophies for the value shown in the programmes, total £1250? I came back and said that he would give you £1000, and you refused to sell them. I have to tell you now that he agreed to pay the full amount, but I was going to get £250 for myself out of the deal." I was shocked and bitterly disappointed, I knew riders and athletes did sell some valuable prizes, although strict amateur rules forbade that practice.

At the time in question houses were being built at controlled prices of £1150. The specification was excellent, a friend of ours had purchased one. The £100 balance would have furnished the house. Eileen and I had been through four lots of rooms, a small terrace house in a very poor area of the city and were now living in a flat above a shop. After fourteen years of marriage we were still struggling. Nothing could put the matter right. On reflection, writing this in 2005, a house of the type described would now be in the £200,000 price bracket. Of course, I still have the trophies but, woefully, the market value of these is not a lot.

The winter was very trying. Dad had struggled through. We had found a dear friend who offered B&B. All was well. Occasionally Dad would pop out and see some of his old friends, including the bookie. He would come back with some steaks or chops or fish, saying, "That one is yours, that one is Tom's and this one is mine: small, medium and large." We had a lot of fun with him. But early in 1959 we had a phone call to say that Dad had collapsed and was in the General Hospital. He had suffered with heart problems from when I was a boy, but he now had cancer of the prostate. Sadly, after wonderful care, he had his seventy-third birthday on January 12th and died on January 29th. I was at his bedside, talking about horse racing. I told him of the meeting that day. His remark was, "I'll never see the Galloping Gold Bricks again." He started gasping and struggling. I called for a nurse and was immediately asked to go. Shortly after I was told that I had lost my old pal. He was an inspiration, my motivator, the strong disciplinarian. We loved each other.

CHAPTER 17

1959

World
Championships
in Amsterdam
as Track Team
Manager

It was a shame that Dad died early in 1959 because by the middle of the year I was honoured by being appointed team manager for the World Championship Track Team. The Championships were to be held in Amsterdam. Dad would have been very proud.

I was, of course, delighted as the team included Norman Shiel, the holder of the pursuit title, having won it for the second time in 1958, Mike Gambrill, a superb rider of that time and another world class pursuit rider, and the sprinters Lloyd Binch and Karl Barton, both in scintillating form at home. One worry was that in *Cycling* for May 27th, Shiel had disclosed his reluctance to race in any more pursuit events.

It was going to be difficult to get the co-operation of some of the team. I had only finished my career in 1953 and some of the team were being prepared by other men around the country. In particular, Shiel worked with one of the finest men in the country, Eddie Soens of Liverpool, who had been a tower of strength in encouraging some of the most formidable riders, road and track. He had been behind Norman Shiel when he won both of his World titles.

I was personally friendly with Lloyd Binch, who had travelled with me in 1952 to South Africa, and we had maintained a very close friendship. In fact, Lloyd had for some time been criticised for his failures in World Championships when his record in Grand Prix wins both home and abroad was something to be proud of, plus his years as British Sprint Champion. When Lloyd heard of my appointment he stated very clearly that he would win the World Title for me, saying that he respected me and that I, in turn, understood him. In an interview for *Cycling* during the season, Karl Barton mentioned me as his mentor. All seemed well, subject to Shiel's decision.

Come the time, we travelled well. There seemed to be a reasonable atmosphere and, of course, I was known by all the team members.

A report in *Cycling* said:

> One long opening day, when 12½ hours of racing from breakfast to tea time, then through the evening until 1.00am Saturday, sufficed to end abruptly the British challenge in the 1959 World Amateur Track Championship in Amsterdam."

In preparing for the pursuit, I was told that the track measurement was such that the ride would be a full 8-laps, and the distance was 48 metres short of the full 4,000 metres. I spoke to Norman first and asked about a schedule for the ride. His reply was, "Don't worry, Tom, I've been here before. I am the current World Champion and I know what I've got to do." I then went to Mike Gambrill, who gave me a similar answer about not worrying.

Shiel had been put down as No 1 to ride the qualifying round. I had no lap times to call out to him and left him to ride his own race, with his experience. His time was 5 minutes 8.3 seconds. Gambrill clocked 5 minutes 8.2 seconds. The other riders now had something to aim at. Eventually, the fastest time was 4.53.8 by Rudi Altig. The last qualifier clocked 5.6.3. Our two riders were nearly 15 seconds off the pace. I was then blamed for not arguing Shiel's case to demand last man off as the title holder, but Norman had not asked for any change.

In the sprint, Barton and Binch progressed through the first round. In the second round Binch won. Barton failed, but had a repechage ride to get back in, which he won. But, as the race had a re-run due to a crash, in winning it Karl had to get up again within five minutes to ride against Gruchet of France. When the French boy attacked, Karl could not find the effort required. The quarter-finals put Binch against Gruchet, a ride Lloyd should have had no trouble in winning. Taking his first ride (it was to be the best of three) under my instructions, I told him to attack hard down the back straight. He won easily.

It was then decided to have three hours of motor paced riding. Binch went out of the stadium on his road bike and, meeting Gasperella, the reigning World Champion, had a chat. When Lloyd came out for the next ride he remarked, "Gasperella said, 'Binch, you and me for the final, yes?'" On repeating this to me, I said, "Yes, but you've got to beat Gruchet and then there is the semi-final."

As Lloyd was riding I stationed myself in the back straight. Arie van Vliet came to me and said, "Hey, Godwin. Binch, he is good enough to be World Champion, but he is crazy, he does not think good."

I had once again asked Lloyd to dictate the race, but he always believed that a good sprinter should win from the back in the home straight. Needless to say, he allowed Gruchet to take him into the banking, low down and quite slow. A kick into the bend, then he eased, another kick in the home straight and Gruchet won – not once but twice, because Lloyd would not go for a long sprint. Binch had a better acceleration even than Reg Harris, but his brain refused to work right. I, of course, went to console him. He was in tears and said he had let me down.

CHAPTER 18

1960
The price of failure

Following the disappointments in Amsterdam, we travelled on to Leipzig in the then DDR (German Democratic Republic) for further racing. On my return from Leipzig I submitted this report to the NCU:

It may well be that the British team failed again in Amsterdam, this story has been told with all the facts known to English journalism. My first appointment as track manager to the British team may not have brought any honours back, for this I am sorry, if in any way I failed.

What I can report however, is something probably of lesser importance but to those concerned it was a marvellous tonic.

Immediately following Amsterdam a team of British riders, eight in number with myself proudly in charge as manager, met up in East Berlin, five riders coming direct from London, namely K Craven, R Gambrill, N Tong, D Handley and T Millard, in addition, N Shiel, M Gambrill, K Barton proceeding direct from the title races. If I was proud at the commencement of this trip then as the days went by I can find no suitable prerogative to use to explain my later feelings.

After 14 hours by train from Amsterdam for four of us and a flight from London for the remainder, we found a 3 ½-hour coach trip awaiting us on our journey to Leipzig where the international match against the D D R had been brought forward, this was a surprise and gave little time for settling in.

However, from the outset, team spirit prevailed, on the whole trip not one mis-word was heard by any team member.

The results at Leipzig no doubt are known, but when one remembers that the British team won four of the six sprint matches, then Karl Barton in his first serious attempt equalled Nev Tong's 1,000 metre D D R record, with 1-11 7/10. At the end of his ride he collapsed with his legs seized up, such was his effort, but regardless of this he later teamed up to race for the first time with Dave Handley on a tandem. This event was won in two wins of three events the first run finding the British pair disqualified, the final run showed Handley and Barton being in world class with an 11 sec 200 metre time, a hope for Rome.

Nothing, however, could deter our boys. The individual pursuit saw Gambrill (M) giving the best show of his career at the distance, 5 min 2.6 sec. This same ride at Amsterdam with a short distance being used would have been worth a 4.55. His opponent was W Jager. Following this, Shiel rode Kohler, also a World Championship pursuit rider, in a most exciting match. The initiative changed hands from time to time, but Shiel showed his class by riding a fast finish to win in 5.6 4/10. The tandem rides followed. They were a joy to watch, two sprinters whom people consider at loggerheads, here were Handley and Barton riding as a pair from a very happy team and enjoying it."

In winning this international match, Britain became the first country to beat the DDR in three years. Among their victims were Russia, Hungary, Poland, Chzechoslovakia, Switzerland, Belgium and Denmark. One can imagine how the team felt about this victory.

An extra match was fixed at Gera on Sunday the 16th, the track 250 metres, cement with steep banking and sharp turns.

In a sprint series there was a disaster thrown in. Handley punctured, ran to the fence and grabbed it to save himself, but sustained a severe dislocation of the right thumb. Barton, a prince of sprinters, on this trip won races in such fabulous style that even his opponents were seen to put their hands to their eyes because of his daring and skill. He set a new track record of 12.3 in a second round and equalled the same in a thrilling final. In an initial heat, Barton purposely allowed Tong to win, saying he would qualify via a repechage heat.

Ken Craven in his debut as a 4,000 metre pursuit rider and on a tarry 250 metre track, had us all screaming with delight as he forged ahead during this race, he was, however, beaten by the smallest of margins and in a manner that augurs well for his future on the track.

Tony Millard, another new boy, won a special star handicap with Norman Sheil setting a fast pace. It was grand to see this boy being blooded with a victory in a strange country, but very unfortunately there was more misfortune. K Barton riding hard from scratch came to grief on the steep banking and sustained severe abrasions.

On went our whistle-stop tour, another long coach journey was made to Dresden, the last meeting, and what a climax to the trip. The team were in high spirits, nothing could prevent what was going to happen, even with Handley now out as regards riding, but a marvellous asset to the team with his friendly demeanor. Barton was heavily bandaged, but once again his devastating sprinting that he had shown through the series brought victory. In the final he beat Lewandowski, a powerful top class sprinter, once again a track record in 12.3 for the last 200 on a flat cement track, winning his race in the finishing straight.

In an Italian pursuit R Gambrill as lead-man gave us a lead in half a lap, followed by a "not in form" Tong and a slightly worried Millard and at this point England were down. But Barton, No 4, was fighting to get Shiel and Gambrill into a winning position. The pressure was on, the D D R last man losing a wheel, Sheil carrying on to give Gambrill a slight lead which, with a superlative effort, he opened up a five second victory, another record.

But more to come, in a special 800 metre handicap, Millard fighting hard with Shiel again setting the pace, came into the finish with a lead which was snatched from him on the line, but yet another place for a new boy.

The final event, a 100-lap madison, saw the most exciting event of the trip: Sheil and M Gambrill teamed up against 11 German teams, and Craven-Tong, Millard-R Gambrill, both the latter teams retired, the first mentioned team, however, went on to tear the field to pieces, a field of riders whose pride and joy is their natural aptitude as Madison riders. Never have I witnessed two men fighting so hard for victory, a lap gained half-way with only one other team with them. The German lead team was gaining victory after victory in the sprints. Our boys were well down on sprint points, but this was not good enough, on hurried instruction they were told they must get another lap and this on a 400 metre track. Gambrill and Sheil went in a workmanlike manner to break away again, shedding their near rivals and eventually pulverising the field by making contact with the tail end. They ran out clear winners for their efforts in yet another track record time by 1 min.

Anyone who was fortunate enough to see the team on the conclusion of the meeting must have realized that the team spirit was of the highest order.

This part of the trip was a great success, the organization was excellent, nothing was spared to give us our needs and I feel that the team would wish me to give a hearty thanks to Jim Wallace and his wife for their efforts. Without Jim we would have been in many difficult situations.

May I conclude by saying, if every team manager has such a grand bunch of boys to handle, then his worries will be few.

On our return from East Germany, I was shocked to get a letter from George Pearson, then Editor of *Cycling Weekly*, in which he explained that Reg Harris had criticised my appointment as team manager, stating that I had no qualifications for the job and that I was responsible for the dismal results in Amsterdam, the failure of Sheil and Gambrill etc. He stated that Benny Foster should have been in charge, but Benny had taken on the responsibility as manager for a professional team in that year.

I was asked if I wanted to reply, but I said I would not lower myself to get in a slanging match just to push the sales of the book. I had no respect for Harris as a man - as a bike rider and world champion, yes. Reg never did anything for the sport in an honorary capacity or as a volunteer. His motivation was money, and I am sure he was paid to belittle me. As for George Pearson, I always called him 'THE LITTLE RAT,' scuttling round for scraps, hoping to make a meal out of it. Fortunately, I got support from Mick Gambrill, in which he explained how I lifted the riders' morale on the German trip and applauded our success.

Tom Simpson also expressed his admiration for the manner in which I handled his disappointment in not winning the professional pursuit. He had broken down, saying he did not know if he would continue to race as a pro. I told him he had only just started, that every sportsman suffers from low morale, he had to forget what had happened and look to the future. In a very different frame of mind, he rode the road race and surprised himself and many others by finishing fourth. Other people wrote in about the unfair criticism, stating how much work I was putting into the sport and the improvement in the Midlands because of my guidance.

The outcome, however, was that I was immediately dropped as a team manager and the responsibility given to Arthur Maxfield, a member of Racing Committee for the 1960 Olympics in Rome. I was shattered to say the least, but I had no intention of ending my dream. I desperately wanted to continue working with riders, with the aim of getting world beaters for the country.

CHAPTER 19

1962

The first BCF
training course for
trackmen – World
Championships
in Milan
– Commonwealth
Games in Perth

My work continued with group training sessions. I was getting media attention and because my main training sessions were on Sunday afternoons it was written up in the press as:

TOMMY GODWIN'S SUNDAY SCHOOL.

Other coaches in the country were working in isolation, but we all wanted to get a National Coaches Course set up. Meetings were held and reports sent to HQ. About this time a man named Peter Itter was full of enthusiasm on Racing Committee and gave us all the support he could.

The 1960 Olympics were another sad disappointment. Our teams pursuit squad of Gambrill, Hoban, McCoy and McLean failed to qualify in the top eight. GB teams had won Bronze medals in this event at the last six Olympics. Karl Barton was 16th in the kilo with 1.11.7, the winner clocked 1.7.3. Handley and Thompson in the tandem event failed to progress beyond the quarter-finals. On the road, GB finished 14th in the team time trial, ten minutes down on the winners Italy. The road race was again a race too far and too fast for the GB squad. Strangely, there was no comment about the team manager from either Reg Harris or George Pearson.

Reinstated as team manager for the 1961 World's in Zurich, I took with me a team with seemingly good prospects. Dave Handley, who had finished third in Leipzig, was No 1 seed, the other two finalists having turned pro. Binch was in the team but not as a selection by the committee, as he was deemed to have had enough chances and failed. He was allowed to travel at his own expense, or rather from public donations by friends and fans of a superb sprinter, he having won the British Sprint Championship seven times and numerous Grand Prix. A third sprinter was named, Harry Jackson, a complete bike rider in every sense. His main interest was in the individual pursuit, with Barry Hoban as No 1 choice in this event.

Sadly, none of the riders named progressed very far. In the analysis afterwards, it had to be agreed that the Continental teams were being professionally prepared. They had state backing or industrial companies connected with the cycle trade contributing heavily to the national teams. Here in Britain everything was so amateur. The need was for an official squad training system with funds to allow riders to travel and be accommodated without having to find the money out of their own pockets. It was mission impossible at this time.

I continued my enthusiasm during the winter months with local riders, encouraging them to take part in regular physical training courses, circuit training, even swimming, to emphasis the importance of all round body fitness. The coaching scheme was growing in many ways, and a basic plan was laid down to find volunteers to pass an examination qualifying them as club coaches.

To my surprise, I was asked by the BCF if I would take over the organisation of a training course for riders interested in road racing. Lilleshall Hall National Recreation Centre had already been booked and Brian Robinson, a famous rider who had left his home in Yorkshire to prove his worth on the Continent, was to be the main attraction to encourage youngsters to pay the £6 for a 5-day course. George Ronsse, a World Road Champion of the past, and Ron Coe, a very successful Independent in GB, were to assist. I came on as course organiser, also to explain the benefits of track racing for road men and to pursue what I have always believed in, the need for general all round fitness, including the importance of correct foods. I had arranged for regular daily supplies of fresh fruit, bananas, oranges and apples, free daily supplies of milk from the Milk Marketing Board and Horlicks drinks and biscuits.

I had obtained cine film of the human body and had the good fortune to find a qualified instructor from H M Prison Service, George Popplewell. He described and explained every aspect of the human body, sometimes a bit heavy for youngsters but very well accepted. It gave them some idea of what the body required, how you could under perform and how you could perform better with common sense and care.

Most important was Popplewell's 'Formula for Success', applicable to all forms of sport.

$$SUCCESS = 3S + A + 3T$$

WHERE

S1 = STAMINA		T1 = TECHNIQUE
S2 = SUPPLENESS	A = ACCELERATION	T2 = TACTICS
S3 = STYLE		T3 = TENACITY

S1, S2 and S3 can all be described as physical states
A1 is also physical but is inherent in the body's make up
T1, T2 and T3 can all be classed as mental states

All the above were then explained in detail and many training manuals cover all these points today. I have the full manuscript in the original report by Bryan Ward. But it is my intention only to impress the quality of teaching on the first ever course under British Cycling Federation jurisdiction.

I was now coming to terms with what I always believed was necessary, and the hope that coaching would be accepted by young people in the sport of cycling. In my opinion coaching has still not been accepted and taken to by the masses.

The current GB squad of track riders is very limited, and almost a closed shop to one and all. It has certainly proved the value of experts in different fields. Today coaching involves physiology, nutrition, technology, computers – every last detail is considered, and success is the result. We had similar concepts in the 1960's but no funds to call on.

Some of the best young riders of that time who attended, 31 in all, sang the praises of the instructors and the quality of the course. They went home very happy, with plenty of enthusiasm for what lay ahead. I still treasure the complete report so well documented by the late Bryan Ward.

The 'Brian Robinson Course' was the start of a new era. From this innovative idea training courses blossomed, and were to have a huge impact on the sport of cycling.

Indeed, so successful was the course for roadmen, I immediately set about organising one for trackmen in May of the same year.

Cycling reported the first course as follows:

TRAINING FOR TRACK TITLES

A REPORT ON THE FIRST BCF COURSE FOR TRACKMEN

SPORTING COMMENT

By John Matthews

May 16th 1962

Two weeks ago 37 trackmen of varying standards of proficiency, ranging from teenage novices to Britain's past – and possibly present – world championship and Empire Games representatives, spent five days at the first national training course for trackmen organised by the British Cycling Federation.

"And about time too," you might say.

For we all know that an intensive, official training scheme, concentrating coaching on our keenest or most promising riders, is the way to end the decline in track racing standards and catapult us back in to the position we held only a few years ago, with world class riders to attract the critical crowds back to the grandstands. But that's enough of that!

By all accounts it was a good course. Dave Handley, who was assisting as an instructor, and promising pursuiter Dave Bonner both commented: "It should have been three months."

In charge was Tommy Godwin, six times a national track champion between 1944 and 1949, who has organised the two roadmen's training courses held at Lilleshall. His assistant was Eddie Soens, recently named to go with Godwin to the Empire Games in Australia.

From my visits to the roadmen's courses, I felt they were, if anything, too free and easy, which seemed a pity. On such a course most riders would respond to discipline.

Course Discipline

The trackmen's course, which was held at Lilleshall Hall, Shropshire, from the morning of Monday April 30, to late afternoon Friday afternoon on May 4, had that discipline.

Those on the course were up at 7.30 am, made their beds, then had a brisk walk, or short ride, round the grounds before breakfast at 8.15. At 9 am they were in the lecture room, listening to Godwin and Soens on training tactics, equipment and feeding; Handley on Sprinting; or Bryan Ward, the polytechnic all-rounder, on weight and circuit training (which was a report on George Popplewell's talk on the last roadmen's course).

From 10 to 12 they were out on road machines for a 30- to 40-mile round trip in the nearby lanes. Then back to Lilleshall in time for a shower and lunch.

At 2 pm they boarded a hired coach to take them the 14 miles to Aldersley Stadium, Wolverhampton, where their track machines were stored. There, on the corporation track, they had carefully planned training for 2 ½ hours.

Warm-up sessions in groups of 7 or so with the speed increasing towards the end of an 8-mile work-out, were followed by sprints and pursuits. Throughout, Godwin and Soens, armed with a lap-chart, megaphone, whistles and watches, kept careful control.

On the second day, I saw Joe and Dan McLean (Melling Wh), Dave Bonner and Paul Burgess (Old Portlians) ride together for the first time in a 4,000 metre pursuit. After a pep-talk by Soens, they went out and clocked 5 min 5 sec against I Alsop, D Butler, M Ives and D Plummer, which was said to equal the track record set up two years earlier by a well-drilled squad. On Thursday the same two teams (except for T Pennell in place of Plummer) each clocked 5 min 3 sec. Progress had been made!

In the evenings there was a discussion group from 8 to 9.30pm. After that, they could do what they liked, which meant that one night they watched Karl Barton's colour slides, and two nights they watched Dave Handley's cine films, taken on their foreign trips.

Many of those on the course were from the Midlands, but 10 were from the London area, one (T Moore) was from Wales, three (the McLeans and C Smith were from Liverpool, three (B Gunn, G Smith and D Plummer) were from Yorkshire, and one, C Dale, had come all the way from Trinidad earlier this year.

Of the up-and-coming riders on the course, Godwin was most impressed with: Bonner and Burgess, whom he sees as prospects for the Tokyo Olympics, Geoff Smith, a sprint hope, and Trevor Bull from Birmingham, whom he believes could develop into a pursuit and sprint star.

Now, Godwin – who is Britain's track team manager for the world championships and the Empire Games – is planning more get-togethers for the "possibles." They will meet on six week-ends before the world titles, and then on another two occasions before the Empire Games.

He hopes to get the actual selections together for another week at Lilleshall.

For only six guineas all-in, 37 trackmen spent five days training intensively, benefiting from the fact that those around them were keen to learn – including those that have worn Britain's colours abroad such as Alsop, Barton and Church.

But it is a pity our most recent world champions, Reg Harris, Cyril Peacock and Norman Shiel, were not there to give some advice.

Again, in *Cycling* Reg Harris was given two full pages to give his views on what should be done about training. He proposed extended training camps, professional coaches from Italy, Continental riders to show how it should be organised and tracks to be used, especially Fallowfield of which he was at that time the owner. He remarked, pointing at me, that to possess coaching abilities one should not have to be a champion at that particular sport.

Everything that I and many other enthusiasts in the country gave in the way of time was done voluntarily. We were working desperately hard to create a National Coaching Scheme. Reg Harris never attempted to set up any scheme to help young riders but was always ready to put people down who did. The sheer impracticality of doing all he suggested was obvious. It would have cost thousands. At the training courses we held the riders paid six guineas for five days.

There were continued training weekends for riders showing form, and on August 20th Racing Committee selected teams for the World's to be held later that month. For the track team, specialist sprinters, were cut out, the emphasis was on individual and teams pursuit. There was also a strong women's team.

I was fortunate to have worked with Eddie Soens in getting the riders in shape, and we had been announced as Team Manager and Assistant Manager for the Commonwealth Games in Perth later in the year. It was still the prerogative of the Committee to pick the teams, based on reports from the training sessions. As yet they were not ready to give responsibility to the coaches or managers. We were given five days to fine-tune the team. It was written in *Cycling* that the Italians had probably been doing this for months.

Our trip was, as usual, arduous: train – boat – train from London to Milan, endless hours cramped up, with no sleeping berths. On arrival in Milan, railway officials would not clear the huge collection of bicycles, suggesting that we were bringing them in to sell, and Italy did not want to see this happen. I had to send the team to the hotel and then, after six hours, was given clearance. Requests for transport proved very difficult and by the time it was finally settled I got to the hotel just as the team were sitting down for the evening meal.

When the team came and saw the Vigorelli Velodrome, then the mecca of the sport of cycling, they could not believe it: a 400 metre track with a smooth wood surface. After riding the first workout all of the lads and girls were absolutely fascinated. It was not difficult to get them working.

In the men's individual pursuit, Jackson was the better of the two British riders but could still only qualify as No 14. McCoy, the second rider, was matched against an absolute flyer from Denmark, who returned a 4.54, at that time in the sport a superb time, which he beat in the semi-finals with a 4.51, a world record. In the teams pursuit, the British boys qualified in 7th place, beating France, but the fastest time was 4.29.9 and GB was 4.36.

The report in *Cycling* said:

> The first team time trial on Sunday morning proved a tremendous morale booster. By evening when Britain faced Russia in the quarter-finals they were a confident unit. Gears were raised for the generally expected fast conditions.
>
> Russia won the ride but lost a man under the pressure, and the gap they had opened just could not be closed by a very smooth working GB quartet, our time 4-35, the fastest ever by a British team. West Germany won in world record time 4-26 against Russia 4-31.

We were proud in the camp by virtue of a Gold Medal won by Beryl Burton and a Bronze Medal won by Jean Dunn in the Women's Sprint Championship.

We made a visit to a local restaurant to celebrate the girls' success. During the evening some Italians, who had obviously been to the track, watched as I got up to propose a toast, and as I finished one of them came to me and said, "You are the manager of the team?" I replied, "Yes." He immediately put his hands to his eyes and imitated a sob, with shoulders heaving. "You were sad for the team." I realised that he had been watching my reaction to the boys riding so well and not winning. He then asked his friends to toast me, saying as he bumped his chest with clenched fist, "You are like the Italians, emotional." A good night was had by all.

I realised, as many other people had, that we could only be moving in the right direction. We were getting squad training recognised, riders were keen to attend at their own expense. We were getting respect and discipline. We were motivating young riders to believe in themselves, and things could only improve. The national coaching scheme was moving on and sixteen divisions throughout the country had been successful in getting club coaches through the qualifying examination that had been laid down.

After the experience of the World's we now had to get down to preparing track men and road men for the forthcoming Commonwealth Games in Perth, Australia, during the month of November.

The team was selected after 'The Meeting of Champions' on September 8th. Barton won the sprint title, Harry Jackson the individual pursuit, John Clarey the 10-mile Title – all were selected, along with Charlie McCoy, Joe McLean, Roger Whitfield, with other riders to be named. The road team was: W Mason, K Nuttall, Bob Addy and K Butler.

All of these riders made a formidable squad. The selected road men had been winning a number of events through the season.

Eddie Soens had been chosen to join me in handling the team, and I could not have chosen anyone better. We had been friends and rivals in the past. Eddie had proved himself a wonderful coach to countless good riders. We were fortunate at being allowed to have a week together as a team at Lilleshall. Eddie and I laid down a programme of training and a bonding session for all the riders to get to know each other. There were training rides with road men and track men so that they could find out each other's qualities. The plans for squad training included talks on faults and mistakes, pressure training, relaxing, controlled diets etc. Eddie and I believed we were taking the first steps towards better teams, with discipline and respect throughout the team by man management and good organisation.

We knew we were in for a true test. Our riders were just finishing a long and arduous season, whilst the Aussies were just coming into their track season.

On our arrival in Perth we found the competitors' village ideal. We were housed in brand new bungalows, which would be on the market after the Games. An excellent food hall provided meals to suit the most discerning food fadist. There were also facilities in the accommodation to make snacks and drinks.

The extreme heat of the day meant that road training had to be done early morning at 6.00am to allow riders to get in three or four hour sessions. The track riders had one and a half or two hours on the road with track training in the afternoons or early evenings. A strict 10.00pm curfew was agreed and the whole team responded.

One evening I had been invited to a meal with some wealthy local business people who I had met at a formal reception at the British Ambassador's residence. I had been in conversation with them and had been asked if I could come to their home. After a very pleasant meal, drinks and conversation I suddenly realised that the curfew time was fast approaching. I asked, "Can someone run me back to the village?" There was some laughter and kidding, "You're are not serious?" I insisted, saying, "If no-one can take me, can you call me a taxi?" The host realised that I was serious and agreed to run me back.

Getting to the gates and through security, I ran up the road to the bungalow, opened the door to find all the lads sitting up ready for bed but waiting for me. Eddie Soens immediately said, "I bloody told you the bugger would be here at 10.00 o'clock!" I was just in time. Had I not returned I am sure I would have lost some of the respect I had gained.

However, at the Ambassador's reception earlier in the day I was having a chat when a rather impressive middle aged lady walked across the room towards me. She obviously saw the letters 'ING' on my blazer and on getting near to me she said, "Sailing?" I said, "No, Cycling." "Oh," was her next remark, upon which she turned and walked away without another word. So much for our sport!

We did have one item which might have upset the team spirit we had created. One day McCoy and McLean, two Liverpool Scousers, asked to be excused from road training, saying they were feeling the strain. Permission was given. On our return (Eddie and I used to go out on all road sessions on a motorbike, with Eddie, an enthusiast, on the front and me on the pillion) we were informed by Barton and Jackson that the large wardrobe had been removed from their room and replaced by a small one. Eddie immediately said, "Come on, let's go and see the two scroungers." He knew what the two lads had been up to.

I was very upset that this sort of thing could happen. I told them to move the two wardrobes back to their original places, only to be laughed at. My reaction was, "If you don't do as I say, I'll knock you flat on your back." Eddie backed me up with, "You take the big one, I'll take the lad." Eddie's past included amateur boxing, and I was pretty useful. Needless to say, the job was carried out. I warned both riders that I would include it in my report and advise that neither man be selected to represent GB again.

After a spell things were back to normal and team spirit renewed.

In the actual competition we finished with Gold in the road race, Wes Mason winning in brilliant fashion. Karl Barton took Silver in the sprint. There were Bronze medals in the kilo, individual pursuit and 10-mile for Roger Whitfield, Harry Jackson and John Clarey respectively.

We had the misfortune of Clarey crashing badly one day in training. He was kept in hospital for a few days but assured us he would ride the 10-mile. There was every possibility that without his crash he would have been more confident and could well have won the event.

Having had a lot of time together and starting to see improvements at the World's and the Commonwealth Games, riders and press were coming round to the idea that we were on the way with the system.

A report in *Cycling* headed 'GAMES LESSONS' said:

> Although Australia did far too well for the peace of English minds, the Common-
> wealth Games in Perth may be voted a successful fixture. It was good to hear team
> manager Tommy Godwin say on his return last week, 'Nobody could wish for a better
> team'.
>   The final score, however, Australia four gold medals, England one, shows the road
> to World and Olympic titles will be long and hard.

Duke of Edinburgh
and TG at Common-
wealth Games Road
Race, King's Park,
Perth, 1962

We had been honoured by Prince Philip visiting the Games and coming out
to the road race in King's Park. On visiting us at the feeding station, he asked
what we were doing. I explained about feeding and drinks and said each rider
had made notes of what he would need during the race. I showed him a little
book and started flipping pages:

Rider 'A' - such and such food, a shot of strychnine."

Quick turn of page, next:

Rider 'B' – sandwiches, fruit drink, caffeine,

Another page:

Rider 'C' – food and a hot black coffee with cherry brandy.

All the lads had been having a bit of fun. Prince Philip said, "I fancy the coffee and brandy."

Whilst he was watching the race riders were approaching for drinks time.
I gave one drink to Alan Dansen, an English lad who had settled in Perth and
was helping out, and named the rider it was intended for. Alan started running, looking behind to see the approaching rider. Suddenly there was a bump.
He had run into the back of Prince Philip. He dropped the bottle, issued a few
choice remarks then realised who he had run into, whereupon Prince Philip
said, "Oh, I buggered that up, didn't I?"

CHAPTER 20

1963

National training
courses for
roadmen and
trackmen – World
Championships in
Liege

I got back home seriously wondering whether I would still have a business to run. My dedication to the sport was taking me away continually. My wife, Eileen, was still keeping things ticking over, with only a young lad full-time and some volunteers to help.

However, there was correspondence in handfuls about the coaching which I was trying to establish. Bryan Wootton from BCF Headquarters was a tremendous help, but requests from all over the UK were piling up.

There was only about a month to Christmas, a very important time for new bikes to be sold for children who had asked for them hopefully. Getting over Christmas and all that brings into our lives, I was once again on the move. I was organising the 1963 Roadman's Training Course at Lilleshall with Brian Robinson, the top man with all his Continental experience. This was to be followed by a Trackman's Training Course in May. There were also plans to have regular track training sessions through the season, preparing riders for National titles and the World Championships, the latter to be held in Belgium.

A very important Roadman's Course was held in mid-February with many of the leading exponents of the country present, in particular Wes Mason, the Gold Medal winner in Perth. Obviously, his visit in preparation for the Perth Games had made its mark and Wes wanted more. So too did international road race winner Hugh Porter and Independents John Woodburn and George Shaw. There had been 56 applicants, but only 30 were accepted.

Due to very bad weather there was very little riding done. However, we had workouts in the gym and lectures by Brian, which were repeats of his talks in 1962. During one of the sessions, I remarked that I had seen one rider who I thought might develop into a top class pursuit rider. I pointed him out. It was Hugh Porter. He immediately stood up and said, "Prove it." I replied that it would take a lot of work, learning to ride to schedules, being patient and coming to track regularly. Little did I realise that this meeting was going to develop into a lifelong friendship. Hugh worked very hard and as the season progressed it was decided he would enter the National Individual Championship to be held at Fallowfield in the last Saturday in June.

The weekend weather was terrible. On the Friday evening only the qualifying rides for the pursuit were run, the eight fastest proceeding to the quarter finals. No fast times were registered but Porter was very convincing and in the final against Jackson won comfortably. I was very pleased, of course, and Hughie said, "What do I do now?" I said, "Wait until about Tuesday or Wednesday and you will have a letter from HQ telling you that you have been selected for the World's in Liege, Belgium." This, of course, happened. We were both on cloud nine.

A report of my appointment as National Coach appeared in *Cycling*, March 27, 1963:

FIRST NATIONAL COACH
from Connecticut, USA
by John Matthews

Tucked away on page 75 of the British Cycling Federation Racing Handbook, at the end of the lists of affiliated clubs and associations, is a modest two-line announcement which says:

NATIONAL COACH
T C Godwin, 10 Silver Street, Kings Heath, Birmingham 14

When the 1963 Handbook was released on March 7, that announcement – for those who spotted it – contained what could be the most important news for British cycling since the days when one man on a bicycle decided that he would like to go faster than the next.

A national coach…the dream of everyone who has seen how the Continentals thrive by being *directed,* and how, because of it, powerful men like Guido Costa can dictate ruthlessly to amateurs – first in his own country of Italy, then in Denmark and now, I understand, in Mexico – just how, when and where they should ride, train, eat and sleep, if they want to make good for their country.

A national coach…Supremo of selections and international racing campaigns. The man who not only finds the raw material but moulds it as he will to produce an international worthy of wearing a national jersey. The man entrusted with the task of improving cycling facilities and performances. The man who, by producing successes, would increase the appeal of the sport to youngsters and encourage more to take it up. From the encouragement and advice of all, and the international honours for the few, would come greater general interest in the sport.

That has been a dream for years.

Behind the scenes, the Federation has been working intensively to obtain a grant from the Ministry of Education to pay for a full-time coach. Anxious for an application to be approved, the Federation has been cautiously considering ways in which to approach the Ministry in order to stand a good chance of their application succeeding.

Some knew who would be asked to accept the job, but nothing was finalized, no agreement reached. In fact, less than a week before the handbook appeared I was told plans to name the coach had broken down. It would be at least a month before any news was available. Then the handbook, after delays at the printers, appeared.

Red faces at the Federation; hurried telephone calls; and then came conformation that Godwin had accepted the position.

It is, however, an honorary position – and although the terms of reference were discussed at a special meeting in London a fortnight ago, and the Ministry of Education is now considering an application for a grant, until funds are made available and a contract is signed to make it a paid appointment (which the BCF aim to do as soon as possible) it seems that it is little more than official recognition of the title Godwin has earned through his valuable work on the week-long national training schemes run since 1961 by the Federation.

But the decision is made. The first national coach in cycling is Thomas Charles Godwin: Electrician turned cycle-dealer, former international trackman, England team manager, Rover RCC club member for 24 years, a disciplined impressive man who says what he thinks and has no time for committees. A good man for the job – but, oh! The irony of it! A man born in America!

Born in Bridgeport, Connecticut, USA in 1920, he was brought up in an atmosphere of sports colleges, which he believes accounts for his intense interest in establishing a co-ordinated scheme in this country.

At the age of 12 the Godwin family returned to England. At 14 Tommy had his first cycle. His father – a tough 17-stone disciplinarian – wanted Tommy to be an

Olympic athlete. But when he got over his disappointment at him taking up cycling, he did everything to get Tommy to the top. He organized his training and racing thoroughly. All he demanded of his son was that he should follow his instructions, go fast when he told him to, stop when he told him to, ride when he told him to, rest when he told him to. The perfect coach. And it produced results.

At 17 he competed on a 27s 6d road machine in the BSA Sports – his first race. Godwin rode in his first track meeting on a racing bike in 1938. It was the BSA Sports meeting in which he had his first taste of competition a year earlier. In four events (two handicaps, a sprint and a "devil take the hindmost") he scored two wins and a third. He wanted to win all four. For the next 12 months he trained to do just that. And in July, 1939, at only his third ever meeting, his second on a racing machine, he won all four events. The training system, and dedicated partnership of father and son, had been proved.

Two weeks later he competed in his first open event as a novice. He was off 84 yards. Before he got on the track the stewards warned him that if he did not go through and win they would get him suspended. Such was the price of ability! A month after his first open event he finished third in the national five-mile championship.

War stopped his hopes for the 1940 Olympics, and an electrical apprenticeship at BSA kept him busy.

Then came the titles. For three years, from 1944 to 1946, he won the national five-mile championship; in 1945 and 1946 he won the national 25-mile track championship; in 1946 he became the first British rider to compete in a world pursuit championship. Not really knowing much about pursuiting, he rode a 1 inch pitch chain – yet he reached the quarter-finals, where he was beaten by the eventual champion. In 1947, he again reached the quarter-finals.

It was a disastrous year – he lost his two national titles in a week. But that year he won prizes valued at £394, excluding trophies, which was higher than at any other time in his career.

In the Olympics in London in 1948 he gained a bronze medal in the kilometre time trial and was a member of the England team which gained third place in the team pursuit.

In 1949 he won the national individual pursuit title but was dropped from the world championship team. A year later he rode in the world championships and the Empire Games in which he finished 3rd in the kilometre time trial.

Racing Committee confused everyone with their selections. Porter as Champion and Dave Bonner, who had registered the fastest time during the season, had been selected for the individual pursuit, also Beryl Burton in the ladies pursuit. The rest of the selected riders, a mix of sprinters and pursuit riders, were not given any definite events to ride, but I could put them in whatever event I chose, sprint or pursuit. Needless to say, no joy in the latter.

On out arrival at Rocourt track Hughie could not believe what he saw. It was a big, dirty looking cement track, surrounded by concrete walls. He said, "Flash, all I need now is a spear, a helmet and a shield and I could be a gladiator." However, things improved once he had got on the track for a warm-up session, and knew all the names of riders entered, and also that there would be a qualifying ride to find the fastest eight. All preparations were carried out and the big day arrived. Hughie's question was, "What do I do now?" My answer was, "You ride a 5 minute 5 seconds or a 5 minute 6 seconds and you qualify." He said, "I've never ridden better than 5.15 at home." My answer was, "Well, if you don't do that ride, you're on the way home."

Surprise, surprise, he returned 5 minutes 5.5 seconds. He asked me, "How did you know that?" I told him that I had registered a 5-12 in 1951 for second fastest time, and things have obviously improved. "Then, what happens now?" "You ride a about 3 seconds faster and you are in the semi-final." He returned a 5-1, and as he rode to me he put two fingers in the air and said, "You were wrong by one second."

In the semis he put in a fantastic ride, Walschaerts 5-4.27, Porter 5-4.45. The other semi times were, Moskvin 5.9.03, Frey 5.12.84. Hughie won the Bronze, beating Frey, but what a wonderful performance, a first time at the World's and a medal. Prior to the Championships and subsequently I was shown as his mentor and advisor.

Beryl rode superbly to retain her title, beating Yvonne Renders, a Belgian girl and a really tough opponent.

We returned home with some honours once again, Beryl Burton with a Gold, and a Bronze for Hugh Porter. It felt good to meet people who had been critics of the state of the sport in this country.

The winter months were very hectic. I was travelling around the country where courses had been set up to interest young riders in the benefits of a coaching scheme. Obviously, everyone in sport had in mind the 1964 Olympic Games to be held in Tokyo.

Early in that year I had laid down the plan for regular training sessions at various tracks around the country, and invited riders interested to attend for the purpose of evaluating abilities for different events. Many names stood out, of course, but riders and coaches who thought they had the quality were invited to go through varying tests. A very good squad was soon established and performances and times recorded for all events: sprint, kilo, tandem (still included at that time), individual pursuit and teams pursuit.

During the winter 1963-1964 Hugh Porter had been invited to ride in Japan in a mock Olympics programme. He came home as winner of the individual pursuit and a Gold in the teams pursuit as a member of a mixed nation team. He, of course, was brimming with confidence and looking forward very much to returning for the real thing. It was a morale booster to members of the squad when they were given an opportunity to ride in a teams pursuit work-out with Hughie. My demands or requests to him to turn up at most raining sessions did not go down too well as he missed many road races. He was, of course, an established winner of classics on the road.

As the season progressed the team 'possibles' rode at open track meetings where promoters would include events that I asked for. This soon proved to be invaluable to all. The strength of the training was soon proven. With any combination of from eight to ten riders, two teams of four would bring out fast times and close finishes. I was so confident with the riders we were working with that in May I confirmed a statement earlier that if we did not win medals in the Olympics, I would quit my job as National Coach and Team Manager.

CHAPTER 21

1964

World
Championships
in Paris – the
Tokyo Olympics

We had been told by Racing Committee that we would have a full track team for the World's in Paris, but may have to double up in events in Tokyo. Karl Barton was showing superb form in his sprinting. In June a pursuit team of Porter, Jackson, Bull and McKeown returned a time of 4.49, the second fastest time in the country. I was able to announce that our target was 4.40, or even 4.35 on the right day.

In the July 4th issue of *Cycling* I was quoted as saying:
I think it is possible that Hugh Porter may well do the fastest ride in a straight competition in the forthcoming pursuit championships." He had already been confirmed

as the choice for Tokyo in view of his win there in the winter.

I was asked,

What sort of ride can the British Champion be expected to produce?

My reply was:

I think a ride in the 5.7 range, and to qualify inside a 5.10.

This being published, Hughie phoned me, quite upset, asking why I had said this. I replied, "They asked my opinion and that is what I gave."

On the day the programme was quite unusual. The riders had to qualify in the morning, four to go through and the conditions not good.

Hughie rode against Jackson and qualified with a 5.9.9 as predicted. Jackson on 5.17 was a non-qualifier. Bonner was 5-15, Derek Harrison 5.15.3, Cromack 5.16.2. It was Porter v Cromack in the semi-final. Porter clocked 5.17 with no distress riding to win. Cromack 5.26. In the other semi-final there was a surprise, Harrison beating Bonner with 5.12.9 against 5.15.3.

I was told by Hughie after the qualifying ride, "You can forget the 5.7." After the semi-final he had gone into the dressing room for a rest and light massage. There was a message over the public address system: "Will Tommy Godwin please go to the dressing room." It was a request from Hughie. I went in and approached him. He remarked, "I'll have a go at that 5.7." I replied, "Don't bother, I was 50% right, in any case."

Going with him to the start, we had our usual banter, me kidding him about his change of mind, but telling him I would be in the back straight with the schedule. Whilst shouting out his progress – you're on a 5.7, you're up on a 5.6 – an official walked past with a friend who was not a cycle fan who said, "How can he shout that? He doesn't know the time" The official said, "I shouldn't go and say that to him, unless you can fight." The finish times were: Porter 5.7, Harrison 5.15.8. So now we had our top pursuiter on song and our No 1 sprinter in a class of his own, with a team now fast approaching world class.

There was a report on July 18th from Leningrad, where an Olympic-style omnium was held. In a teams pursuit between USSR, East Germany, Poland and Bulgaria, USSR won in 4.40 with East Germany second on 4.47. The kilo was won in 1.10.9, second 1.11.3 and third 1.12 on a superb cement track. Herne Hill was renowned for slow times on a bumpy tarmac surface.

The week after the headlines read:

Jackson v Bull new record, Britain's Olympic track hopes show great form.
  Jackson on his home track took four tenths off Bull's record, the new record for
½ mile SS 56.4 seconds. Only minutes later Bull equalled the new record.

We were now at a stage where everything was falling into place, the regular squad sessions proving their worth. I was now beginning to feel all my ambitions would be realised in the near future.

August 8th was the first open meeting at the new Kirkby track in Liverpool. The highlight was Roger Whitfield, a new member of the squad, who set a new 1,000 metres TT record with 1.11.5. On August 15th teams were selected for the World's and the Olympic. The road and track, men's and women's team for the World's looked formidable.

I was more than pleased with the Olympic selections for the track, although I felt fully justified after intense, regulated and disciplined training. I had not been connected with the roadmen in their programme, but the names of those selected looked a well-balanced team, with riders suited for any type of course.

On August 22nd an article in *Cycling* said:

Our pursuiters best yet – good enough?
  The pursuit team recorded 4 min 41 sec at Nottingham against the South African team, and the track is not recognised as a fast track.

On the programme was a kilo ride. I asked Bull if he wanted to ride. He said, "No, not after that team ride." I asked for volunteers. Jackson and Whitfield agreed and returned 1.11.5 and 1.12, very happy.

One sentence in the *Cycling* report read:

All credit to the team and Tommy Godwin for his season-long confidence, and his inspiration.
  They look happy together, they are really determined to justify the selectors' underwriting of Tommy Godwin's confidence.

So to Paris for the World Championships. All the year's work was to come to nought. It was a great shock to me, the team and the selectors, and a disappointment to followers of the sport. Our sprinters failed in the first round. Hugh Porter and Roy Cromack failed to qualify in the first eight. An excuse can be made for Porter. I, along with others, wrongly convinced him to step up on his gear and this proved to be fatal. In the teams pursuit we qualified well in fourth place, but this put us against France, the home nation. In the ride, as it was very close right up to the finish line. I and many others claimed our third man over the line was in front of the French third man, and a bit of favouritism showed. We came home in shock and knew that we would have to pick ourselves up in time for Tokyo.

It was now my job to boost the morale of the team, albeit no-one was ashamed at what had happened in Paris. Porter, indeed, realised that his failure was due to the mistaken decision to raise his gear, a point he would later prove. The team knew it was the favouritism shown to the French team that

Myself and Chas Messenger – invited to visit the home of the mother of my car driver – Tokyo Olympics 1964

had beaten us in the quarter-finals. We and many onlookers disputed the result given. In fact, the impression that the British team made on the officials was to prove advantageous to us in Tokyo.

We left for Japan in early October, a happy and confident bunch. The journalists had been very good to us, in spite of our misfortunes, and still stood behind us and the manner in which the team had been prepared and selected, with one exception. It was sad to read that Racing Committee, or the Chairman Wally Gray, had dropped Les West from the road team. His riding throughout the season had been brilliant, and his capability was beyond doubt. A niggling injury was somewhat blown up. There was no medical proof forthcoming and some anonymous report said that he was swathed in bandages, which was untrue. No official of the BCF contacted him at any time about his condition.

On our arrival we found everything first class in the way of accommodation, The food was excellent and the team soon settled in. It was, however, a sad start when after the evening meal the road team was missing from the village. I had, as usual, set a 10.00pm curfew, and was very determined that this would be adhered to. As the evening moved on the track team prepared themselves for bedtime. I waited patiently in the corridor from the entrance and, fortunately, just at 10 o'clock the road team with Chas Messenger at the head came through the door laughing and playing silly boys.

Asking where they had been, the reply was, "To a strip club." All the riders went to their rooms and, unfortunately for me, I was sharing a room with Messenger, the road team manager. Behind closed doors we had an exchange of words and a very unpleasant atmosphere developed between us. The following day Messenger opened a massive wooden chest and distributed 'goodies,' as he called them, that he had pinched off the Milk Race. His sharing out was two for the road boys, one for the trackies – as trackies did not work as hard as the road men. So much for team spirit.

Track training went extremely well. It was vital that McKeown and Whitfield had a kilometre test to select who would ride the event. During the season at home they had both broken the national record, and both were justified in expecting the ride. In the test, Whitfield returned a 1.11.6, McKeown 1.12.8, with timing by Reg Grimsell, a grade A timekeeper, and other watches being used to confirm. Whitfield was selected. The team of Porter, Bull, Jackson and Sandy were riding well, and our final serious ride before the competition took place was to be held in the last ten minutes of our allotted training time, when the track would be clear.

At 5.20 I was lining the team up when two Italian riders due to commence at 5.30, their scheduled time, rode onto the track. This would interfere with our plan. Suddenly, there was a loud voice, that of Guido Costa the famous Italian coach, telling the riders in no uncertain terms to vacate the track. The British team set off and clocks held by Costa, Derksen (Holland), Gerarden (France), all national coaches, went into action. Our boys gave a flawless display, a time inside 4-40, which I expected, and a medal winning time. All three coaches were full of praise, "Anglais formidable etc" We left the training session quite buoyant, and I visualised a ride near to 4.35 in the competition.

My situation now was to keep both teams relaxed. What was sadly missed was the presence of Eddie Soens. He, in place of Chas Messenger, would have been the ideal situation. Bill Shillibeer, who had in the past twelve months travelled as a masseur with cycle teams, had been contracted to the athletics team stationed 26 miles away in Tokyo. Bill did visit twice to try and support us. The only answer was for me to advise the boys that I was capable of light massage and this was added to my work load, but did give some satisfaction to the lads.

Sadly, none of us could have imagined the unexpected. Hugh Porter, three days before the individual pursuit, complained of a severe cold. We tried to control it, but it seemed as if he would have to withdraw. He was determined to ride, his ambition was, of course, was Gold, and normally he was very capable of achieving it. In the qualifying ride he was fifth, and in the quarter-finals he was beaten by Isakssen, 5.01 to 5.04. The final was won by Daller in a time 5.04.75 to 5.05.96.

We had no medical contact at all, and I had to approach the French team to ask for their help. Dr Dumas, the very well known Tour doctor, came to examine Porter and firmly stated that he must not ride in the teams pursuit. The replacement had to be either McKeown or Whitfield. My decision was for the latter.

We had been honoured and respected by the UCI officials when we found we had been matched with the West Germans, the current World Champions. This, in the seeding process, was ensuring us almost certainly a place in the semi-finals. Our riding in Paris had been noticed.

Full of confidence before the start, we had a schedule of inside 4.40. Hughie, obviously, was sadly missed. He was the power house in all our training rides.

But there was one more act of fate. In a change Whitfield swung up from the lead and prepared to drop onto the rear man, Sandy, who was very nervous and twitchy, as in Paris. Sandy got his front wheel inside Jackson's rear wheel, could not control the inevitable and crashed just as Whitfield dropped off the banking. With no chance of missing the falling Sandy, Whitfield made contact and did a complete somersault, leaving the team in disarray. At the time the British team were very close to the Germans, who qualified with 4.42. Italy were fastest with 4.39.

The British team were allowed a re-run. First of all, Sandy said he would not ride again, but, after a very serious discussion, I told him he must ride. Whitfield complained about his wrist hurting. I set to and taped his hand and wrist, then pulled his track mitt on, which was very tight, for support. He had a ride on the rollers and decided he would ride. The outcome was we failed to qualify by 0.63 of a second. Roger was taken to hospital for x-ray, to find that he had fractured his wrist in two places.

It was the end of all our work, all our dreams, a season of training, proving ourselves to Race Committee with the record breaking performances which had been demanded. Times for every event were laid down, which were to be achieved or there would be no selection. The press were behind us, giving every support whenever they heard of our continued performance.

The road race was due to follow the track events and there was to be one more misfortune for one British rider. He was in sixth place as they came in for the finishing sprint around the last corner but was brought down in a crash with another rider.

My immediate reaction to the total disappointment was to declare my resignation as Team Manager and National Coach. I had stated clearly in May of 1964 that if there were no medals I would resign. I was approached by Peter Bryan of the *News Chronicle*, one of the few journalists I had any respect for, and he asked me, begged me to reconsider my decision. But my reply was, "You journalists would rip me apart if I did not stick to my statement." He held back from reporting to his paper to give me time to reconsider, and in doing so missed what he called a 'scoop'.

The realisation that I had severed all my connection with dreams and ambitions swept over me. I had made so many sacrifices, and my wife, Eileen, more so. Hours, days and weeks away from business had taken a terrible toll. Some of the team members, the track lads in particular, tried to console me, but they too were in shock. There had been such a strong desire, belief and an ambition in their minds because of what we had done to prove that organised training was vital and acceptable.

Among the riders I have worked with, the prince of them all must be Karl Barton, not only a quality rider but intelligent and invaluable in communicating with the riders for me. Hugh Porter was top for sheer dedication, and was later to prove an absolute winner in individual pursuit riding. His contribution in teams pursuit was amazing. Trevor Bull, following Hughie, always had a dream lead-out and recorded fastest half-lap times regularly. Harry Jackson was the complete trackman, any distance, any discipline, and he was a dangerous opponent. Whitfield, McKeown, Sandy had proved themselves against all others in repeated training sessions.

I expect if there were happy memories from Tokyo, one had to be my brother Bob flying over in a USA military plane to be with me for a few days. We had last seen each other in 1946 when he decided to go back to his birthplace to serve in the US Army instead of the British as a conscript. He did sign up as a regular, reaching the rank of Top Sergeant, and now lives in Hawaii. The other pleasant thing was Hugh meeting Anita Lonsbrough in the plane on the outward journey. On watching them for a short time, I mentioned to some of the lads that this was a match and it would be serious. Some of them kidded me and asked, "How can you say that?" I replied, "Intuition."

The Olympics we had experienced were the forerunner of the present highly commercialised modern day extravaganza. We all brought back souvenirs, but none equal to the large Olympic flag I was given by team members, one of whom had climbed to some great height to obtain it illegally. Ever member of the squad had signed it and it is still a cherished memory of the occasion.

On our return home all Olympians were invited to attend Buckingham Palace. The Queen and other members of the Royal Family met us on arrival. I had the pleasant duty of introducing each of the team individually to Her Majesty, and I felt very proud indeed.

CHAPTER 22

1965

'Monday night is Madison night'

Now the situation of settling back to normal life. The business, our livelihood, had been neglected by me but had survived by the dedication of Eileen and one mechanic/salesman. The strain on my wife must have been incredible, bearing in mind that she had been through a life threatening illness only a few years before. But she always knew how proud I was to represent the country in sport.

I could not cut myself off completely and continued coaching locally, but then got terribly involved with the administration of the sport. I really believed that I could do something to see that future teams got more support and better forms of selection, so that therer was less chance of ridicule.

Working at division level was one thing, but to be proposed as a delegate to National Council and then eventually to get voted onto Racing Committee was the ultimate.

Nothing had been done immediately to find a new National Coach. But early in 1965 a list of prospective candidates was drawn up: Karl Barton, Charles Ruys, Bill Dodds, Chas Messenger and Norman Shiel. In March the news came that Norman Shiel had been appointed, with a four-figure salary, believed to be £1500 per annum, plus expenses. But from the outset he stated that he would be a coach who did no coaching. *Cycling* quoted him as follows:

> I shall have no time to mess about with teams or individuals, that will be the job of divisional coaches. In fact, (I shall be) a coaching advisor/administrator, going into schools and local authorities to popularise the pastime of cycling etc. I am going to be a salesman, and this is going to be a selling campaign.

He also said:

> I'll be frank, I don't think we have world championship material in British cycling. It would be a waste of time to send anyone to represent the country. We will not have a world champion within the next five years. But this is not my job, I have to find the material and pass them on to Benny Foster and Chas Messenger to work on.

Apparently, a late application by Eddie Soens for the post of National Coach had not even been considered, but he was the man who had prepared Shiel and many other Liverpool lads to the highest level. He would have been the ideal man to prepare teams for international competition.

My own interest at this time was to encourage schoolboys and juniors by getting permission to organise a series of circuit races in the numerous parks in the City of Birmingham. The City Fathers gave me their blessings, agreed with the whole programme as laid down and also agreed to sponsor the final Madison race in a series which I had also proposed. Both ventures were completely successful and created tremendous enthusiasm in the sport.

The 'Monday Night is Madison Night' caught on rapidly. A half-hour event for juniors of second and third categories on a gear limit of 84" followed. The last race of the evening was a senior 1-hour event with a gear limit of 88", and there were filler events in between. Special team vests were supplied, with team numbers, available before racing and to be returned at the end of the programme to be cleaned before the next promotion. Riders were ordered to present themselves well. With clean white socks, clean shoes and helmet. Inspection was made and riders could be refused a ride if not well presented.

Early in this year Benny Foster had come back into the fold as British Track Team Manager, and had involved a number of top riders in joining him on a trip to the Continent to race in Holland and Belgium. Very foolishly, without funding, he had been forced to use a paraffin delivery van as the means of transport, with Heath-Robinson seating, all packed in like sardines. The riders made light of it and raced with commitment and determination, having some success. On their return home Benny was summoned to a meeting with BCF officials, who had been informed of the ridiculous scheme. The result was "Benny Foster Quits" headlines in *Cycling*. Immediately after there was an announcement that Eddie Soens had got the Track post. "I'll have a go, it's a bit late," was the typical reply from Eddie.

The title races were to be held in San Sebastian, Spain, in September. That only left July and August for the team to get used to another manager and he to impose himself on them. The result was chaos.

Unexpectedly, with Burton and Porter tipped to perform well, Beryl did not qualify and Hughie was eliminated in the second round. A complete failure of the track team.

The road team also failed.

I had decided to go to Spain as a spectator, and at my own expense, taking with me a young man I had been preparing individually, a lad named Tony Slatter.

Just prior to the World's I had organised a special track meeting on the Monday following the Continental-based pros competing at Crystal Palace. Amongst the top riders was my dear friend Tommy Simpson, who had arranged with the other riders to come and put on a show for me as a personal favour, their fees not being prohibitive. Other names were Barry Hoban, Michael Wright, Bill Lawrie, Dave Bonner and Albert Hitchin.

> Tommy Godwin's devoted work to put cycling on the map in Birmingham was more than rewarded last week when the 'Continental Professionals' stayed over from the Corona Grand Prix to star in his weekly Salford Park promotion. *(Cycling)*

At this meeting Tony Slatter, the lad I have mentioned before, was called on to make up a pursuit team with Porter, Bull and Whitfield, all Olympians. Slatter was a 17 year old junior, but his team returned a 5.3 ride to beat 'The Rest', who rode 5.7.

For the Madison, the final event, Brendan McKeown, usually Porter's partner, had not made an appearance. Hughie was concerned at not getting a ride. I said, "I can only recommend young Slatter," to which Porter replied, "I'm not going into the event with him." I said, "No ride, then." There was a change of heart. Hughie said, "Okay, I'll give it a go, but if we begin to look foolish, I'm out." After three changes Hughie shouted, "Tell him to slow down, I can't catch the bugger." The outcome was that they finished third to Cromack-Bull and Cox-Watkins. Hughie was more than pleased with the lad. Tommy Simpson

My dear friend
Tommy Simpson

said, "Who's that ginger haired lad riding with Hughie?" I told him that he was
my special lad and that I was preparing him for the future. "Well, he can come
over to me in Ghent any time he wants for a month or so, and I will show him all
I know to help him on his way."

Back to San Sebastian. Tony was with me, enjoying the atmosphere. There
were so many people in the sport that I knew and Tony being introduced. It was
inspirational. After the sadness of the track results, and so much expected, we
looked forward to the road races, the pro one in particular. On the day, I suggested we walked around the circuit and to make sure we were near the finish
line at the right time. As we moved around I suddenly met up with Guido Costa,
the famed Italian Team Manager, and stopped to have a chat.

I introduced Tony, who knew of the great man and shook hands. Costa
said, "Godwin, the boy, he cyclist?" I said, "Yes, I am preparing him specially."
"Momento." A whistle and a call to an old Italian guy, a few words in their own
language, and the next thing Tony was ordered to turn around with his back to
this weathered soigneur. He proceeded by placing his hands on the lad's shoulders, moving down his back, hips, thighs and calves, "Formidable." He then
asked Tony to sit on a nearby table and ran his hands up the calves and upper leg,

smiled and grunted. Guido Costa then said, "If the boy wants to come to Italy for six months, pay only to travel, he can live with the Italian team, all equipment will be found, a road machine and a track bike, and he will be looked after very well." Sadly, this did not happen. When we got home his stepfather and his mother would not allow it to happen. They said he was making too much of cycling and telling them what he must do and not do according to Tommy. It was a wonderful opportunity lost.

The pro race continued. As it neared the end with about one and a half laps to go, Tommy was away with Altig, and as he passed he said, "Get to the finish, I am going to win this one." We got to the finish, but not in the VIP area. I then asked someone which hotel the team was staying at. I was told, and where it was situated. Just at that time a cyclist from our area back home came by in his car, stopped and I asked him if he could take us to the team hotel. He was only too happy. On arrival, Vin Denson and some other team members said that Tom had been whisked away in a helicopter. He was wanted back in Belgium for a Crit the next day, but he asked them to pass on his regards to me. I later received numerous photos, one signed for me personally and the others for whatever use.

Our trip had been a very happy one, and we were proud to be English.

Back home my regular promotions were drawing good crowds locally, and riders were coming from London, Welwyn, Derby, Coventry, Leicester etc. But the maintenance of high standards of presentation had placed another big responsibility on my best mate, Eileen. She was washing and ironing 44 vests every week and never complained. We were at the time living in a flat above the shop. Her clothes line was a pulley line across the workshop roof, which I had installed. But Eileen had to climb out of a window and stand on the roof to hang out her washing.

At the end of the season we had a big meeting, and had invited teams from Holland, Belgium and Germany to ride the final Madison. I received a telegram from the German Federation to say they had sent laurel wreaths for the winners and they were being flown into an airfield some twenty miles from my home. I did go and pick then up. They were superb in quality and I did appreciate the thought behind it. As it happened, a West German team won the event, with a Dutch team second and another German team third.

1965 had been successful for me personally. I had rid myself of the demons of 1964 by getting involved with yet another facet of our sport, promoting, and it had been a memorable inspiration.

CHAPTER 23

1966

British Training
Camp, Majorca

In 1966 I was surprised to be invited by Ernie Clements and Mr Mayo of Falcon Cycles to be the manager of the first ever British Training Camp in Majorca. It was an idea put to Billy Holmes at the Corona Grand Prix at Crystal Palace in 1965. A course of six weeks duration, with groups coming in and returning home at intervals. I could not be there for the opening week and Brian Robinson, who I had worked with at Lilleshall and other training weekends around the country, agreed to take the responsibility for one week. Billy Holmes became most respected for the work he did. He was inspirational, demanding and led by example. But he also paid respect to Brian Robinson and myself for the encouragement and advice we gave on style, ambition, sacrifice and respect.

Tom Simpson arrived, with foot in plaster, and was the icing on the cake. The youngsters in the camp at that time were enthralled to be in the same room as the great man. But, as usual, Tom's wonderful sense of humour always won the day. After settling in he was asked his opinion:

Marvellous, marvellous, marvellous! What more can I say?

The spirit was tremendous, Holmes, Bernie Taylor, Nigel Dean and Dave Burwood, all on their second fortnight, They are backed by Tommy Godwin, who, as keen as he always is, has been recharged by the 43 young men.

Tom and I had always had respect for each other, and Helen, his wife, enjoyed the close relationship we had developed.

One evening Helen said she would love to go out for a stroll. I immediately volunteered and, as we got up, Tom asked, "Where are you two going?" Helen replied, "For a walk." Tom got up, grabbed his crutches and followed. Helen whispered, "Let's walk fast," with Tom shouting, "Wait for me," and sounding rather worried.

Tom had been very observant of me and my methods and knew that there were times when discipline was necessary in training, which I have always been a stickler for. Before Tom and Helen left he asked if we three could have a quiet drink and a chat. The outcome was that he had made up his mind that on his retirement he was going to invest in and develop a training camp. He said, " I want you as the camp manager. I was taken aback and said "What, with all the Continental men you know?" He replied, "I have never seen a more strict disciplinarian than you anywhere in the sport. Who knows what might have been the outcome? I was very proud and realised our friendship would have been lifelong but for the dreadful day to come. I miss him very much. Helen and I have kept in touch over the years and she has found happiness with Barry (Hoban).

I returned to Majorca for many of the training camps that followed, but the memories of the first one are the most vivid.

Remaining very obsessesive with all that the sport offered, there was always a new idea cropping up to improve what was happening. I had formed a new club, the Birmingham RCC, after the demise of the famous Rover RCC and the Wyndham RCC. My reputation in the sport was such that numerous riders resigned from other clubs to join the new one, which appeared to offer better chances of improvement and success. At one point the club boasted four national championships in one year: road race, 5-mile grass, teams pursuit and motor paced.

The meeting with Geoff Bull, father of Trevor Bull, was a godsend. He and I worked so well together in the training sessions, promotions, committee work, our personal relationship was a pleasure. Our respective families were responsive to all of this and gave us tremendous support in every way.

During the 60's the spin-off from all the coaching began to work wonders with local clubs. Solihull CC in particular benefited as much as any. With a strong membership and the response from many of the riders, the track training sessions were invaluable. Time triallists, roadmen, and pure trackmen all improved immensely, and they respected what was being done for them. Solihull CC won the National Teams Pursuit two years running, 1965 and 1966. Trevor Bull, Graham Webb, Roy Cromack and Andy King in 1965, Barry Moss replacing King in 1966.

In July of 1966 I encouraged Bull, Webb and Cromack to attempt breaking records.

A report in the Solihull *Awheel* magazine states:

> The Golden Trio gave an amazing display of talent and dedication, the meeting organised impeccably by Tommy Godwin at Salford Park, when they set up two National Records.
> Trev Bull attacked the one mile record of E V Mills of 2 mins 1.2 secs, his 1.59 also beat the longer standing professional record of W J Bailey, 2 mins 5.6 secs.
> The "Black Raven," Graham Webb, went for the one hour record held by Les West, during the ride Webb beat Cromack's 10 mile record by 4 secs, 40 seconds off West's 25-mile record, and went on to top 27 miles and add 583 yards to that for the hour record.

In 1967 Graham Webb and Trevor Bull joined the Birmingham CC, feeling that I could help their aspirations. Graham Webb has always thanked me for the interest I showed in him. That year he was selected for the British Team for the World's Road Race, and won the Gold Medal. He turned pro immediately after, and due to getting in the wrong hands never benefited from his success as he deserved. For some years he was lost to us on the Continent.

I received a call from the Federation that they had Graham's World Championship Diploma, could I take the responsiblitity of getting it to him? I agreed and the Diploma was sent to me. I had it nicely framed and it took pride of place in my lovely Trophy and Memorabilia room, of which I am very proud. One day some years later I had a surprise visit from Graham at the shop. I told him I wanted to take him to our home. When I showed him the treasure he said, " I want you to keep it, Tom, for all you have done for me." I tried to convince him to take it with him but no, he refused. He left me and I went straight back to the shop. About an hour later I had a call, "I'm sorry, Tom, but my wife has told me I should have it." I agreed and it was taken.

Some months after there was a package from Belgium containing a replica of the Diploma, about 14" by 11" in full colour and a photo of Graham in his championship jersey with sponsor's name, Mercier – Hutchinson. Now both suitably framed, they are a wonderful token of respect.

Another young upstart about this time was Mick Bennett from Solihull, who had been coming down training and riding track league. One day he came to see me to tell me he was riding in the 1,000 metre junior championship on the Wednesday meeting, and he was going to do a 1.15. I said, "You will do a 1.17, and I'll be waiting for you as you finish and watch you collapse as you get off your bike." He rode, returned a 1.17+, and as he stepped from his bike his legs gave way. I laughed because I had been through it all and I had seen many riders after a kilo.

I told him on that evening, and at seventeen years of age, that he would be a great bike rider and would ride for GB in the pursuit team. How true that prediction was. My association with Mick has been long lasting. I have helped him many times when he needed a shoulder. He has shown his respect in many ways.

CHAPTER 24

1969

Team Manager,
Copenhagen

Getting to the end of the 60's, I was a little surprised to be asked by the Federation if I would take a team to Copenhagen in 1969. I queried my position, not having managed a team since 1964. I was told that they knew I had a soft spot for Denmark, which was very true. I had ridden with success there. I went to Copenhagen in 1945, in the September, and had raced both at Aarhus and Copenhagen since then. I agreed and was told that the team would be Hallam, Keeble, Whiteside and Brockhurst.

From this I had my doubts. As far as I knew, they had never been together before as a team. The journey was train from London then boat and train to Copenhagen. A long journey, but during the trip I talked a lot about training and teams pursuit in particular.

Arriving at our destination, we settled in at the hotel and then made a visit to the track. There were various rides, with me trying to find the right order. Hallam, of course, was the top man. Keeble was smooth and fast. Gradually we got some rhythm going. I was organising all the food, times to relax, work-outs etc.

Come the day, there was a work-out in the morning and the meeting was in the evening. I had asked for the meals I wanted them to eat, at lunchtime a light lunch of fish and salad. I was asked about steak, but I said, "No, you don't eat steaks before the meeting, but I will order them for eating at the track restaurant after the meeting."

Everyone took a rest after lunch, then a light tea and down to the track. On arrival we were given programmes. Records show that the Danes had never been beaten in the teams pursuit since 1945. They had beaten the team that I went with that year. French, Belgian, Italian and German teams had all gone to the wall. I was not too optimistic. But I had geed the boys up and had worked on a schedule of 4.45, from figures shown of previous rides.

I talked personally to Ian Hallam, telling him I would call for a full lap at sometime in the ride. I was surprised when Whiteside came to me saying, "I don't think I will finish the distance, Tom." My reply was, "Thank you, I don't want you to finish but at about 3 laps to go, I want you to do the fastest half-lap of your life and then get out." Ian Hallam's brother Stuart had travelled with us at his own expense and was very excited, but I told him not to interfere with anything.

On the programme, the Danish team were to start in the home straight, I disagreed and spoke to Mr Breyerholme, the boss, that this was unfair as I knew the shape of the track gave an advantage. He agreed to a toss of a coin, and we still lost. I had warned the boys to take great care at the start.

In the race the Danes, who, incidentally, were the Gold Medal teams pursuit winners in the Mexico Olympics in 1968, got away to a fast start, very smooth. Our boys settled in and held them about a team's length down up to half-way. Stuart was getting impatient. I warned him not to say a word. Then just after half-distance I leaned forward as the Brits went through, "Now, Ian." A nod and at the corner Ian went through, closed the gap and the teams were level. Then as they neared the end I shouted, "Billy, now." Whiteside raised his level and at the end of his half-lap swung up and out. Our boys were now flying, with Keeble and Hallam smooth and Brockhurst giving his all. The result was a win, the first team to beat to the Danes in twenty-three years. I was so pleased, one of my finest moments of motivation, the boys came to me so excited.

They went on to ride in other events, getting places and winning events in this hotbed of track racing.

I mentioned steaks at about 11.30pm. "No, we want to go back to the Tivoli Pleasure Gardens." "Bad luck, they close at midnight." Back to the hotel, full of fun and very proud. The trip home was a joy to experience. You do get critics in sport, some very personal, but if you can ride these and come out with proof of your ability, then all is well.

CHAPTER 25

1970

World Championships in Leicester

Whatever happened at Racing Committee meetings during the close season, I will never know, but I was asked to be Team Manager for the World's to be held in Leicester, thanks to the hard work and inspiration of Benny Foster. As a championship series it was a wonderful occasion and success. Details of the Championships are well covered in Benny's own book, *The Benny Foster Story*.

Amazing, but I had the responsibility of organising all the training sessions for the track team, especially teams pursuit. I still have records of all the half-lap times and the numerous riders who were given a chance. My best pal, Eddie Soens, was regularly with me, especially when working out at the Leicester track.

The results in the title races included a Gold medal for Hugh Porter in the pro pursuit, a Silver medal for Ian Hallam, classed as a protégé of Norman Sheil and a Bronze for Beryl Burton, not fully recovered from an accident with a car, in the ladies pursuit.

Tommy holds up Hugh Porter for his lap of honour after his World's professional pursuit gold win at Leicester

Gordon Johnson, a surprise winner of the pro sprint, gave me a wonderful opportunity. He was riding a Carlton frame at the time, a small company which had been absorbed by Raleigh. I was on very good terms with some of the Raleigh management. I immediately ran across to Mr Woods, the Advertising Director, and said, "What about a revenge match?" His reply was, "How much will it cost?" In return I said something like, "I don't know, but I know a man who does." I rushed over to Jan Derksen, Mr 'Ten Per Cent' of that period, and explained what I had suggested. He gave me a figure of £1,000, a lot of money in those days, but for this I got three top sprinters and some other riders. I set up a pro-am meeting two weeks after on a Wednesday evening.

The whole thing was a great success. We were allowed to keep the gate money for further promotions. Geoff Bull and his family along with Eileen and my daughter Kay arranged a lovely buffet after the meeting for Raleigh officials and VIP's. Mr Wood wanted to pay for all of this, which I refused and said it was our way of saying thanks. The out come of all this was that early in the next year I received a cheque for £2,500 to organise some more meetings. Which, of course, were carried out in an excellent manner and were very successful.

CHAPTER 26

1971
World
Championships in
Varese –National
Championship
Week

Once again, in 1971, I was asked to take on the responsibility of Track Team Manager, which I accepted. The Championships were to be held in Varese, Italy.

The whole thing was a fiasco. Once again the hotel booked by the Federation was in the most inconvenient place imaginable. It was miles away from the track, stuck on the top of a hill, which meant riders going out for a road session had to be an Indurain or Armstrong to get back to base.

At an early track session in a string work-out, Mick Bennett foolishly took the lads up to some Dutch riders before switching out, a show-off trick. The following riders hit the riders in front, injuring two of the team squad, Ray Ward and John Patston. Ward was in hospital with a cracked pelvis. Patston carried on riding but could not recover well enough to compete. It was necessary to bring in Dave Lloyd as a reserve, but he was due to ride the team time trial.

At one session, after having made the decision, I asked the team to warm-up, and we would do a 6-lap ride to get a schedule for the qualifying ride. I was outside the track as they warmed up, a wire fence between us, when suddenly the team came to a stop, moved towards me and announced, "We are not going to ride the 6-lap, it's too hot." My immediate reply was, "When the tail starts wagging the dog, that is me finished. Are you going to ride or not?" The answer was, "No." I said, " You've just finished a team manager's career. I will not be at the start. I will not be telling you anything during the race and I shall put in my report exactly what happened." They did ride but not very convincingly and got knocked out in the next ride.

I was approached by Hugh Porter, who asked me to come to his room. He opened up by saying something about my behaviour and attitude, and then went on to tell me I put riders under too much pressure. He said, "All you want is gold medals." I said, "That's my job." He then advised me to go out with Barry Brandon, his sponsor, get drunk, find some female company and come back relaxed. To which I said, "If that is your idea of a team manager, you've got the wrong man."

I never handled another cycle team again. At that time I was fifty years of age.

Later, the basis of what I had formed and worked with, Hallam, Bennett and Keeble, went on with different fourth men to get Bronze medals in the1972 and 1976 Olympics, taking us back to what so many British teams had achieved in the past, and a Silver in the World's.

Never did I realise at that time that it would take thirty years to win medals, Gold, Silver and Bronze, at the Olympic Games and World Championships at the cost of millions of pounds. In my time all the effort put in was voluntarily and had to be self-financing by riders, coaches and team managers. Yet, on reflection, my dreams, ambitions, dedication and sacrifice started it all in 1958.

Bitterness, regret, envy and hate could have turned me against all that I held so dear. I am still proud to be shown respect by some of the young men that I have worked with, offering advice, motivation, suggestions and talking of sacrifice, dedication, ambition, even directing them into careers that they had never considered. I have had men in their fifties come to me after many years of no contact, just a chance meeting, a firm hand shake, a hug, an emotional gasp and then, "What you did for me not only in cycling but also what you taught me about life…"

Mick Bennett was a case of a very successful international whom I had helped when he had a health problem and was told to forget cycle racing or it would kill him. But an interview and tests by a very eminent specialist, arranged by me, encouraged him to go on. Mick talked to me about his career. I made a suggestion and some years later the opportunity I had suggested came along. He took it and has gone all the way. He once said, "I owe a lot of thanks to you for what I have got in life." When one gets this type of testimonial in the twilight years of life, everything seems worthwhile.

But, strangely enough, I was not deterred by this setback. I had been involved with team management, coaching and committee work for some twelve years. I have always been enthusiastic about everything to do with cycling.

The promotion of the sport had grown over the years, and particularly at Salford Park, Birmingham. I had always had special support from Geoff Bull, the father of Trevor Bull. Our respective families enjoyed helping us in the presentation. At one of our big meetings a suggestion was made that my daughter, Kay, joined by Jenny and Chris Bull would dress in matching outfits and arrange a formal presentation of awards, accompanied by music. Benny Foster mentioned in his book that his idea of the Ford girls at the 1970 World Championships was a copy of what he had witnessed at Salford Park.

We had been promoting on behalf of the Birmingham RCC and the Solihull CC for some years. In 1968 we presented the first ever multi-National Track Championships, first at Salford Park and then at Leicester, Saffron Lane, in 1969. This gradually developed into my suggesting holding a National Championship Week, which would include schoolboys, junior, ladies, amateur mens and professionals in all disciplines. We called a meeting at Leicester to discuss this item between myself, Geoff Bull, Bill McCormack, Benny Foster, Derek Bowyer and Sue Matthewman. Ideas were bounced about, with enthusiastic discussion and then decisions. I really thought that as it was my brainchild, I would be selected as chairman. But Benny Foster informed me that as I was Chairman of Standing Committee, ie Racing Committee, I was not allowed to chair a sub-committee.

Benny was appointed and I was never given a position in the organising structure through the years. But I was always acknowledged as the person responsible for the idea. I was always treated cordially and mentioned at the opening of the Championships and asked to assist in medal presentation ceremonies.

There is no doubt that Benny Foster had all the ideas of showmanship. He could force his way into meetings of company directors, make his point and come out with contracts and support almost unheard of in the promotion of our sport. His greatest success was in showing not only National Championships but also World Championships in 1970 and 1982 at the wonderful venue in Leicester. We owe a lot to the man, for his genius, his enthusiasm and the personal sacrifice he made.

Benny was not the most popular of men, as he rode roughshod over many people. He and I crossed swords on a number of occasions. He once said, "Why do you always want to punch my face?" I replied, "Because you always poke your nose in where it is not wanted." But he always came up with, "Well, we are good mates and we soon make up."

In July of 1971 we promoted a Raleigh Championship meeting, which included the return of Reg Harris at the age of fifty-one to ride in the pro sprint. Harris rode well against pros who were mainly racing on the road. But included in the field were Gordon Johnson of Australia, who had won the World's pro sprint at Leicester in 1970, Trevor Bull and Reg Barnett. The result was Johnson the winner and Barnett second. Reg Harris beat Trevor for the Bronze, which rather surprised me as Trevor raced at Salford regularly and was capable of faster 200 metres than were returned in the races.

At this meeting I was approached by Reg, who asked me if we could sit down and have a talk. We had not spoken to each other for some years and I was not keen on the idea, particularly because of the way he had undermined my ability as a coach and as a team manager, always trying to put me down. However, I decided to agree to his suggestion and sat down with him. He immediately said, "Can I have my say first?" I replied, "That is as I expected."

His opening remark was, "You once called me something in a race at Herne Hill which upset me badly." I knew exactly to what he was referring. It was in a Madison race. He was going in as the sprinter and he won the first one. As we went into the second sprint Reg was leading into the home straight when I rode up beside him saying, "Come on, you b------d, if you want to have a race." I was aware that he was, in fact, an illegitimate child. His first wife, Flo, had told Eileen many years before. Obviously he wanted an apology, which was given. He then asked if we could get on friendly terms again and invited Eileen and me to visit him at his home for a meal, which I accepted.

A date was fixed and we duly arrived to be met very warmly by Reg and Jennifer. Reg, in Eileen's eyes, was the typical country squire, wearing a tweed jacket, smoking a pipe and, after greeting us, sitting very relaxed in a large sitting room chair. Once we had settled in he asked if we would like to look at the other rooms in the house etc.

On moving around we were introduced to the dogs, Dobermans, then shown his wine collection. When we were taken upstairs I noticed a four inch cube of marble with a gold figure on top about two to three inches high. There was a small engraved plate on the base. I stopped to read it, when Reg said, "It's the top of the Vitonica Cup," a famous trophy which was awarded for the sprint event at the Manchester Wheelers Meet. Reg had kept the top when he sold the cup itself back to the Manchester Wheelers. The Vitonica is no longer competed for, so the Cup was re-engraved and is now the Muratti Cup, which is still competed for.

I had refused to sell my Muratti Cup, but Reg was not one who had much sentimental attachment for anything. He then asked, "Have you still got your trophies?" I answered, "Yes, Gold and Silver, I would not think of parting with

REG· HARRIS
BRITISH SPRINT CHAMPION
1944·45·46

Reg Harris

them." I was then surprised when he remarked, "Yes, everything I won, I sold and now that I've got money I can't afford to buy any of them back."

It was at this time Reg was with Draka Foam. His attempt to break into the cycle manufacturing world had failed. He had also left Raleigh. He told us the story of how he had been sacked because of his underhand arrangement with Campagnolo, a company he had arranged a deal with to supply Raleigh with their components. But, in the tie-up, Reg had a deal which brought him a small percentage of all sales to Raleigh and they were not aware of this.

1980
Charitable work

In an Evesham '25' and
wearing Birmingham
RCC colours – still
racing in 1982

My love for cycling has never left me. But because of my interest in helping others, I became very dedicated as a Rotarian, having been invited to join after my return from Tokyo in 1964. I was always keen to give support in any fund raising project, and also assist in schemes for disabled or visually handicapped.

On one occasion a speaker at Rotary was a war veteran, a Mr Walter Thornton, who had lost his sight after being brought down while flying a Spitfire. I became very heavily involved with the Queen Alexandra College for the Blind situated in Harborne, Birmingham. As a result, the instructor at the college, a Mr Miles, who I knew, had an idea of a workshop for the visually handicapped to become cycle mechanics. I supported the idea wholeheartedly and approached Raleigh and other firms for assistance. Machinery, tools, components etc flowed in to create a wonderful and successful training school, which is still operative. A Tommy Godwin Trophy is awarded annually for the best young mechanic.

When I was sixty I decided to ride the Lands End to John O' Groats to raise funds for the college. After a rather adventurous eight days I achieved this and, through Rotary and personal friends, raised £3,000 in sponsorship, in those days a reasonable sum.

A number of years after I got involved with SOS, the 'Stars Organisation for

Spastics,' not PC today and the name is now changed to SCOPE. It was again through Rotary that I got involved. A young lady came to talk about her job as a fund raiser for the charity. She mentioned that she had received permission from Birmingham City Council to organise a wheel event in the city centre. After her talk I approached her, volunteering to help in any way possible. We arranged a meeting to discuss matters. On her arrival she informed me that the Birmingham event was not going ahead but she had been offered the Tour of Britain, the Milk Race, to raise funds.

On the day of our meeting I went to my golf club, met some friends and was introduced to a Mr Colin Jones. I started to explain to a distant relative of mine that I had become in volved in this fund raising for SOS and remarked, "I don't know what I am going to do." Immediately Colin Jones, who had remembered me from my racing days, said, "Can you use a quarter of a million bags of Cadbury's chocolate?" To which I replied, "Yes." He went on to explain that he worked for the firm which did the promotion work for the company, and followed on by saying, "I may not get it all for you as many of the supermarkets will want a cut." However, for the first Milk Race we had supplies for every finishing point on the Tour.

For the first two days sales were poor then I hit on the idea at Weston-Super-Mare that I would do a market trader's job. With the assistance of some wonderful ladies from the local WI, my wife and I filled tables with heaps of bags of chocolate. The normal price was £1.40, our price 75p a bag. That day we sold £1,250 worth of chocolate. This became the norm thereafter, and we continued selling huge amounts at every stage finish.

The first year was a great success, but the two following years were even more so. Due to a change in the retail price, we lifted our price to £1 per bag, which was easier to operate as we didn't have to give change, no worries. We repeatedly sold in excess of £1,000 a day and, with other items supplied by the organisation, over the three years we raised well in excess of £100,000. During this time Eileen and I had the pleasure of meeting Dame Vera Lynne, Bob Monkhouse, Richard Whiteley and many other stars of the entertainment world. Unfortunately, the Milk Race, as such, finally came to an end when the Milk Marketing Board pulled out of sponsorship.

CHAPTER 28

1987
Retirement

During all these years of endless devotion to cycling my family life and business life did in some ways get neglected. Our daughter, Kay, born in 1948, had passed through her first fourteen years and had enjoyed school life. She had been very enthusiastic and had achieved such good marks that she had earned herself a place at King Edward Camp Hill School, a very satisfactory step. She had a wonderful feeling for her mother, who had been steadfast in Kay's development as a person.

After four years at King Edward's Kay passed with very good marks. But she had been told after her second year by one teacher that she would never attain university level because she was too interested in sport. Under this impression Kay did not apply for university but chose a teachers' training college in Cheltenham, St Mary's. When final examination results were delivered she had two A's and a B, and we received a phone call from the Head asking us to meet with her. At the meeting it was explained to us that Kay could get into any university in the country and that we should get her to change her mind. I said that the school should take that responsibility as they had misled Kay about her ability.

Kay did not change her mind and had a successful time at St Mary's. She also found an interest that would fulfil her sporting enthusiasm. The twin college for men in Cheltenham, St Paul's, encouraged basketball. Kay got involved in this, so much so that from around twenty years of age she developed into one of the top players in the country. She went on to play for a club team, who became national champions, and to play for England. As a club or England player, she visited USA, Holland, Belgium and other countries.

The reason for including these facts is only to say that Kay was in the Olympic squad selected to go to Montreal in 1976. On March 17th, the eve of her twenty-eighth birthday, she was playing with girls from the school where she was teaching when she was brought down by a very big youngster and the result was a badly broken leg. It was so bad that she carried it through her life until she was fifty-five before anyone would operate. Her young life was ruined with regard to participating in sport actively. But, being very determined, she has succeeded in life in many ways. I would have loved to have seen my daughter as an Olympian.

As she has progressed in life and her chosen career she has had the experience of deputy headship, a job she successfully applied for before her thirtieth birthday and was selected from six applicants. Kay has been to her mother and me a wonderful support in our lives and invaluable in our happiness.

I began to realise at fifty-five years of age that I was being unfair in my obsession with the sport. I had had a successful racing career then coaching, team management and getting heavily involved with the admin side, even to the extent of chairing the National Racing Committee. I finally chose to resign from that post in the middle of a year term because of the lack of enthusiasm, dedication and sacrifice by some committee members to improve the situation for the young riders of the future.

My own enthusiasm had been costly and the business had suffered. But once I made the break, things changed for the better and in the next eleven years turned around favourably. Our retirement came in 1987 at sixty-six years of age, ending thirty-six years of looking after the cycling public and club folk, with a comfortable retirement assured.

One of the first things arranged was a visit to my place of birth, a suggestion made by Eileen before I retired. She had said, "You will never retire, you will stay in the business until you die. If you do retire, I promise I will go to America with you!" My reply was, "You will have to fly, you know." She said, "I'll risk it." It was wonderful to go back after fifty-five years and to seek out places I remembered, and Eileen enjoyed it all.

CHAPTER 29

1995
Looking back

Below: about to try a
few laps of the new
Manchester Velodrome
Right: at the
Velodrome again
having been presented
with the belated
championship medals
by Hugh Porter

My interest in the sport has never waned. I marvel at what has happened in our cycle racing world, such as the development of the machine in Chris Boardman's early years, the technical and scientific interest now, the inclusion of nutritionists and psychologists and the amount of money involved. Elite riders are now fully paid professionals, travelling the world doing nothing but racing and training, with a very skilled back up team. I look back and think of the early training camps. All the same ideas were built into the scheme but no money was available. I realise now that it has taken forty years to develop and achieve what is now being accomplished.

Some of my happiest moments as a result of being a successful amateur have come in my later years. At seventy-five years of age, after some fifty years of waiting, I was honoured by being presented with five solid gold medals for National Championships won in the late 1940's. At the time of winning the titles it was explained that gold medals could not be struck so soon after the war. I was offered silver-gilt, which I refused, and even money to the value.

The NCU was the controlling body in racing until the BCF was formed in the 1960's. My wife, Eileen, just mentioned one day to an official of the BCF that I had never received my medals. The matter was taken up and a special die had to be made to the NCU design of the era, which resulted in some of the

most treasured items in my sporting memorabilia. I was most grateful when the presentation was made at Manchester Velodrome, and to receive them from Hugh Porter was most emotional. We were and are still are very good friends.

I still so enjoy being asked to carry out duties for the sport and other events. Once established and showing a willingness to co-operate, the media appreciate a personality who will respond to their wishes.

In 1998 I was approached by members of the local famous cycling club, the Solihull CC, to ask if I would consider taking the presidency of the club. I hesitated when thinking of the names who had brought honour to them in the past. I insisted I would only accept subject to some of their past members being asked to agree to my nomination. At the annual meeting it was passed unanimously, and I was notified accordingly. Having now served for eight enjoyable and exciting years, and with a membership in total of over 200, I am very proud.

My relationship with the club is such that when I was awarded one of the greatest marks of respect for my contribution to sport and the community, that of the Gold Badge of Honour from the BCF in 2001, it was arranged that the formal presentation be made at the Solihull annual dinner in January 2002. For the occasion, the President of the Federation agreed to do the honours.

The years have passed on, and I have been adding on pages of fond memo-

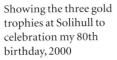

Showing the three gold trophies at Solihull to celebration my 80th birthday, 2000

ries. In the earlier pages, and with some regularity, I have mentioned my age. As I come to the concluding chapter of what is truly a life's story, I am within two weeks of my eighty-sixth birthday.

I would like to mention that in the year 2005 I was awarded from the Birmingham Sports Council, of which I had been a member since its inception, a framed address:

> In recognition and appreciation to THOMAS CHARLES GODWIN for your lifetime contribution to sport in Birmingham.

In this year of 2006 I have been invited to be an Ambassador for the City of Birmingham to the 2012 Olympics.

Finally, for all that has been achieved and experienced, I am very deeply indebted to my wife, Eileen. Her love, dedication and support have been

With a City Councillor in 1993 when Manchester was bidding for the Olympics

beyond belief. She has sacrificed her interests to encourage me in all that I have undertaken. Our marriage has been tested over sixty-two years, our happiness is immense, always working together, and may it continue. We are blessed with a wonderful daughter, a son-in-law of great character and a grandson of whom we are very fond.

As a footnote, I have always been a very physical person, enjoying helping others. I love people and can pick up with anyone I meet. Especially if anyone has a job that needs doing and they are too busy. Sometime after my retirement at sixty-six years of age I went to visit a man I had known in business. He is an expert craftsman with wood, some of his work is mind boggling, and he is always extremely busy. On my visit I remarked how untidy his workshop and wood store were, to which he replied, "Do you want to tidy it up for me?" Without hesitation, I said, "Well, I can certainly make it look better than it is." Needless to say, I have spent many happy days carrying out mundane duties.

On my mentioning that I was writing my life story, he asked, "Will you include that I am perhaps the only man in the country to have a Double Olympic Medallist sweeping my workshop yard."

As I reach the end of my memoirs I have recently read a wonderful interview with Bradley Wiggins and how he describers his development in the sport. In the 2004 Olympics in Athens he won Gold, Silver and Bronze, along with other medal winners in the team. An earlier report mentioned that each medal won by the team cost in the region of £68,000. His ambitions are now for the Tour de France and future Olympics and his declaration is that his son will never want for anything. A far cry from the amateur days that I described earlier.

Good luck to all the competitors and may they have continued success.

Index